CW00539396

SOLID AIR

THE LIFE OF JOHN MARTYN

By

Chris Nickson

ISBN: 0615534856
ISBN-13:978-0615534855

SOLID AIR: THE LIFE OF JOHN MARTYN

First published in 2011

By Creative Content Ltd, Roxburghe House, Roxburghe House, 273-287 Regent Street, London, W1B 2HA.

Typesetting by CPI Rowe

Cover Design by Michael Page and Daniel at HCT Design

Cover Photograph Suzanna Cramtom

Solid Air ...The Life of John Martyn

CONTENTS

INTRODUCTION

At the beginning of October 2003, websites run by John Martyn fans were giddy with the rumour that John was set to play a pair of shows at a pub close to his home in rural Ireland in November.

The big man was back - and to those who loved his music it seemed like a miracle.

In April 2003, John Martyn's right leg had been amputated below the knee. It was an item that didn't make the music press, although plenty of friends and well-wishers, including Eric Clapton, heard the news and sent their good wishes to him in hospital. In time, he was fitted with a prosthetic limb and discharged from hospital.

One man, one operation, carried out successfully. It wasn't the end of the world; millions around the globe had survived similar things and continued with their lives. And there was no doubt that John was a survivor; the pendulum swings of his career over almost four decades had proved that.

But this was different. John was in his mid-50s - and to come back, especially from something as traumatic as this, took a wealth of energy and spirit, things that could have been in short supply.

The gigs that marked his return took place on November 7 and 8 at Connollys of Leap, a tiny bar out in West Cork, known for the music it staged, with acts like Roy Harper and Hothouse Flowers passing through its doors. It was hardly a high-profile venue, but there was enough pressure on John without any visibility. The BBC were filming the first night for part of a documentary on John. He hadn't played live in two years and even though John was a veteran performer, with longtime keyboard player Spencer Cozens and bassist John Giblin backing him up, there were nerves.

i

For several months he'd been undergoing physical therapy, getting used to his prosthetic leg - but he chose to perform from a wheelchair. It offered safety. This was a test for him, a full performance of 14 songs, ranging from favourites like "Solid Air" and "May You Never" to newer work and a selection of covers, like Portishead's "Glory Box," and "Suzanne," wrapping up with the old standard "Goodnight Irene."

Fans travelled not only from all around Ireland, but from across the globe for the shows, to show their support for John and to welcome him back. His nerves vanished once he began playing. After all, this was what he did, the way he defined himself to the world, through his songs and his music. Doing this was vital.

"John told me he had to get back to playing," said an old friend, singer-songwriter Bridget St. John, who'd visited him at his Kilkenny home during the summer and who spoke to him after the Connollys shows, "it's the only thing that makes him feel great." And he was satisfied with the results, she noted, saying "I know his gigs went great."

It was the kind of confidence boost he desperately needed after all that had happened. There'd been trauma, physical and mental, and he needed to re-establish exactly who he was.

"Whatever he's doing is in balance," St. John observed. "I think as long as he has his thing in balance, it's fine for him."

Obviously, it worked. He was certain enough of his abilities to book a 15-date UK tour in April and May, 2004. That would come around the same time as the BBC were airing their documentary in March, with his name fresh in people's minds.

In many ways, it was set to be a longer test run to see just how viable continuing as a performer might be. The schedule wasn't easy, but still better and less gruelling than many John had undertaken in the past. There were no long distances to travel between dates and he'd be surrounded by his band, musicians he knew well and trusted, and who were used to him and his foibles.

There was also the small matter of a new album. His last release has been *Glasgow Walker*, all the way back in 1999. Since then, any John Martyn material that had appeared on record shop shelves had been repackaged, or old gigs spruced up for CD release. Welcome fare, some of it, but there was nothing fresh.

However, before his leg problems had become really bad, John's band had laid down fresh tracks, working from his material. By now they were old, of course, but they could form the basis of an album. And while John was at home, undergoing rehabilitation, he'd recorded his guitar and vocals. Initially it seemed that it wouldn't happen in time for the tour, but maybe after, once he was used to working again. He'd undergone a lot and had plenty to say. But in April 2004, just as the first dates were getting underway, the brand new *On the Cobbles* hit the shops.

The idea of John away from music was unthinkable. It had been his life since he was 16 and first playing folk clubs in Scotland, under the wing of the late Hamish Imlach. He'd dedicated himself; he'd had drive and ambition. He'd started out playing folk music, but quickly accelerated past that barrier, adding electricity, touches of jazz, avant-garde, and whatever he wanted to create his own sound.

While John the musician forged ahead, John the man could be a little more problematic. He loved his drink, and while he could be charming, there was also a temper that lurked not too far below the surface. He was volatile, which could result in knock-down, drag out fights and a few instances of burning personal bridges and sabotaging his career, setting him back several paces on the path.

But at 55, and settled with his partner Teresa, who seemed a good match for him, perhaps all that was finally behind him. Living in the peaceful environment of Kilkenny, away from the razor bustle of the music industry, he'd maybe come to terms with and was at peace with himself.

He'd enjoyed a number of revivals since his critical heyday in the '70s, when a gushing Martin Carthy actually kissed his television on seeing

John appear on *The Old Grey Whistle Test*, declaring, "It's so good to see our John again!" (an apocryphal story, but Carthy admitted its truth). At the end of the '70s he worked with Phil Collins and put out a pair of commercially successful discs. He revisited his old songs in the early '90s, finally finding some small slice of acclaim in the US, and he won plaudits for *The Church with One Bell*, his 1998 album of covers. The chillout movement hailed him as a godfather, and he'd recorded a version of the Beloved's "Deliver Me" with Sister Bliss from Faithless.

On each occasion, there was a moment of holding the breath – could John finally break through this time? But great reviews and touring somehow never translated into mass market acceptance.

And John had done his share to pull away from commercial success. After *Solid Air*, he didn't capitalise on the album's excellent reviews. Instead he turned around and released *Inside Out*, probably the most uncompromising disc of his career. Recorded in a short burst, it offered little of the comfort of its predecessor, instead aiming for the avant-garde jugular with the centrepiece track "Outside In." Perhaps the closest it came to capturing the calm night spirit was the stoned vibe of the opener, "Fine Lines," but from there it was a jagged course. It wasn't the move of someone determined to become a star; it was someone set on being an artist. Why else would he gradually move away from acoustic music, which had been very good to him, to the band format that remained his trademark for more than the last two decades? Because that was where his muse took him.

Being true to his musical heart might not have made him rich; it hasn't always translated into great music. But it kept him honest. Even when he revisited his "classic" material in the early '90s, it wasn't wholly to use those songs as a springboard back into the wider public eye. He'd been playing them with the band, and they'd changed – this was a way of capturing that - and having celebrities like Genesis drummer/singer Phil Collins and Pink Floyd guitarist Dave Gilmour on board certainly didn't hurt.

As trip-hop became the fashion in the mid '90s, John made his own foray into the style with *And....* But he was never subsumed by it; instead, it became another arranging tool in his arsenal. And on *The Church with One Bell*, his album of covers, he never blindly followed the styles of other songwriters; everything was refracted through his own prism.

Virtually from the beginning, John was praised as a formidable guitarist. From his second album on, as he began to develop his own style and work outside standard tuning, it was a well-deserved reputation (the capo-shifting "Seven Black Roses" off *The Tumbler* offers a perfect example, as does "The Easy Blues" from *Solid Air*). But he was also an innovator who explored the nooks, crannies, and possibilities of echo and effects, beginning with "Glistening Glyndebourne" on *Bless the Weather* and progressing, reaching something of a climax with his work on *One World*, which integrated all the facets of his creativity perfectly.

From there, after the transitional *Grace and Danger*, his guitar work became one facet of a band sound. Still sharp, and more than capable of some cutting solos, he subordinated his sound to become another member of the group.

However, he did concentrate more on his vocal style, which was very much front and centre in the sound. Starting with *Bless the Weather*, he changed his folkie singing into something more relaxed, with slurred lines that were meant to sound like a tenor sax – he even stated that was his intention. It meshed perfectly with the music he was making, but by the '80s he needed something a little different. What he developed was something cleaner, still with the smoky ambience, but offering more of a focal point (even if it wasn't necessarily any easier to decipher the lyrics).

There's no single arc to John's career, no path that's readily traced. Instead it's a series of bumps and dips, high points and low. And it's important at times to separate the man and his art; in John's case, the two definitely aren't always the same. But that's true of most people - we're all a mass of contradictions. It's what makes us human

JOHN MARTYN 1948–2009

CHAPTER 1 – The Young Man

Glasgow still wears its Victorian past proudly. The Civic Hall is a monument to the opulence of the 19th century, when Scotland was a proud part of the British Empire and the wealth – for some – seemed never-ending. With its marble walls and frescoed ceilings, it was a solid statement of Glasgow's bourgeois place in the world.

But while the gentry seemed self-satisfied, there was little joy for the working class. The city reached the peak of its industrial production in 1900 and the First World War was a boon to its heavy industry, but the working man and his family saw little of that.

Still, people flocked to the place and, by the start of World War II, its population had risen to 1.1 million, many crammed into the tenements, or flats, built far too long before.

Nothing could be done immediately, with the press of battle occupying minds and bodies. But even before the first servicemen returned home in 1945, plans were being presented that would make Glasgow into a modern, vital city. The Bruce Plan, named for city engineer Robert Bruce, proposed new transport routes, housing in the outlying areas that would be less dense than the crammed inner city, and industrial estates where factories and businesses could expand. A year later, the Clyde Valley Regional Plan echoed these ideas, suggesting that almost a quarter of the population should be rehoused, decentralising living areas and industry, something that was sealed with the passage of the New Towns Act. In 1947, East Kilbride New Town (the New Town part was soon dropped from the name) was designated, with a goal of providing living spaces for 40,000 Glaswegians. Within another 12 months work had begun on the peripheral estates of Castlemilk, Drumchapel, and Easterhouse.

The idea was good, a paternalistic endeavour to give families a better life. But for many, wrenched from close-knit communities, it proved less than ideal, as it would all over Britain as the new towns sprang into life.

Glasgow had long enjoyed a dual reputation. The city's burghers represented Calvinist rectitude and propriety. Its working classes were louder and more boisterous, with a love of drink and violence. It was all stereotyping, to be sure, but that was how people saw it.

McGeachy was John Martyn's true family name - and pre-war Glasgow was the home of the McGeachy family. It's not the most common name north of the border, and seems to have Scots-Irish roots, coming out of the surname McGough in Ulster's County Monaghan. But there were McGeachys in Ayrshire in the 1800s.

The family was quite respectable, with a 13-room house in Glasgow, a mansion by any standards. But John's father was a dreamer, a man who didn't, or couldn't, fit easily into society. The family was religious – Presbyterian - and he had ideas of becoming a Doctor of Divinity, but they came to nothing. Instead he ended up working for the Scottish Bible Society, packing bibles for missionaries to use in their conversion work overseas. It was a life that ticked by – until World War II began.

He fought and did his duty, but the experience changed him irrevocably. Seeing death and destruction firsthand stripped away all the illusions of society and proper behaviour; it made him cling to life. After so many dour years, he wanted lightness and fun.

And what offered more fun than show business? He was blessed with a good, natural voice, and he began to use it, starting out as an amateur in Glasgow before turning professional.

It was hardly the most secure profession and it wasn't one he could make a living at north of the border. He made his way south, to London, the centre of entertainment, and that was where he met his wife-to-be, another singer, a trained soprano and a refugee whom John described as "Jewish Belgian."

They settled in New Malden, Surrey, outside the hubbub of the capital, but still with access to its stages, and that's where John was born on September 11th, 1948, christened Iain David McGeachy (Iain is a Scots variation of the name John).

John's parents had success on a small scale. His father sang on the British Forces Network and trod the boards on vaudeville stages around the country. But it was a form that was already entering its death throes. Still, they tried, and one of John's earliest memories is of being on the road with them.

"I remember being in a caravan in Lanarkshire, being completely entranced by it. They did a show once with Roy Rogers and I was introduced to Trigger and I remember I much preferred Trigger to Roy."

The marriage wasn't happy or settled and the couple had separated by the time John was five. His father returned to Scotland, while his mother continued to live in the south of England; as a youngster John led a schizophrenic existence, shuttling between the two parents, spending most of the year with his father and grandmother in Scotland and two months in the summer with his mother near London.

In many ways, that shaped him. Different places required different masks and accents to fit in. So he became equally at home with a rough Glaswegian brogue and a plummier Home Counties voice, able to switch between the two at will. It was a child's way of surviving; it allowed him to blend in to the scenery without necessarily letting anyone become close.

"A friend of mine told me, 'You're just trying to keep people away from you,'" he said in *Scotland on Sunday*. "I think that's true. I put on accents, I put on a front, because I'm a very private person."

The two places couldn't have been more different. The Home Counties was virtually a synonym for middle-class security and values. While most families there didn't qualify for the opulence of the stockbroker belt, it was, by and large, comfortable. Glasgow, on the other hand, was the home of the hard man, where you were expected to hold

3

your own from a very early age. And if you couldn't...well, bullying was the order of the day. It was the survival of the fittest, with the rest left to get by as best they could.

John's father did try to instil love of music into his son and there was plenty of it in the house, as aunts and uncles dropped by, playing the piano and singing - a mixture of hymns, popular songs, and traditional Scots melodies. John began violin lessons, but abandoned them for the more masculine pastime of rugby.

"I went from violin to rugby," he recounted to dotmusic.com, "because violin practice was on a Thursday, the same night as rugby practice, so the violin didn't last long." He became comfortable in a place where "you went out and kicked a few heads, or you were looked on as a pansy."

Violence didn't come naturally to John, but he hadn't "got the capacity for being trodden on...I don't like being taken advantage of. There were fights in school all the time and knives were bandied about."

Secondary school was the Shawlands Academy, within walking distance of home, where John went for five years, the last of which (at least in warm weather) supposedly saw him arriving deliberately barefoot, living on a late beatnik cusp as his musical interests blossomed..

The summers in England were more genteel, but in their own way just as difficult. John's mother had remarried and lived in Surbiton, but when John visited, he couldn't stay with them, "because my step-father didn't like me," so he stayed with his aunt and her husband, who lived in Hampton Court.

For all that he was the product of what used to be termed a "broken home," young John didn't care. By his own estimation, he had a great childhood. He was principally brought up by his grandmother. In a *Mojo* interview he characterized her as "probably a better mother to me than most modern-day mothers 'cos she brought me up with that Victorian thing" – real hands-on parenting, with mustard baths and foot massages, and washing his hair with carbolic soap. His father was around to teach him the things a growing Glasgow boy needed to know about fishing, bike riding, sex, and distilling spirits.

Drink was all around, even at home. His whole family drank. His grandmother, wanting to retain some respectability, would imbibe quietly and secretly in the kitchen, from egg cups instead of glasses, the bottle carefully concealed out of sight. It was a drinking culture and John was already indulging by the time he was 14 and out on his paper round.

He might have put on a tough face, but under it all was a sensitive, highly intelligent boy. He learned to read when he was just four and found chess and algebra to be suitable hobbies. He loved art and claimed that from the age of nine he tried to persuade his father to buy him prints of Chagall paintings. Down south, his mother introduced him to the magic of Debussy's music and he was enthralled. He'd inherited his love of music from his parents, even if he couldn't be seen playing something like the violin. Rock'n'roll was completely established by the time he was a teenager, but it never seemed to move him. Instead, a defining moment came from a most unlikely source.

"To my eternal shame, the thing that inspired me to pick up a guitar was a single by Joan Baez called 'A Silver Dagger.' It was the first time I'd heard finger-picking guitar and I just loved the sound. And then I took an interest in folk music and discovered Davy Graham, who still remains the founder of that movement."

Joan Baez was 19 when she released her eponymous debut on Vanguard Records in 1960 (it appeared on Fontana in the UK). "Silver Dagger" was the opening cut, a traditional song that would become her concert trademark for many years and which showcased her gloriously clear soprano and finger picking. Where might John have heard it? It was hardly jukebox material. Radio seems the best bet, although folk music was hardly a featured style on the BBC, which enjoyed a radio broadcasting monopoly in those days.

When it appeared, John would have been 12, just approaching his teens. But it wasn't until three years later that he heard it – and it was a direct catalyst to starting him playing. Nor would he have probably heard much of Davy Graham at that young age, as Graham was still very much a cult figure in London-based folk circles.

Davy Graham, the product of a Scots father and a British Guyanan mother, had quickly established himself as the guitarist's guitarist in London. He was the young icon of a scene that was beginning to hum. And he was an artist who absorbed influences not only from folk and blues, but also jazz and music from around the globe. He could play like a dream, distilling everything inside in magical, expansive ways, and creating at least one classic in "Angi," which he wrote for a girlfriend, but which is better known in versions from Bert Jansch and Paul Simon.

"He had an album called *Folk Blues and Beyond* on the Decca label in 1965, which was formative for me. Amazingly advanced player, he swung like whoa."

Although John was taken with music, he had no driving ambition to become a musician; playing started out simply as fun, although it quickly became obvious that he had some facility on the instrument. He began attending a folk club, Clive's Incredible Folk Club on Sauciehall Street, one of the main thoroughfares through Glasgow, run by Clive Palmer, who'd become one of the founders of the Incredible String Band. It was there he finally saw Davy Graham perform live, along with others like Josh McCrae (whose "Messin' About On The River" was a staple on the radio show *Children's Favourites*) and a few American performers.

It was a friend of John's father, a luthier named Willie Sinnit, who introduced John to Hamish Imlach. Imlach became John's teacher. Imlach, John said, "was not a fabulous musician, but he had a great attitude. I liked his guitar playing." And it was from him that John learned many of the basic guitar licks and how to play ragtime – one of the staples of a folk apprenticeship in the '60s.

When John was sixteen, it was Imlach who gave him his first taste of playing for an audience. John hadn't been playing long, no more than three or four months, when Imlach played a concert near John's home and John naturally went. However, the opening act never arrived, "so they were stuck for somebody to play for half an hour. They asked people from the audience to do a couple of songs and eventually they shoved me up there and everybody liked it."

It was a low-key start, but also a revelation. John could actually do this. And he certainly needed to do something. He'd dreamed of becoming a doctor or an artist, but he'd left school and had already managed to be kicked out of art school "for being nasty and silly, and I didn't have much money – I was earning my money playing darts in those days, making about two quid a day." Not that he was too broken-hearted. His image of art school was that "it was going to be bohemian, listening to Rolling Stones records all day and smoke dope and drink coffee. That was going to be my lifestyle and it didn't work out that way. It was worse than being in school, to be honest."

So when Imlach suggested, "Why don't you come round and do a couple of songs in my set for people and maybe earn a few quid for it?" John was more than amenable.

And he was introduced to a whole new world – Imlach's world, where music and politics rubbed shoulders.

As the '50s turned into the '60s, folk music had undergone a revival of sorts, led by singer Ewan MacColl. His view of folk music was quite political and he drew heavily on the heritage of different countries of the British Isles and urged his followers to do the same. A network of folk clubs began to spring up, enough for some performers to make a living. Labels, like the fledgling Topic, issued folk albums by some of the new artists like Shirley Collins.

Hamish Imlach was one of the leading lights of the Scottish revival. A giant of a man, weighing almost 300 pounds, he was an anti-nuclear activist and a comedian (Billy Connelly was one of his many protégés). While many of his songs were deliberately funny and often explicitly scatological, he was also a serious traditional folk singer, making the rounds of the clubs in the '50s and '60s. In fact, he wouldn't record his first album, the self-titled *Hamish Imlach*, until 1966 (for Transatlantic); by then he was a famous figure on the folk scenes both north and south of the border. In addition to his singing, Imlach was also a very committed socialist, and that influence had also remained with John through the years.

Imlach proved to be a goldmine of information on music "and simultaneously introduced me to socialism, because that was the driving force at the time. Folk music was folk music; it was for the people and quite deliberately so. Through the socialist aspect of the music, I was introduced to a lot of the great black musicians. We used to pool our money and bring over these guys, like [the Rev] Gary Davis, to play at the clubs in Glasgow...that was the only way we could hear them."

It was a good, solid apprenticeship for John, who was getting in on a burgeoning scene. It was 1964. Another Scot, Bert Jansch, was already making waves both as a guitarist and songwriter down in London, a year away from his own debut record, and something of a hero to those back home – John almost certainly saw him when he made his annual visits to Surbiton and when Jansch returned to Scotland to play.

"Everyone in Scotland was very in awe of the London scene," John would recall in *Zig Zag*, "like that was the thing to do if you wanted to make it...that's where you went. Then I listened to a Davy Graham album and that completely blew me away. I went to see him in a folk club called Cousin's and I came back full of the whole thing about London."

The capital was calling and John was ready to answer. He returned to London, stars in his eyes. This time he didn't stay with his mother or aunt; instead he tried to make it on his own. He slept rough in Trafalgar Square, moved on regularly by the police. It didn't last long. He might have had an infinite belief in his abilities and potential, but the simple fact was that he wasn't ready yet. He hadn't been playing long enough or hard enough to have developed an individual style.

He gave up and returned to Glasgow and worked on a building site for a couple of weeks. But the twin ideas of music and London were inside him, coursing through his bloodstream.

"John was totally consumed with his guitar work," recalled Clive Palmer, then already part of the nascent Incredible String Band. "A very restless character, and quite moody, but they all are, aren't they?"

The Incredible String Band, which then consisted of Palmer and Robin Williamson, had been working on their sound at Clive's Incredible Folk Club and attracting a varied crowd. Billy Connelly would come down to see them, as would Mike Heron, who soon became the group's third member. Their music was folk, but utterly different from anything anyone else was doing – a psychedelic vision of folk.

"Alex Campbell and Imlach were playing all this 'endemic' pro-Scottish, anti-English folk music," John recalled in *Classic Rock*. "Nothing wrong with that, but Clive and the Incredible String Band embraced all this other stuff. He made it all right to listen to stuff that wasn't 'pure'."

It wasn't long before their reputation began to precede them, and they were playing outside Glasgow. Les Cousins in London, then *the* club for up-and-coming folk acts, booked them. And to John, that made them successes on a par with Davy Graham. He'd seen the band, and was intrigued by what they were doing.

"John was a big fan of the String Band, and started to play a bit," Palmer said. "But he was also a good friend of Hamish Imlach, and we got to know each other."

John often became their support act, opening for them on small folk club gigs and earning three or four pounds. A friendship of sorts grew up between John and Clive Palmer, in part because "I think he was an admirer of mine, as he was of a few other people. And he was developing a new style of playing. He was probably influenced by Bert [Jansch], and the String Band, and then he started to develop his own style."

John did indeed admire Palmer: "Those were wild times," he recalled, "and Clive was a remarkable man, a great musician and down to earth, absolutely no bullshit, taught me lots of things to play."

The friendship between the pair grew to the extent that rumours persist that the two of them shared a shed as living quarters for a while – something Palmer denied, although he admitted that, "it's possible we might have spent the odd night in odd places when we were travelling. Mind, I can't be absolutely sure – and it doesn't really matter, it's all part of the mythology."

They did, however, spend a lot of time at Palmer's flat in Coronation Buildings, Edinburgh. There was no money for the gas or electric meters, "so we pitched a tent in his front room. We went busking but it was too cold to play." According to Martyn legend, one night as the pair took a shortcut home through the Royal Highland Show, they killed a ram and dragged its carcass back to Coronation Buildings, where they – and many other musicians "all had ram chops for weeks!"

Within what was still a small Scottish folk scene, John was beginning to make a name for himself. He was like a sponge, absorbing everything he heard. But the name he was going by was still Iain McGeachy. Scots it certainly was, but as someone pointed out, it was also a mouthful. He needed something more easily remembered and less obviously Scottish if he was going to make it in London - and his ambitions still lay there. Iain became its Anglicised counterpart, John. And the Martyn? According to legend, it came to him when he looked across the room and saw a Martin acoustic guitar (an American brand that's still the instrument of choice for many acoustic guitar players, including John). And so Iain McGeachy was reborn as the sleeker John Martyn. He knew what he wanted from life; all he had to do was get there.

He began setting up his own folk club tours in Scotland, then ventured over the border to the North of England. Palmer often went with him.

"I drove him round on a couple of tours of Scotland and England, and I played a little bit on the tours. We just did it for a diversion, he was starting off, doing little club gigs and building a reputation. He worked very hard for it, and it was quite difficult. He was always a very determined player, he used to practice a hell of a lot. He never put the guitar down when I knew him." He was a driven man, with a fixed goal, "and I think he had a chip on his shoulder. He was very determined to be successful."

Even at that stage, on the cusp between seventeen and eighteen and still learning the skills of the instrument and only just beginning to get inside the music, John was looking fixedly ahead.

"My impression of him early on was that he was so ambitious that he really didn't have time for anything else," Palmer observed. "He was going in a straight line towards being successful in his terms. He reminded me a lot of [tennis player] John McEnroe, he was an exact copy. Ambition taken to extremes. But it's like that sometimes with people, and that's what makes them successful. He came from twiddling around on the guitar to making a name, and it wasn't that easy then. You had all the established guitarists and he had to compete with them, so it was quite a feat."

Even then, in the go-with-the-flow '60s, John's temper sometimes got the better of him.

"He used to fall out with people a bit," Palmer remembered. "A little highly-strung. I think he was just a very restless character. He had a very short fuse; he could get wound up very quickly about things. I think some people gave him a bit of a wide berth. But he was always very pleasant to me."

Although alcohol would soon become a constant in John's life, Palmer said, "I don't think he was much of a drinker back then. A bit of dope and a bit of booze, but not to any great excess." In part, that might have been because there was so little money around, but also because music offered him enough energy and diversion, as "he was playing and composing a few things when we were touring. We didn't spend a lot of time socialising."

For all that John seemed independent and footloose, dedicated to becoming a musician, summers still meant Mum and Surrey. But that was fine; it gave him a chance to investigate the London scene, which was really where everything was happening. It was 1965, and Bert Jansch and Davy Graham were the top dogs at Bunji's and Les Cousins, the two clubs that formed the backbone of the acoustic clubs. They were folk clubs inasmuch as the performers played acoustic guitars, but it stretched the definition of folk. The String Band would play there sometimes, driving down from Scotland, but mostly it was anybody and everybody, the scuffling talents and no-talents who mingled around Soho, hoping for a break - or just an audience.

Located at 49 Greek Street, Les Cousins was the king of them all. It was a basement under a Greek restaurant, where Andy Matthews (affectionately known as Andy the Greek), the son of the restaurant's owner, opened up and treated the performers well – often they'd retire upstairs for a free meal, courtesy of Andy's father, a welcome full stomach after days of probably eating nothing.

John played floor spots – where members of the audience get up to play a song or two - a few times over the summer, but it wasn't until the String Band played there that he finally met Matthews.

"I just asked him and asked him and asked him for a gig. And he said, 'I've never heard you.' So I said, 'Fuck you, man, I've played in your club about five or six times, why haven't you heard me?' So he said, 'Alright, you can do an all-nighter.' So I did an all-nighter with Davy Graham, and that was it."

John was properly blooded on the London scene at its most auspicious venue. By the standards of the time, he was well on the way. But there were other forces at work, too. It might have been 1966, and John now almost eighteen, but in those days that meant he was still a juvenile. Both his parents had been musicians, but all that meant was they knew how difficult a path it was to tread, how uncertain and insecure. John had been a smart (if sometimes unconventional and awkward) boy at school. At one point he'd aspired to be a doctor or an artist. The artist idea obviously hadn't worked out, but there was still hope the doctor part might.

It was probably family pressure that made him apply to university. But apply he did, and he was accepted for a place, to start in the autumn of 1966. If nothing else, with a degree he'd always be able to get a good job, as - in those days - it was a guarantee of strong employment. If he wanted to play guitar, fine; this way he'd "always have something to fall back on."

Before heading off to college, though, there was still a summer down south to enjoy. And John was going to make the most of it.

CHAPTER 2 – The Start of a Career

Playing the folk clubs was a pleasant way to make money. It didn't pay much, but at seventeen John's expenses were few. He had relatives and friends he could stay with outside London. Cigarettes and alcohol seemed cheap; someone always had some dope. The people were fun, the girls occasionally nubile. And every gig helped him improve as a guitarist. For a teenager without any responsibilities, it was as close to a dream come true as he was likely to get, even if the dream was due to end in September.

Several of the artists he played with had records out and were acquiring huge critical reputations – talents like Davy Graham, Bert Jansch, and John Renbourn. Donovan was scoring hit single after hit single – he'd turned into a pop star. It even had ramifications overseas; Paul Simon had been hugely influenced by his brief time immersed in the London folk scene.

New clubs were opening all the time. There was even one close to John's mother, called the Kingston Folk Barge. It was aptly named, because it was, quite literally, nothing more than a barge moored on the river. A completely amateur place, it could only hold a tiny audience - and it was debatable whether it should even have been allowed on the water at all. The place, John remembered, was "run by an alcoholic called Geoff, who used to drink methylated spirits and red wine....he's now become a traffic warden, and the barge was towed away as a derelict."

It was visited by "a fat man called Theo Johnson," an energetic hustler who was, perhaps, looking for the next big thing. He had a connection of sorts to the music industry. He'd produced a pair of albums of rugby songs for the young Island label, both of which had done well.

Island was run by Chris Blackwell, the son of a white Jamaican plantation owner. He'd started the label in 1959 as an outlet for West Indian music and soon scored a hit with Laurel Aitken's "Boogie In My Bones" – an auspicious beginning. Unlike many whites in what was then the British colony, he interacted with and had respect for the black community; a group of then-reviled Rastafarians had saved him from drowning and, when he ran a scooter rental business, it was the Rastas who'd exhibited the most honesty in paying.

In 1962 he moved to London, realising that there was a huge West Indian market for music there in the immigrants who'd arrived since 1948. He operated from a small office and drove all over the country, selling records to shops from the boot of his car. He'd made licensing arrangements with a number of Jamaican labels (indeed, he released an early single by Bob Marley – incorrectly credited on the label as Bob Morley – in 1963, a full decade before Island issued their seminal Bob Marley and the Wailers *Catch A Fire*) and in 1964 he hit the big time as "My Boy Lollipop" by Millie Small became a huge hit in both Britain and the US.

Ska, the '60s sound of Jamaica, was popular with British Mods, as was American soul, and Blackwell strove to take advantage of that side by starting the Sue label, which focused on obscurities from the States.

Island became the biggest label for ska and its successor, rock steady. But Blackwell had greater ambitions. While on tour with Millie Small in 1964, he came across the Spencer Davis Group in Birmingham, which featured not only Davis, a former teacher from Wales, but two brothers, Steve and Muff Winwood. Steve, then just fifteen, was a prodigious talent, not only on guitar and organ, but with a soulful voice that belied his Midlands origins. Blackwell signed them, but leased their tracks to Phillips, who released them – with great success – on the Fontana label. It was certainly apt that they covered "Keep On Runnin'" by another of Blackwell's acts, Jamaican Jackie Edwards, for their second single, scoring a massive hit on both sides of the Atlantic.

To expand, Blackwell needed money. So, on subsidiaries, he issued whatever might sell - and that included albums of bawdy rugby songs. They could be recorded very cheaply and the profit was good.

By 1966, although Island was massive in the British West Indian market, he was ready to begin repositioning himself and nose into the very lucrative white market. There were plenty of opportunities in the new rock bands and solo artists who were constantly popping up and, with some good judgement, there was money to be made.

His first attempts didn't work out too well, as singles by the now-forgotten VIPs, Chords Five, and Freaks of Nature testify. Nor did his first white LP release, *Sunshine Superfrog*, by one Wynder K. Frogg. That was the pseudonym of Mick Weaver (not the same as Mick "Blue" Weaver), a jobbing keyboard player. Its instrumental covers were hardly going to set the world on fire.

Blackwell was looking for talent. In John Martyn, Theo Johnson believed he'd found some. Legend has it that Johnson told John, in classic fashion, "I'm going to make you a star!" But as John remembered it, during the summer of 1966 he was in Surrey, "in Kingston-on-Thames, and I was playing – well, learning to play, really. I used to go to a folk club and someone asked if I'd like to make a record. I though he was joking, but I gave him my mother's phone number, because I was living in a place without a phone."

Of course John didn't believe a word, but what did he have to lose by giving out a phone number? Like anyone else playing music, the idea of making a record was a dream. It was what other people did, not him. And even though he was ambitious, he'd agreed to go to university. The next few years of his life were set. He'd still be able to play music, but for fun, not money. Like everyone else involved in music, he would have heard the tales of disreputable managers: people who promised the earth, but couldn't deliver.

The one thing he didn't know was that Johnson really did have a connection to Blackwell and that Blackwell was young and hungry for good artists. Nor did he know that Johnson had secretly taped him performing on the Kingston Folk Barge. He took that tape to Blackwell, who was impressed enough to offer a contract.

"My mother came flying round one day and said 'A guy wants to take you to see a record company.' So I went up to see the record company and, unbeknownst to me, he'd already taped one of my songs ('Fairy Tale Lullabye') from the club. Blackwell really liked it."

"I liked his voice," Blackwell confirmed. "I remember Theo Johnson. He was a huge guy, and he rode a tiny little motor scooter. Maybe he did the rugby song albums, I don't remember. I can't think why I'd know him, so maybe that was it. Those happened in 1965, and we signed John in 1966, I think, that makes sense. I remember I was living on the corner of Earl's Court Road and Cromwell Road when I first signed John." But he confirmed, quashing a longstanding debate, "[John] was the first white artist Island ever signed. I'd signed the Spencer Davis Group, but not to Island Records, they went to Fontana."

Just like that, he offered John a contract. Suddenly the dream of the last two years was coming true. He might not have been the first white artist to *release* a record on Island, but he was the label's first white singer, a landmark in the careers of both Martyn and Blackwell. John said, "How do you think I felt? Top of the shitheap, cock of the rock, thank you very much!"

John could kiss the thought of university and academic application goodbye. He was going to make a record. He had a label, a home.

He was also a lot savvier than people believed an eighteen year-old should be. Not long after he'd recorded his first album for Island, Johnson presented him with a management contract. Reading it carefully, John discovered that it gave Johnson 45% of John's earnings for the next decade – not a healthy situation at best, and extortionate at worst, "so I told him to stick it." While John called his reaction intuitive, it was sensible. After that he only ran into Johnson two or three times.

Prior to that, however, Johnson would produce John's first record, *London Conversation*, and rent John a room in a flat he owned in Richmond. John, still on a high from having a deal, was writing material for the disc and trying it out at places like Cousins and Bunjie's. That was where Robin Fredericks, a young American singer-songwriter, met him in July, 1967.

She said, "I needed a place to stay and John, who has always gone out of his way to support and encourage other songwriters, offered me a room in the flat where he was living. The flat belonged to … Theo Johnson. Johnny Silvo [a folk singer] and Diz Disley [folk-jazz guitarist] were living upstairs, so it was a bit of a music scene. People came and went freely. There was an itinerant Italian poet sleeping on the couch. Someone was usually playing a guitar in the front room. There was no money, so we lived on dry toast and tea. Nevertheless, rather large chunks of hashish and brownie mix would mysteriously turn up from time to time and I was put to work in the kitchen baking snacks that would knock your socks off!"

At the time, John was "learning to play sitar for one of the tracks [on his upcoming LP]. It seemed from the moment he picked up the instrument he could sit, Buddha-like, and improvise endlessly." In the end, he only used it sparingly, on "Rolling Home." With India in the air, as the Beatles took up with the Maharishi, and George Harrison using the sitar on Beatles' tracks, it was perhaps natural that musicians would be drawn to the instrument.

Inevitably, with musicians in the flat, there was plenty of song sharing going on.

"A couple of days after I arrived," Fredericks recalled, "we were in the front room swapping songs, when I played 'Sandy Grey' for him. He immediately said he wanted to record it. I'm sure John already had more than enough material of his own to fill the album, but it's typical of his generosity of spirit that he would help promote another songwriter when he himself was just starting out. It's something he has done over and over again."

Fredericks was on her way to France, where she'd meet a young Nick Drake, who was slowly pulling together ideas in Aix-la-Chappelle. She'd also encounter another British singer-songwriter across the Channel, Bridget St. John.

"I met her in the South of France in the summer of 1967," St. John said. "I'd gone there as part of my French course at University, and didn't do any studying at all. There was a little American community there. When it came time to come home, we decided to hitch back together. I remember arriving at my parents' at five in the morning, so we stayed in the boiler room until my parents were awake. She must have said, 'I know this really neat guy.' He was living with Johnny Silvo and Diz Disley in Richmond. I remember going there for the first time and meeting him and hearing him play at Bunji's and Cousins. That was my introduction to that kind of world. I never knew to go to those clubs at that time, other than up in Sheffield, where I was studying. The first summer I met [John], he helped me buy my first steel-string guitar, because I only had a nylon string before that. He was sort of my first musical friend that helped me discover more about different things. I'd watch him for different tunings."

Friendly and helpful as he was, John's focus had to be on one thing – that first album.

Outside pure pop acts, no one expected a new artist to be an overnight sensation. There was room, and time, to grow and develop over the course of several albums, for an artist to discover his voice. As Bridget St. John noted, "We weren't blitzed with so much, so we found what was actually inside us, instead of feeling like we had to sound like this, or copy this. Maybe we just had a little more solitude and a little more space...I think record companies were a lot more careful what they put out. They saw me as growing, and I'm sure Chris Blackwell felt the same about John."

It's certainly true that there was a great deal less music released than there is today. Unlike now, it was possible to take everything in. And while there were prejudices for and against different styles by listeners, the pigeonholes that defined music were far fewer. The pirate stations that operated off the coast of Britain offered an alternative to the BBC and once Radio One began in September 1967, former pirate DJ John Peel had airtime for less conventional music, giving everyone who listened a chance to experience those alternatives.

Also, in those far more primitive days of recording, budgets were much lower than they are now. A pop single would be recorded in three hours, not a minute more (due to union fees for musicians). Bands – certainly other than someone like the Beatles - didn't have the luxury of months in the studio, tinkering and experimenting endlessly. It was a case of in, slam it down, and out again. Of course, the technology was relatively primitive, with eight-track boards just beginning to creep in to the most advanced places and changing the possibilities of recorded music; most places still operated on four tracks.

John's album was definitely of the chop 'em out variety. With his discoverer, Theo Johnson, producing, it was recorded in mono in a single day, he said, "within two weeks of the first meeting [with Blackwell], at the reputed cost of £158." The bulk of the material was John's, kicking off with "Fairy Tale Lullabye," the song which had garnered him a contract in the first place. Robin Frederick's "Sandy Grey" (rumoured to have been written about a young Nick Drake, whom Frederick knew) was in there, too. "Cocain" represented the traditional side, performed in a very Bert Jansch-influenced style, and there was a Bob Dylan cover ("Don't Think Twice It's Alright"), which was almost *de rigeur* for the time.

Released in October 1967 on Island ILP 952, *London Conversation* received good reviews, but could hardly have been said to have changed the world. That John was a good guitarist was beyond dispute, but mostly what he displayed on the instrument was potential. It was easy to spot the influence of Jansch and Graham in his agile style, which still depended more on the right hand than the left, picking hard and fast. The songs were, for the most part, very much of their time, the product of a young man. The exception was "Rolling Home," where John played accomplished sitar (in a Western rather than Indian manner), accompanied by an uncredited flautist.

The vocal slur that would become one of his trademarks was still a few years away. If anything, singing was John's weakest suit. It was tuneful enough, but wispy, with no real force behind it. The phrasing was obvious; he was still very much learning his craft. And he was still an apprentice at the craft of songwriting, too. There was a broad romantic streak running through the songs – something he never lost. But they remained very rooted in the singer-songwriter sensibility of the time, folkie and innocent and sometimes even twee, which was perhaps understandable, given that he was only nineteen when the record came out.

It was someone growing out of adolescence and learning to cope with adulthood, as evidenced by the groping, uncertain thoughts of "Who's Grown Up Now" and "Ballad Of An Elder Woman." At the same time, he played and sang with the kind of assurance and confidence that set him apart. Maybe it didn't contain anything as good as Jansch's best songs, and some of the images from "Fairy Tale Lullaby" were just excruciating (and it was far from the only such song – "Golden Girl" more than gave it a run for its money), but the talent was plain for all to see. His playing was more accomplished than anyone that age had a right to be - still derivative, but with buds of individuality poking through. His experience hadn't caught up with his ambition yet, so many of the songs were projections rather than personal insights – "London Conversation" was a perfect case in point, with "Ballad Of An Elder Woman" not far behind. But only by stretching himself could he find his limits - and at that age the world seems limitless.

Among the rest of the material, "Back To Stay" stood out as the most complete piece. It arrived fully formed, a delicate work that was unassuming on the surface, but whose words reflected the confusion of growing – both up and apart. "Rolling Home" was a slender idea expanded more than really necessary by the topical use of the sitar, making "Who's Grown Up Now" something of a relief. It was "Back To Stay" from another, musically less successful angle, an experiment in writing that didn't quite come off. "This Time" could almost have come off a Bert Jansch album; Bert's style was apparent, even down to the picking style. And it would hardly have been a proper album by a young singer-songwriter without the obligatory Dylan cover; in this case "Don't Think Twice It's Alright" filled in the appropriate blank.

However, the LP certainly contained something that remained with John throughout his career – the sense of the romantic, wanting complete, total love. It's there on "Back To Stay," a revel in true love - even the cover, which shows John sitting alone on a rooftop, unkempt, dressed in denim and plimsolls, playing his guitar against a backdrop of chimney pots. But that image is countered by the youthful cynicism shown on "Run Honey Run" and his version of "Don't Think Twice It's Alright," perfect songs for someone on the point between adolescence and adulthood. John hadn't come into his own yet; he was still very much the sum of his influences.

In other words, the songs were very much a mish-mash, from a person on the brink of something, pushing out in all directions at once, and not sure which one he was going to follow. But that was fine; it was only to be expected. Very few and far between are the singer-songwriters who can come out of the blocks fully formed. Unsurprisingly, *London Conversation* didn't sell in huge quantities. It should have been the calling card to help John get gigs, but while it was useful in London, in the provinces few people had heard it and outside the capital he sometimes still had to perform with the more established Hamish Imlach. Who, after all, had heard of John Martyn?

"I went back to Sheffield for my last year of college," said Bridget St. John. "If he was playing in the neighbourhood, he'd come and stay at my digs. I remember one time he appeared there with Hamish Imlach."

Perhaps the biggest problem was that his record wasn't easy to find. It was out, but hardly any shops had it in stock. Unless you knew about it and ordered it, the chances of accidentally discovering it were small.

"I remember going into Island about six or seven months after the recording of *London Conversation* and saying, 'I'm sorry, I don't see my record in the shops'," John said. "In those days I was very ambitious and enthusiastic, and I said, 'We don't seem to be getting anywhere with this.' They said, 'Well, okay, we'll give you some money and we'll keep the publishing.' I said, 'If you keep that, it'll be very difficult for me to get a record.' At that point Blackwell took notice, because back then you weren't supposed to be that intelligent. So that was the start of our friendship and since then we've been the best of friends."

While John was playing everywhere and anywhere around the country, trying to capitalise on his hard-to-find LP, the whole scene really centred around Cousins (as Les Cousins became known), the small basement club in London's Soho. Anyone who was anyone played there and to be given a headlining show meant you were recognised as either established or up-and-coming.

For so many acoustic musicians, Cousins became a home away from home. Playing there would mean playing to a large number of friends. It offered an arena for trying new songs and working out fresh ideas.

"Things didn't have to be so polished; you could go up and play a song you'd just written," St. John explained. "Whoever was playing at Cousins, we'd go; we just wanted to be listening and out."

They were all young and eager, learning from each other; there was a sense of camaraderie, not competition. Everyone helped everyone else. The music business hadn't yet become cutthroat, more concerned with the bottom line than the music. The people in charge at the big labels might have been out of touch with the new generation, but they'd started progressive offshoots, run by people who were aware of what was happening. And the upstarts like Island were willing to take chances. They realised genius rarely came right out of the box. Or, as St. John put it, "they knew you hadn't actually reached your height when you'd only just written 12 songs." Careers were an investment and artists needed time to develop and grow into themselves: "If you're allowed time, you feel like this is *my* music."

Cousins became more than a place; it became a home for the musicians. On any given night, various artists would be spending time there, some playing, others just watching, chatting with friends, and listening.

"It was much more relaxed, the gig thing," St. John said. "We'd go to the restaurant upstairs that was run by Andy the Greek's father. We'd have a tremendous meal, and it was all such a community. Even within this big city of London it was very homey. It was wanting to hear all these different people."

One factor that aided the growth of this community was that all these people *could* come together in London. Obviously it was the home of the music business, the place to be heard and taken seriously for aspiring acts, but for many it was where you served your apprenticeship. While people endlessly reminisce about the '60s as a special time, there definitely was a glow about it, an openness that's since become formulaic and constrained. London did offer opportunities then. As the capital, it was England's most expensive city, but in the days before gentrification, expense was relative.

"Rents weren't as high," noted St. John, "so you didn't have to do other things, you could hire the people whose music you loved."

St. John herself moved down to London in 1968, after finishing her degree. She was still close to John, but had also become friendly with Pete Roche of the Liverpool Poets, who might have written poetry, but whose style was much closer to rock'n'roll – a bridge between popular music and the arts. They gave a tape of her songs to disc jockey John Peel, who, with business partner Clive Selwood, was in the process of starting up his Dandelion label and "that all happened so fast." He signed Bridget, and her single "To B Without A Hitch," backed with "Autumn Lullaby," became one of Dandelion's first two singles in 1969. That same year, her *Ask Me No Questions* was the label's debut LP (with John's composition "Back To Stay" included and John playing guitar on two tracks).

She was one of the Cousins crowd, happy to hang out inside or, on fair nights, to sit outside and talk until late. There was no rush by record labels to snap up these artists. The fertile club scene acted as an incubator, allowing them to work on their styles, to develop ideas, until they were ready. In many ways John was lucky to have been recorded so early. *London Conversation* was good, but there was still little to distinguish him from the crowd. Still, he was playing constantly, gigging more and, most especially, keeping his ears open.

His playing and writing were both evolving and tightening, and his facility with words was increasing. He had good songs and he was ready to return to the studio. Although *London Conversation* hadn't sold too well, it had been cheap to make, and Chris Blackwell, whose move into rock was beginning to pay off handsomely, was willing to keep taking a chance on John.

So, in the autumn of 1968, John began work on his second album, to be called *The Tumbler*.

"Al Stewart produced *The Tumbler*," he recounted in *ZigZag*. "I don't know why that is; I think it's because somebody said I should have a producer. Chris Blackwell, I think, said that. Probably Al volunteered, because I don't ever remember asking him. I don't think I would have been so silly. But we recorded the album in one afternoon, which is quite interesting, I think. Things were very simple in those days."

Al Stewart had arrived in London from Bournemouth (although he was born in Glasgow) in 1965 and quickly established himself in a residency at Bunji's Coffee House, before becoming the MC at Cousins. He'd appeared in a couple of BBC television shows and even on two religious radio programmes, releasing his first single in 1966, which featured session man and future guitar god Jimmy Page. His first album, like John's, arrived in 1967. But it wasn't an acoustic, folkie affair; Stewart's highly autobiographical songs were clothed with full orchestral arrangements. Three years older than John, their careers were running on almost parallel lines.

Stewart had appeared on John Peel's *Night Ride* radio show and so had John. John had chalked up his radio debut on July 10, 1968, performing "Come Along And Sing Of Summer," "Fairytale Lullabye," "The Gardeners," "Memphis Blues," and "The River." The first track would be on *The Tumbler* as "Sing A Song Of Summer," and "Memphis Blues" would become "Goin' Down To Memphis" on the album, but it was a mix of the old and the new in the session.

In fact, in those last few months of 1968, John was all over the radio. There was a September appearance on *Country Meets Folk*, and he was back with Peel on November 12. Accompanied by flautist Harold McNair, who would bring some light, jazzy touches to *The Tumbler*, he performed new material – "Different From The Back, Mr. Jelly Roll Bakers Blues" (which wouldn't appear on disc until 1973, transformed into "Easy Blues"), "Dusty," "Hello Train," "Flying On Home," and "Seven Black Roses." Most of these songs were from the upcoming LP, which was to be released in December – and John celebrated its arrival with another gig on *Country Meets Folk* three days after Christmas.

To call *The Tumbler* a transitional album is probably fair. Parts of it, like the ridiculous "Sing A Song Of Summer," with its hippie-dippy lyric, are completely of their time and saved only by the guitar work. His finger picking on the track (in open tuning) shows a huge advance from the first album, though, and the first inkling of the way he would sound in the 1970s. Just forget the words and listen to the fretwork.

In addition to McNair, guitarist Paul Wheeler (a close Cambridge friend of Nick Drake, whom John had yet to meet) offers some sympathetic second guitar on some tracks, with Dave Moses on bass. It's McNair's contribution that's the most significant, however. Born in Kingston, Jamaica, he was a jazz player, on both sax and flute (he was not Caucasian, in spite of the assertion in a *Record Collector* article). Even before John signed to Island, he'd released a solo album on the label and played on Donovan's *Wear Your Love Like Heaven*, in addition to later being a member of Ginger Baker's Airforce in the early '70s (McNair died in the '70s).

McNair displayed an easy empathy with John, capturing the moods of the songs and offering embroidery or counterpoint to "The River," "The Gardeners," and "Fly On Home."

"He did a lot for me, in that he opened me up," John said, and it's certainly true that from this point John began moving away from folk-based music. But it was quite obvious that his range was already increasing. "Goin' Down To Memphis," the good time "Fishin' Blues," and Jelly Roll Morton's "Winding Boy" were pure blues, the former exhibiting some good slide work (which John never really bothered to pursue later), showing that John was aware of the history and form of the blues. The first two were cobbled-together constructs of standard blues verses, both credited to John, but the Morton piece was relatively obscure. The two instrumentals on the disc stood as testament to the leaps and bounds John had taken as a musician. "A Day At The Sea" was complex, requiring the dexterity of someone fluent and confident on the guitar. But it was "Seven Black Roses" that stood out as the party piece (John would still occasionally play it almost a decade later at shows). The fingering was easier, but it also required moving the capo up and down the neck to make key changes while playing - no easy task. It was showy, pure flamboyance – but it worked.

There were themes of travelling ("The River," "Hello Train," and "Fly On Home"), nostalgia ("Dusty," his reminiscence of going to Hampton Court during the childhood summers spent with his mother) and songs very much of-their-time ("Sing A Song Of Summer" and "Knuckledy Crunch and Slippledee-Slee Song," both of which exhibited a childish naïveté typical of British hippiedom of the period).

But the true formation of a songwriter was falling into place. There was nothing startling about a song like "The River," but it showed a sure grasp of the way a song should be constructed and contained some strong lyrical images. "The Gardeners" was much darker, a strange vision of evil that seemed out place amongst the warmth and nostalgia that characterised so much of the disc. And like much of the record, it showcased John's guitar technique more than his voice, as if he still wasn't completely certain whether he was a guitarist or a singer-songwriter. But he was still making the youthful mistake of putting too many words in a line, overwriting his lyrics. It was something he'd grow out of quickly, but on the disappointing "Hello Train" it was firmly in evidence. Perhaps the best song was "Fly On Home," where his fretboard virtuosity was least in evidence, the chords strummed, rather than fingerpicked.

The blues songs barely count; they were simply exercises within a form, a chance for him to show what he could do. His extensive knowledge and command of the genre was apparent, but there was very little in them that showed his future creativity.

John's singing voice was definitely stronger, which may have also been due to Stewart's production work (it's worth mentioning the backwards effects he used sparingly on 'Hello Train') and there was some individuality in the phrasing. In every way he was far more confident than he'd been on his debut, just twelve months earlier. He still had a long way to go, but he'd certainly taken the first steps on the journey.

Where the cover of *London Conversation* had been a cityscape, *The Tumbler* was more pastoral, a still youthful John in white shirt and red velvet waistcoat (which had been made by Clive Palmer and given to John). And it's certainly a more relaxed record; it breathes and lets in more light and shade.

And in spite of its forays into blues, it's a very British record, which was a conscious choice, according to John.

"*The Tumbler* was influenced by my partner at the time, Paul Wheeler, a Cambridge philosophy student, who taught me the value of the British intellectual tradition, in the Graham Greene/Noel Coward sense. We decided not to play the American way, but be self-consciously British in everything. It was great, I enjoyed all that, but its potential for creativity was limited." And what exactly was the British way of playing? In essence, it came down to instrumental ability, since "I never played slicker or faster. It was a show-off British exercise."

But tugging him in the other direction was McNair, "the first fully-fledged jazzer that I had ever encountered. And I was quite astounded by his technique and confidence and his mastery of various styles. It was an inspiration for me to meet someone like that. We were never great fans or anything; he just turned my head around. At that point I was so immersed in faded denims and Woody Guthrie and all that sort of stuff, and the hobo image. To meet something as cultured and refined as your man came as a shock..."

John was sensing the seeds of change. But there was still a living to be made, and that meant playing familiar songs (familiar, at least, to the few who'd bought his records), as well as trying out new material. It was the tried and true that won out for radio sessions. There were two for *Country Meets Folk*, in March and June, 1969, in addition to one for *My Kind of Folk*, also in June, where he performed "Mr. Jelly Roll Baker Blues" and "Fairytale Lullabye" – a song that obviously hadn't lost its magic for him, perhaps as the talisman which had helped secure him a record contract in the first place.

At twenty, any teenage shyness John might have known had disappeared. He'd become effusive, a seasoned performer used to entertaining. He knew people around London and was meeting more all the time.

One of those was a young American singer-songwriter Jackson C. Frank.

Jackson Carey Frank was born in Cheektowaga, outside Buffalo, New York, in 1943. The event that changed his life happened when he was eleven. A fire at school trapped him and though he was rescued – the fire on him was extinguished with snow - there were permanent scars inside and out; Frank was burned over half his body. In some ways, he was one of the lucky ones, since eighteen of his schoolmates died, but the pain remained with him.

As a teen he played guitar in bands, but it wasn't anything serious; certainly, he hadn't dreamed of becoming a musician

When Frank turned 21, he was given access to the $110,000 insurance settlement from the fire (minus the third that went to the lawyers), and decided to enjoy his life. He'd been working on a local paper, but he left that and caught the *Queen Elizabeth* to Britain. His aim, he said, was to buy himself a Jaguar. He was going to live for today and not the future.

On the voyage over he wrote what's still his classic, seminal song, "Blues Run The Game." Frank claimed it was the first song he'd ever written, and if so, he scored straight out of the box.

In London he fell in with the singer-songwriter crowd of Soho almost by accident, and for the first time in years, he felt that he belonged.

"I enjoyed the people," he recounted. "Eccentricity was something that was socially acceptable. It wasn't a matter of you being crazy. Here [in the US] it was automatically a matter of I was crippled, therefore I had a crazy idea in my head, therefore I was going to the mental hospital."

He recorded an album, with another American expatriate, the largely-unknown Paul Simon, producing. *Jackson C. Frank* would prove to be a remarkable document of someone who briefly managed to tap a well of creativity and find release. "Blues Run The Game" would be recorded by many performers over the years, and quickly became a folk standard.

Frank, who would be diagnosed as schizophrenic, certainly acted eccentrically enough in London, according to Al Stewart, who saw him regularly around town with his then-girlfriend, future Fairport Convention singer and solo artist Sandy Denny, and performing at Cousins.

"I mean one day he would be in standard folk outfit of blue jeans and whatever, and one day I saw him in a business suit and a bowler hat... He had this long, ragged yellow hair and he was wearing a pin-striped suit and a bowler hat. He might even have been carrying an umbrella for all I remember. The effect was startling."

He was also a spendthrift, rapidly running through his entire insurance settlement – no mean feat in those days. In 1966 he returned home, eventually coming back to London in late 1968 or early 1969. A tour had been arranged, where he and Stewart would open for Fairport, who were beginning to acquire a reputation on the growing university circuit.

He returned with another new song, "Four O'Clock In The Morning," that Stewart, among others, praised. Oddly, Frank would later have no recollection of the song. Certainly while he was in England his schizophrenia became worse.

"He proceeded to fall apart before our eyes," Stewart said. "His style that everybody loved was melancholy, very tuneful things, this new one, 'Four O'Clock In The Morning' was in that style. But immediately thereafter he started doing things that were completely impenetrable. They were basically about psychological angst played at full volume with lots of thrashing. I don't remember a single word of them, but it just did not work. There was one review that said he belonged on a psychiatrist's couch."

And that was when John met Jackson.

CHAPTER 3 – John and Beverley

John and Jackson and their friends began a series of "fake Leary 'Acid Tests'," a reference to the events held in the US a few years earlier involving LSD – a drug advocated by the late Dr. Timothy Leary as a way of expanding the mind. It was a psychedelic drug and its effect on people with psychological problems was unknown. In some cases, such as Pink Floyd's Syd Barrett, it could prove very destructive.

However, in Franks' case, there seemed to be no lasting problems once the drug had worn off and he could function well enough to play. In addition to his tour with Fairport Convention, he'd scheduled a few other shows, one of them at Chelsea College of Art. John tagged along, more as a friend than an artist, although he was scheduled to play a short set (for which he was to receive £11, good money for a few minutes' work in those days).

Also on the bill was another singer-songwriter, Beverley Kutner, whom John described as "this very sexual lady, with a big hooter and great big brown eyes....and I thought I'd love to fuck that."

Frank had met Beverley shortly after arriving in London for the first time and John insisted that he make some introductions. John was smitten, but he had no idea what the future held.

By the time they met, Beverley had far more experience in the music business than John, and plenty of friends. Born in Coventry, the melodic rock'n'roll of the Everly Brothers and Buddy Holly had been the soundtrack of her adolescence.

But music hadn't been her ambition. Instead, she'd wanted to become an actress and at the tender age of fifteen received a place and grant to a drama school in London. It was a big move for someone so young, but she pursued it, and was soon attending classes with the likes of Francesca Annis and a boy named Mitch Mitchell, who had aspirations of becoming a drummer.

The true bohemian musical scene in the capital was folk music and soon Beverley found herself drawn into that world. She began dating Bert Jansch, who was acknowledged as *the* up-and-coming man. He started to teach her guitar and "he gave me confidence to begin writing my own material."

She formed her own jug band, the Levee Breakers, which played old American songs she learned from import records she managed to pick up at Dobell's record shop and taught to the group. The Levee Breakers played gigs around town, not only in the West End, but out in the suburbs. It was at one of those, in Tooting Bec, that they were seen by bassist, artist, and Beatle friend, Klaus Voorman. He was impressed by what he heard and, being a man of influence, managed to get them a contract with EMI.

The band managed one single, "Baby, I'm Leaving You," and then the label suggested that Beverley become a solo pop artist. At the time, artistic purity won out over commercial considerations. Influenced by Jansch, she turned them down.

By the next year, however, the situation had changed. Beverley and Jansch were no longer together ("He was juggling about five women at the same time and I didn't realise!") and she was performing occasionally at Cousins. That was where producer and entrepreneur Denny Cordell saw her.

Born in Buenos Aires, but raised in England, Cordell had already worked for Chris Blackwell and scored a huge hit producing the Moody Blues' single "Go Now." He'd set up his own production company (which would eventually do very well, with The Move, Joe Cocker, Leon Russell, Tom Petty, and the Cranberries among his future clients) and he saw the potential in Beverley. When he offered her a production and management deal, she didn't run away. Quite the opposite.

The first fruit of their work was also the very first single on the Deram label. Beverley covered "Happy New Year," a song by the then-unknown Randy Newman, with her own "Where The Good Times Are" on the flip.

That b-side was far from the acoustic, lulling singer-songwriter fare she'd been playing in the clubs. Instead, she was backed by some of London's top rock sessions musicians, including Jimmy Page on guitar, bassist John Paul Jones, and piano man Nicky Hopkins – in other words, half of Led Zeppelin. They proceeded to put plenty of crunch into the song, transforming it into a serious piece of rock'n'roll.

Neither that, nor her second single, "Museum," ever managed to sell many copies, but she had records out and all around town other musicians knew who she was. One of those musicians was American Paul Simon, whom Beverley had begun dating while he was in London, before "Sounds of Silence" took off and he suddenly became a star at home.

In 1967, with her musical career going nowhere in Britain, Simon offered her the chance of a lifetime – to go and play in America. And not just anywhere in the States, but at the Monterey Festival, the first of the huge music events of the late '60s. Cordell was now busy with his new find, Procol Harum, who were just enjoying a number one single with their debut, "A Whiter Shade Of Pale," so what did she have to lose?

At Monterey, in front of thousands of people, she performed three songs, backed by Lou Rawls' band, then spent the rest of the summer going around the country with Simon and Garfunkel, opening for them at venues bigger than she'd ever dreamed.

She and Simon remained an item – he even suggested they get married, so she could stay in the US, but she refused, thinking herself far too young to settle down. She did, however, record with the duo while there, on the sessions for the *Bookends* LP, and can be heard – uncredited – on "Fakin' It."

Like all dreams, this one had to end - and she woke with a start when she returned to England. There she discovered that her mother had died while she'd been away and "I just changed then. It shook me."

She was starting over, not only single again, but without a mother to turn to for advice. She was certain of one thing, however: she didn't want to travel down the pop star road Cordell had started her on. Back in London she began writing songs and trying to restart her folk career.

One person who was glad to help her was Joe Boyd.

Although not yet 30, Boyd had established an enviable reputation in music circles. Born in Boston, he'd attended university at Harvard, and began his career while still a student, distributing small blues and folk labels from his dorm room and putting on concerts.

Taking a year off from college, he headed to Los Angeles, finding a job as an office boy with promoter Les Koenig, then, by sheer luck, landing a jazz radio show on KPFK Pacifica radio.

From there he landed another job, taking a blues and gospel tour to England, and shepherding around the likes of Muddy Waters and the Rev. Gary Davis in 1964-65. Liking what he saw in London, Boyd decided to stay, hanging out in the blues and folk clubs around the city.

Back in New York, he talked with a friend, producer Paul Rothchild, and suggested putting some New York folk musicians together in a band, plus a rhythm section. The idea didn't work, but several of the musicians would regroup as the Lovin' Spoonful, achieving great success.

From there, after meeting Jac Holzman, the head of the young Elektra label, he helped put guitarist Mike Bloomfield together with the Paul Butterfield Band, creating one of the great blues groups of the '60s – who happened to end up recording for Elektra.

Holzman offer Boyd the chance to return to London and represent the label – and he jumped at it. He wasn't shy about suggesting artists.

"I brought The Incredible String Band for Elektra and a few other things. I tried...I brought them The Pink Floyd, the Move, Eric Clapton and Holzman wouldn't sign any of them."

It was frustrating and Boyd started moving in other directions. He co-founded the seminal UFO Club on Tottenham Court Road, where virtually every emerging psychedelic act cut its teeth. But his heart remained with his first love, folk music. And as police interference made UFO harder and harder to run, he started his own production company, Witchseason.

Among Boyd's favourite acts was the Incredible String Band, and he produced their work. But he also became involved with Fairport Convention and singer-songwriter Nick Drake, who was introduced to Boyd by Fairport's bassist, Ashley Hutchings.

Hearing Beverley Kutner perform, Boyd was taken by her potential too, and signed her to Witchseason, a company that, in many ways, seemed more like a family. Witchseason had established strong ties with Chris Blackwell's Island Records. By then Island was firmly enough grounded in rock to be the country's premier independent progressive label, which put Witchseason in a good position.

Boyd encouraged Beverley in her songwriting and began making plans to record an album with her. He also tried to gently push her into working with Nick Drake, who'd also recently become a protégé of his, "but he was always so shy."

On meeting John at Chelsea College of Art, Beverley asked him if he'd be interested in playing on some sessions for her. Both as a musician, and also a lad with his eye on the main chance, John agreed – then promptly vanished back to Scotland.

He was engaged to a girl in Glasgow, even if his life in London was footloose and fancy free.

"I was turning into a total freak, and really had few remnants of civilization left, and she was a very straight young lady."

They'd grown in different directions and John went home to break off the engagement. Once back in London, he began working with Beverley, a professional relationship that quickly grew into an intense, personal one. They began writing together and were very soon living together, although Boyd tried to warn her away from John.

There could have been one factor complicating the romance – Beverley had a young son, Wesley, from a previous relationship. But John and Bev loved each other and that was what mattered; the rest would work out somehow.

By now the idea of John simply backing Beverley had become history. They had a partnership – in fact a union, as they married and became John and Beverley Martyn during the first half of 1969.

As Boyd said flatly, "they recorded together because after I signed Beverley, she met and moved in with John. They wanted to be romantic and musical partners."

They played Boyd some of the material they'd been working on - and it was impressive. John joined Beverley as a Witchseason artist and a deal was made with Island for a record. Notably, however, although they were a duo, John was still playing solo gigs, including a radio appearance on *My Kind of Folk* in June, where he played two songs, neither of them new.

Boyd's idea was to record the pair in America, a country already familiar to Beverley, but an entirely new experience for John.

"I introduced them to Paul Harris, pianist and arranger with Stephen Stills," Boyd recollected. "He took them to Woodstock to rehearse and we recorded in New York City."

The legendary Woodstock festival was on the horizon, but hadn't happened yet. Woodstock, upstate from Manhattan, was still a sleepy town, one that had become a favourite with artists, writers and musicians. Bob Dylan made his home there, as did The Band, whose recent *Music from Big Pink* had a profound roots influence on musicians on both sides of the Atlantic.

It was a complete contrast to London - quieter, but still buzzing with a fierce energy. Jimi Hendrix was virtually a neighbour; he'd arrive in Woodstock "every Thursday in a purple helicopter, stay the weekend, and leave on the Monday. He was amazing...a good lad."

Teaming them up with American musicians who could play in both a rock and roots manner (and this was decades before roots music became the fashion) was an inspiration on Boyd's part. There were some excellent players in England, but very, very few of them could swing, especially the drummers. Like so many people at the time, Boyd would have listened to The Band's debut, with its down home feel, yet sophisticated writing and performances.

According to John, the money for the trip didn't come from Witchseason or Island – probably just as well, because it was (by British standards) an expensive trip. Instead the bills went to Warner Brothers, who'd signed John and Beverley for America.

"It was Warner Brothers who paid. Joe Boyd was managing me at the time and he said, 'You're going to America on Thursday,' and I said, 'Oh great'."

One of the first people John and Beverley met in Woodstock was Band drummer Levon Helm, with whom John quickly established a strong bond (Helm and John would record together again in the '90s and they'd remain good friends for the rest of John's life). Given his prodigious talent as a drummer, especially his feel for a song and a rhythm, he was a natural for the drum stool on the sessions.

Another Woodstock resident, Harvey Brooks, was drafted in on bass, and Mothers of Invention drummer Billy Mundi was featured on "Go Out And Get It."

John, Beverley and young Wesley settled into the bucolic paradise and began working with Harris, who had musical director duties for the disc, in addition to playing piano and organ. To have a musical director at all seemed a little strange, but this album was going where few, if any, had gone before. Not only was it mixing British and American acoustic music, it was adding a band into the equation. Harris was a seasoned professional who'd produced electric music for the Doors and acoustic music for Crosby, Stills and Nash.

All in all, the Martyns spent three months in New York, most of it in Woodstock. But the recording sessions, which John described as "very one-off, very swift," took place in New York City – rumour has it that the sessions actually took five days, with another three days for mixing. John Wood, who'd become Joe Boyd's engineer of choice, was flown over to work on the album and Boyd himself produced it, although John was a little dubious of the "producer" label.

"In Joe's case it was more of a discipline thing," he explained to journalist Andy Childs. "He used to just say, 'Well, that won't do.' We used to have disagreements. He doesn't have as free an approach as I'd like to see."

There was never a great deal of love lost between John Martyn and Joe Boyd. Indeed, even as they worked together, not just on this album, but until 1971, when Witchseason folded, there appeared to be a lot of distrust, with Beverley caught very much in the middle.

"I don't think Joe Boyd ever really liked me, and he probably still doesn't," John said (and this appears to be true). "I think he thinks I'm a good musician, but I've always had personality differences with the man."

In spite of bringing in Harris, the album John and Beverley were making wasn't originally conceived as a full band album – and in some ways it isn't, as little pieces like "Woodstock," John's paean to their temporary home, show. The real influence seemed to have come from John's friendship with Levon Helm.

"I very much liked Levon Helm and I was inspired by that. [The band idea] crept in."

It's interesting to note that although Boyd had originally conceived of this as a Beverley Martyn solo album, the final record only contained three of her compositions, against seven from John. Of course, she and John sang together, with the blissful sound of newlyweds, but at times it's impossible not to hear it as a John Martyn album with Beverley Martyn. But it was still a very far cry from the original concept of him backing her up on her own disc. Somewhere along the line, either because of love or the sheer weight of John's personality, it became something different, with John as the prominent figure and Bev as the sidekick, the little lady who was granted some time in the spotlight, a feeling that may have caused some bitterness in her, as if the whole project had been hijacked from under her, although that never seemed to be deliberate. John was ambitious to an extent, but he wouldn't have sabotaged his new marriage to further his career.

As a band album, it was certainly very different. Apart from John's electric guitar work, which was spare – and notably, on the closer "Would You Believe Me?" included his first tentative foray into using the Echoplex unit that would become one of his trademarks during the '70s – this was largely an acoustic album with a rhythm section of keyboard, bass, and drums. It focused on the songs and the performances of them rather than any kind of instrumental virtuosity. Indeed, much of the album hewed to a philosophy of "less is more" – making people like Helm ideal for the sessions (although he only played on two of the tracks; actually, only five cuts actually use drums, in spite of the reputation the record has).

John insisted that it was the first acoustic album to use drums, which may or may not be true; several other similar records from the period utilise drums. Likewise, whether it was as influential as he's often claimed is a matter of debate. What's certain is that it was very, very different, an Anglo-American hybrid that worked very well. The British sense of melody and harmony was set against the sprung American rhythms to great effect – you can make a case for it being one of the precursors of the Americana movement of the '90s.

That John, in particular, had rapidly and hungrily embraced America is quite apparent from the writing, which represented a seismic shift from his previous, precise work. On this album John's songwriting changed dramatically. With the exception of the finger-picked "Woodstock" and the whimsical "Traffic-Light Lady" – just to show he hadn't completely abandoned what he'd been doing before – there was a much looser feel to everything. Most of John's material was strummed, rather than picked, and there was a definite funkiness to pieces like Beverley's "Sweet Honesty," propelled by Helm's backbeat. Beverley's other pieces are gentler, both "Can't Get The One I Want" and "Tomorrow Time" (the latter decorated by both John's guitar and John Simon's lovely harpsichord). While "The Ocean" is credited on the CD reissue to John, Beverley sang it, and it has the feel of one of her pieces. Perhaps it was natural that their work would seem so different, as they were still coming to know each other and both were used to writing – and performing – alone.

Rhythm is an important factor in John's songs on *Stormbringer*. Not merely because of his strumming, but because of the way he interacts and depends on a rhythm section for the disc. It probably finds its climax on "Would You Believe Me?," the most fully-developed piece in this style. John and Beverley's voices blend in a gloriously rough-hewn manner, while most of the accents come from Herbie Lovell's drums. The lyric (possibly about John's former fiancée) show the kind of obliqueness that would become more typical in the future, and the subtle use of the Echoplex , a tool John had just begun to experiment with, lends washes of sound. His lead playing was the most expansive he'd try until the '80s, with plenty of little fills and runs. It sounds almost like an American Richard Thompson, not only in tone, but also style. (Interestingly, at one point he credited the fact that he began playing electric to "a bunch of Chicanos. We were going to be a pre-Santana Latin band" – difficult, since Santana already existed – "and they introduced me to Pharaoh Sanders' records...that opened my mind like you wouldn't believe. Fuck me, it was gorgeous. I wanted that roar and sustain.").

It was a seismic shift in writing style for John, vastly different to the filigreed fingerpicking outings that had characterized his first two albums. "Go Out And Get It" and "John The Baptist" were far more basic, seemingly almost thrown together without any delicacy, very pleasingly raw and filled out by the other musicians. Of these, "Stormbringer" and "John The Baptist" worked best, the former a lovely minor-key piece, the latter one of the disc's standouts, from the casual "I'm John the Baptist/and this is my friend Salome" opening to the way the two voices worked around each other, with Helm's drumming providing just enough push to keep things moving, utterly in the pocket. By "Would You Believe Me?" he'd come close to the feel, if not the execution, of *Music from Big Pink*, filtered through his own consciousness, and with the vocal slur just in evidence on the horizon.

There was more delicacy and craft about Beverley's songs, even if she only had three of them. "Can't Get The One I Want" was decorated with soft strings and piano, an expansive, developed song with sophisticated changes that worked perfectly well without John. "Sweet Honesty" revelled in its gentle funk, a vehicle for Beverley's sensual voice, at this point much more mature than her husband's as an instrument. That was confirmed with the wistfulness of "The Ocean," with its lingering descending melody, and John's electric guitar offering an *obbligato* to Beverley's languid vocal. Beverley looked at melody in an entirely different way from John, as she showed with "Tomorrow Time," where the harpsichord framed an unusual, almost dissonant chord sequence that she managed to tame as an album track, although it wasn't something that could ever have been considered as a single.

It's tempting to see this album as the foundation of the John Martyn sound of the '70s. And it's certainly fair to pinpoint it as the place where the John Martyn vocal slur began, albeit in its early, formative stages. For the first time he sounded comfortable in a recording studio. That might have been because he was working and interacting with other musicians and a real producer, making him feel less naked and exposed than he'd been on his previous discs, where the clothing provided by others for his songs was at best gauzy, if it existed at all. He was growing and inevitably had new ideas for his music and this offered the chance, the people, and the budget to make them real.

And, for all the wariness between them, it might also have been the fact that Boyd was able to squeeze exceptional performances out of John. Neither Theo Johnson nor Al Stewart, his previous producers, were skilled in the art of working with artists in the studio. Boyd was coming into the project thoughtfully, and with a relatively lengthy track record. However quickly the tracks were laid down, it was still much longer than the single day John had been used to (and as someone who'd recorded singles, Beverley had probably operated in the three-hours-for-a-track deadline standard in the pop industry in the '60s). There was the luxury of getting inside, and refining a vocal. The songs themselves weren't complex, by any means. The trick was what you did with them. So, instead of a take that emphasised John's playing ability (the reason Beverley had originally asked for his help), he had to work harder to find and express the emotion of a song.

For the first time on one of John's records, arrangements became important and full credit to Paul Harris for the job he did. He never overcrowded a track and he allowed the songs to breathe. Certainly it was enough to make John think. Previously it had been a case of writing a song and playing it, as it was for any solo artist. Even on *The Tumbler* the other instruments became an afterthought, tacked on to what were essentially solo performances. Now both he and Beverley had to operate as part of a larger unit.

A standard folk album it definitely wasn't. Instead, there was a bite to it and a bit of a sting in the tail. The possibility was that it would alienate those few fans John already had – a little like Dylan going electric in 1965, but on a much, much smaller scale – who liked him as the sweet, acoustic folkie. But, at twenty one, why shouldn't he reinvent himself? There was no reason to put himself inside a single box and stay there. Nor did Beverley come from a folk background. They could start over together musically with a completely clean slate.

It was possibly the first British record to replicate the electric rusticity of *Music from Big Pink*. Certainly it was far ahead of its time, not just in its marriage of British and American styles, but in its feel – no British record had managed that before. At the same time, it was *so* different that no one knew quite what to make of it.

For the era, there was a long gap between the recording session and the album's release, from mid 1969 to early 1970. The LP was preceded by a single, "John The Baptist" and "The Ocean" in January 1970, heralding the new decade with a fresh sound. The entire LP followed a month later. *Record Song Book* called it "one of the most beautiful albums you're likely to hear in a long time," and that was just one of a string of great reviews for a record John called "very innocent in retrospect."

Back in England, John and Beverley were performing live as a duo (not always easy, given a young child at home that precluded concerted touring). They only did one radio session together (on *Top Gear*), laying down "Traffic Light Lady," "Tomorrow Time" and two new pieces, "Give Us A Ring" and "Road To Ruin," showing that writing for the new album was already underway. John also did a solo "Seven Black Roses," which was still his party piece, and later that year guested with Bridget St. John, singing harmony on his own "Back To Stay." Their most high profile appearance at the time was a concert in London that featured a remarkably shy Nick Drake as the opening act. Where John was effusive, a natural communicator onstage, Drake was introverted to a crippling extent. Unfortunately, communication with an audience was a necessity; the music couldn't just speak for itself.

John had come to know Drake through Beverley, who'd been introduced to him by his champion, Joe Boyd. Drake, a product of Marlborough public school and Cambridge, might have seemed like an unlikely close friend for the far more down-to-earth John, but the two quickly developed a close bond.

On returning to London, John and Bev had found a flat in Hampstead, which turned out to be close to Drake's flat, and he became a regular visitor, always welcome and accepted, whether he chose to talk or simply sit – which, according to many reports, he often did.

Stormbringer was meant to bring John and Beverley to a wider audience. It should have done, but in early 1970 it didn't fit into any kind of niche. It wasn't a rock record with plenty of lead guitar. It wasn't prog-rock, which was finding plenty of favour with fans. And it wasn't an acoustic singer-songwriter disc, either. It managed to fall neatly between every stool, which was reflected in its sales.

Not that the Martyns were deterred, by any means. They'd loved Woodstock, especially John, and they came home inspired and full of songs. John even attempted to learn saxophone in an effort to sound like Pharaoh Sanders. After a short while he decided he was "too old to learn the sax, which is why I got the fuzz pedal and Echoplex" (although he'd obviously used echo in New York).

By spring of 1970 they were back in the studio with new material. Once again, Joe Boyd was producing and John Wood engineering at Sound Techniques in London. Paul Harris had been brought over to offer continuity from the previous record, arranging (with John this time) and playing piano.

Yet the songs had a different feel from the material they'd recorded in New York. If anything, they were a little sparer and certainly more atmospheric, as a listen to Beverley's "Auntie Aviator" shows. The bass and drum pattern is minimal, with Harris' piano and Bev's voice front and centre. Even John's guitar is relegated to a minor rhythm role, until he takes off for a swooping electric solo that indicates he'd figured out how to use the Echoplex - and the track builds until it fades. It's a superb song, one of the centrepieces of the record.

Road to Ruin notably also features horns, especially the saxophone of South African jazzman Dudu Pukwana, who's highlighted on the title cut, "Sorry To Be So Long," and "Say What You Can." Introduced by Boyd, Pukwana proved very much a kindred spirit to John, a man who liked to drink a little (although, at this time, John certainly wasn't drinking to excess on any regular basis). He introduced John to African music, from Nigerian highlife to South African jazz, especially Chris McGregor's outfit, Brotherhood of Breath, in which Pukwana played (he also had two bands of his own, Spear and Assegai). Since arriving in England to escape the apartheid regime of South Africa, the musicians had established a reputation on Britain's small jazz/avant-garde circuit, bringing a different sense of rhythm and melody to jazz.

As John said, suddenly "I was listening to a lot more. It was osmosis, really. I'd been to a lot more live gigs and I was hanging out with musicians non-stop, really. So I was exposed to more stuff every day – peoples' record collections, gigs they took me to, gigs I went to."

The music of Pharoah Sanders affected him most. Born Ferrell Sanders in 1940, he started on clarinet, switching to tenor sax in high school, playing blues gigs in his native Little Rock, Arkansas, before moving to Oakland, California to go to college. There he started investigating be-bop and even free jazz. Then he went to the centre of jazz, New York. At first he had no luck and often had to pawn his sax and sleep on the subway. However, in 1964, the great John Coltrane heard him and invited Sanders to join his band. After Coltrane's death in 1967 he began leading his own ensembles, showcasing his own sound - raw, but filled with rich overtones and a tremendous sustain.

Sanders' music hit John powerfully, to the extent that he began using the Echoplex to try and achieve the same kind of sustain on guitar that Sanders managed on sax. From a nice effect, it would gradually

46

become a vital component of his sound. Sanders would also influence John's singing. The slur had started in New York, but he would take it several stages further in an attempt to replicate the sound of a tenor sax with his voice.

All that lay in the future, however. For now there was a record to be made. Wells Kelly, who'd been one of the founders of American chart popsters Orleans, drummed on all the tracks except "Auntie Aviator"; his seat on that was taken by Mike Kowalski, who'd also appear on Nick Drake's *Bryter Layter* (before going on to work with Shuggie Otis, the Beach Boys and Crazy Horse). In other words, that American backbeat, which had been such a vital component of *Stormbringer* would still be in evidence. Fairport Convention's Dave Pegg and Alan Spenner from the Grease Band divided bass guitar duties between them and Pentangle's Danny Thompson played double bass on "New Day," the start of a long relationship between him and John.

However, *Road to Ruin* built on the solid foundation created by the American work. Congas, courtesy of Traffic's Rocky Dzidzornu, were integral and the use of horns (Pukwana, Lyn Dobson, and Ray Warleigh) beefed up the sound with a more formal, Anglicised jazziness.

It was an English take on what John and Beverley had achieved in America. The songwriting was more developed, with three of the tracks joint John and Beverley compositions. Beverley was credited alone with "Primrose Hill," about the area of London where John had lived when they met, and John contributed the light "New Day," which harked back to *The Tumbler* with its flute line over the song, although Bev's harmonies gave the song a gauzy beauty. Old friend Paul Wheeler, who played guitar on *The Tumbler*, wrote the sublime "Give Us A Ring."

It's an album about travelling and returning home, and hardly as obsessed with death as the title and the cover (taken from a brooding Max Ernst print) would indicate.

It was, John explained, "an adolescent's view of mortality, you know the idea, isn't it all fun, we're doomed but we may as well enjoy it: we're all going one way, but we may as well get down to it while we're here."

In many ways, it's relaxed and enjoyable throughout and the basic idea crosses the Atlantic well. However, for all that, it proved to be difficult record to make.

"With *Road to Ruin*, nothing much had happened with their careers, despite great reviews," Boyd, who picked the musicians, explained. "John never really allowed Bev to perform with him, despite that being the original idea, so by *Road to Ruin* there were problems personal and professional."

And Beverley agreed that "John wanted more and more control. I just got pushed further into the background. He didn't want to do gigs with me."

At the time, though, they remained a committed and firm family unit, especially since Beverley was pregnant again.

Almost inevitably, there were tensions between John and Boyd. John was less than impressed by Boyd's production technique, in later years accusing him of just sitting in the control booth and reading a newspaper. And Boyd, in turn, was far from happy with the control John was exercising over Beverley and the music. However, on the recorded evidence, she played a greater role on *Road to Ruin* than she had on *Stormbringer*. The sessions were protracted, taking weeks instead of the days they had taken in New York, with numerous overdubs, rather than most of the material being laid down live in the studio.

However, the results were compelling. *Road to Ruin* was more focused than its predecessor. Even the title cut, which moved from song to jam, worked - John's guitar interacting well with the horns, filling and adding carefully; it was as loose as the record got, an enjoyable romp to finish off the disc (and, possibly, to fill it out – at less than 38 minutes, including a good four minutes of jamming, it wasn't overly generous on time).

By transposing the concept they'd developed in America to Britain, the songs received very different shadings. American musicians, at least the ones who'd been on *Stormbringer*, brought the natural simplicity of country and funk to the table; their counterparts across the Atlantic didn't really have that facility at their fingertips. As a result, the songs on *Road to Ruin* became more ornamented, although Paul Harris and Wells Kelly brought a solid American grounding to the disc. One notable change was Ray Warleigh's sax on "Primrose Hill," which took things in the jazzier direction John had barely begun to explore on *The Tumbler*. Lyrically the whole album was a series of impressions of America and returning home, occasionally embarrassing ("all those groovy guys") and sometime profound. Since Beverley only had one song that was purely hers on the disc ("Primrose Hill"), this could almost be seen as a transitional album between *Stormbringer* and the relaunching of John's solo career. At the same time, it's the mirror image of *Stormbringer*, both in songwriting style and execution. Folk it's definitely not, inhabiting a grey area between acoustic music and pop, with a breezy lightweight style typified by "Parcels."

"Auntie Aviator," lyrically whimsical, was this album's "John The Baptist," musically adventurous, giving John a brief outing on electric guitar to show what he'd learned and how he was developing.

More than anything, though, *Road to Ruin* had the feel of a stop gap. Songs like "New Day" were pleasant, but carried little weight. It was a telling that on an album by two songwriters, the strongest track was written by someone else. "Sorry To Be So Long" attempted to replicate the ramshackle American funk that had served so well on *Stormbringer*, but it became a muddied mess, with everything too busy. Both "Tree Green" and "Say What You Can" were slight compositions, both eminently forgettable in spite of their sweet sentiments.

Not all experiments work, and this was one at best sparked half-heartedly. There wasn't enough material and the songs that existed were far from the best either of them had penned. Even the title track, as a song, was little more than a fragment. It was, however, a precursor of the future, both of John's guitar style – acoustic and the atmospheric electric - and his singing, which had taken on more of the style that would become one of his '70s trademarks. And while the jam that took up over the last four minutes seemed tacked on, it could be seen as a step towards "Glistening Glyndebourne," but without the Echoplex in the central role. Here John was content to stay on the fringes and let the horns blow.

American musician and journalist Brian Cullman met John and Beverley in the summer of 1970, after they'd recorded *Road to Ruin*, and sensed no personal problems between them. Through "a series of very lucky mishaps, without any qualifications whatsoever, I wound up being hired as the London editor of *Crawdaddy*. My one qualification was that I was in London." Just eighteen, he'd been looking for a summer job before college, and "I'd never written anything more substantial than a couple of record reviews for a high school newspaper."

Certainly Cullman enjoyed a charmed life in London. He met the late Australian journalist Lillian Roxon, who introduced him to *Oz*'s Richard Neville. From there his circle widened. It was the era of the underground press and soon he ran into Barry Miles.

"He'd been the London editor and facilitator for *Crawdaddy*. He was moving to New York, I think to write a biography of Alan Ginsberg. Suddenly they didn't have anyone in London, they didn't have any money, and someone suggested me, pretty much out of desperation, and I was made their London editor...times being what they were, I was taken seriously, and I was given licence to go off and talk to anyone I wanted to."

Cullman's interest was folk-rock, especially the stable of artists Joe Boyd had established under his Witchseason umbrella. As soon as he had credentials, he went to the Witchseason office to start interviewing them for the magazine. Witchseason was happy to help, "so the first people I met were John and Beverley, Sandy Denny, Robin Williamson, Nick Drake – Nick I met through John and Beverley – and Richard Thompson. I think I met them all within a week, in June of '70, then spent the summer in their orbit, going to gigs and recording sessions."

According to Cullman, by then "they were in the process of recording *Road to Ruin*, or had just recorded it. They played it for me on a reel-to-reel tape. I'd met Paul Wheeler through them, and I was aware of the cast of characters."

John and Beverley's flat became a nexus. Not only was Nick Drake spending time there, it became a magnet to Cullman too.

"I think I spent a lot of time with them socially, but I was so new to doing everything, and such a puppy. I'm not sure I was clear on the boundaries between being a journalist, being a fan, and being what I wanted to be, which was a fellow musician. So whether I spent more time than they would have liked, I'm not sure – I think they were very indulgent. That summer was a really lovely time, and they seemed really happy, with a nice crew of people around them. Over the years that changed a little, I think. John's guard went up a bit more – Beverley was always very welcoming."

Even around John and Beverley, Nick Drake was quiet. He could be relatively forthcoming when he was alone with Beverley, but with John he sometimes appeared chronically shy. Cullman's relationship with Drake was primarily through John and Bev.

"The second or third time I was at their place, he was there. I hadn't heard of him, nothing of his had come out in the States. He was just in the corner of their living room, rolling joints. John took me aside and said, 'You've got to hear his stuff,' and pressed a copy of *Five Leaves Left* [Drake's debut on Island] on me. John was clearly his protector and champion. I was probably more effusive about it than John might have liked, I think. He wanted me to like him, but not that much! From that point on, whenever there was any kind of social gathering that I was privy to, Nick was always there, but was always in the background."

That John might take Drake under his wing was natural. He was extroverted, in a way Drake could never manage, and respected enough that he was listened to – at least by some. And he recognised Drake's undeniable talents as both songwriter and guitarist. In fact, except for the established greats on acoustic guitar, he was one of the few John could really respect for his abilities. And the fact that he was a good, platonic friend of Beverley's undoubtedly helped. People helped people.

At the same time, John had an ambitious streak. He wanted to be, if not top dog, then up there with the leaders of the pack. He had great faith in himself and what he could do – a necessity for any artist in any field. At the same time, his ego wasn't out of control.

"The person I knew in the few years that I was around him was so warm, so sweet, was incredibly generous and gracious with his time, with his energy, with his friends," Cullman noted. "Modest is probably the wrong word, as he was always very aware of his talent, but he didn't take himself seriously. In fact, whenever I'd start to take him too seriously he'd be the first to take himself down."

John's influences certainly intrigued Cullman. When he visited the Hampstead flat, "I'd snoop through his records to see what he was listening to, to try and figure out where he was. The two people he was most keen on were Hamza El Din, the Nubian oud player – he had a couple of his Vanguard albums – and Geoff Muldaur – he had that Prestige album (1964's *Geoff Muldaur*). I think John had pretty much learned everything on there, and he'd go out and play at least half the songs on it."

There was a certain irony in John's idolisation of Muldaur, since Muldaur and Joe Boyd had been close friends in Boston, and John and Boyd, although they had a working relationship, could never have been called friends.

While much of the Muldaur album was recorded in a standard guitar tuning (EADGBE), John was starting to experiment with alternate tunings. Some, like DADGAD – credited to Davy Graham – were standards on the folk scene, while others, such as lowering the bottom string to D (known as drop D), were part of the blues tradition. According to Cullman, John "did a lot of drop D tuning, and I'd pick up his guitar, at least surreptitiously. Once in a while he'd put it into a DADGAD tuning. When he was sitting around he'd play in a drop D, which he used for a lot of songs from that period." He'd apparently yet to discover the C tuning that would become his mainstay in later days, as Cullman said "if he put it into his C tuning, he didn't leave it in that."

It was a time of transition for John and Beverley. They were happy enough in Hampstead, with plenty of friends around. But Beverley was pregnant, and where they were living was too small.

The era of "getting it together in the country" had passed, but the idea of moving out of London had its attractions, especially as rents increased. Somewhere a bit quieter and cheaper sounded good, especially as John would need to spend more time on the road. Obviously, with a young child at home and another on the way, the onus fell on John to be the breadwinner, and to play solo gigs. While *Stormbringer* hadn't sold well, it had garnered excellent reviews and John's star was beginning to rise. The same fate would await *Road to Ruin* on its release in November 1970.

The downside was that it scuppered the duo plans. Much of the material from the last two albums had centred on the pair of them and, at best, there could only be selected performances with Mr. And Mrs. Martyn together – a situation which continued until at least 1972.

According to interviews Beverley has given, John became more of a "control freak" about their relationship. He felt that a woman's place was at home "and that was that." Beverley began to find herself pushed into the background.

"I remember [John] used to say to me I could be creative staying at home rearing our children rather than making music."

It wasn't necessarily a meanness, or overweening solo ambition. And alcohol definitely wasn't a factor, according to Cullman.

"He smoked a fair amount of weed, but in '70 or '71 I don't think I ever saw him drunk. He would drink and he'd be really effusive and funny, but I never saw him get nasty or out of control. I would see him get stoned, but people would get stoned in each other's homes. It felt like everyone was at the same level, all be a little bit high together. Nick would be the only one who'd be so out of it that he couldn't get upstairs or across the street."

It was around this time, during 1971, that the family did leave London for a more bucolic life down on the South Coast. Hastings was a pleasant little seaside resort whose great claim to fame was its battle in 1066, when William the Conqueror made England into a Norman country and changed the course of history.

They settled into a house in the Old Town, in the centre of Hastings, where John quickly became part of the landscape in the local pubs and shops. Even today there's real affection for him in the area, even though he moved away in 1977. He left a mark on the place.

CHAPTER FOUR – Blessing the Weather

Hastings had an effect on John, too, and a very good one. Getting out of London and being surrounded by the unfamiliar seemed to spark his creative juices. It wasn't so much that he was writing new songs, as adopting an entirely new direction in his music. The jazz he was listening to had a huge impact on the way he thought about structuring a song.

Previously, his work had been very formal, taking the accepted forms of verses, choruses, bridges, and solos. Now he started looking at something a little looser and less dependent on the lyrics, if only because he considered himself not much of a poet. It was the feel of the music that became important, the way the pieces worked together.

His acoustic guitar playing changed radically. He'd begun playing more rhythmically over the last two albums, but that was strumming along with a rhythm section. He no longer had that luxury and he needed to essentially become his own rhythm section. And since necessity is all too often the mother of invention, he developed the string slap, bringing his fingernails down on the string to create a backbeat. Given that he was already an outstanding fingerpicker, the two styles combined to create something that was unique, immediately identifiable as John Martyn.

Beginning in America, he'd also begun to change the way he sang. The careful enunciation of the first two albums slowly faded away. It was still decidedly British, but it placed less emphasis on the words themselves and far more on the way they were expressed. He began to draw out notes and to slur and swoop between them in imitation of the glide of a tenor sax.

Putting everything together, the result was an entirely new John Martyn sound. There was the feel of jazz in there, with everything open-ended to accommodate improvisation. But much of it was firmly acoustic and rooted in folk music, which kept him connected to the audience he'd acquired in his more formative stages.

As if all those changes weren't enough, he'd been experimenting with the Echoplex and learning how to use it effectively within his own style. A kind of taming of the beast, it allowed him to emphasise and experiment with rhythm and the layering of sound; in many ways, it made him into a one-man band, creating the rhythm and topping it with overlapping lines. They faded away, to be replaced by new ones. It freed him to be more than a solo artist. By judicious use of pickups (a transducer in the guitar and another pickup in the soundhole of his acoustic), he could control the texture and flow of sound, moving back and forth between electric and acoustic sounds.

All in all, everything led toward a greater spontaneity in the music. That was the undoubted influence of jazz, but it was also something he'd come across in America, where the speed of the *Stormbringer* sessions had been so satisfying. It was perhaps also a reaction to the grind of recording *Road to Ruin*, where so much had seemed like pulling teeth.

A new town, a new beginning.

Almost.

The original plan had been for John and Beverley to continue making albums together, but things behind the scenes were changing in ways they couldn't anticipate. Joe Boyd, who, while running Witchseason, had effectively been a buffer between the couple and Island Records, decided to move back to the US and work for Warner Brothers, having received an offer he simply couldn't refuse. He sold Witchseason to Island for a pittance and vanished very quickly, leaving a vulnerable Nick Drake at the mercy of the record company, with just a few friends to care for him ("Look after Nick for me, Bev.")

It also meant that John and Beverley were now dealing directly with Island. For John, that was simply a reversion to the way things had been a few years before, but it was entirely new to Beverley. And the company was being run in a slightly more corporate fashion, as business and profits became more serious.

There are different stories about what happened next. The only certainty was that Island decided they didn't want another John and Beverley Martyn album, following the failure in sales of the previous two.

One version has it that the plan was for them each to record a solo disc, and that because of family responsibilities – Beverley gave birth to Mhairi, the daughter she had with John, in 1971 – Beverley's never happened.

The other version, and one that John reiterated over the years, was that Island simply decided there was more of a future in John as a solo act; they didn't want Beverley any more (although she'd still occasionally perform gigs with him, and she did do a little singing on *Bless the Weather*).

Brian Cullman theorised that while "it wasn't that John was being pushed as a solo artist, as he started doing guitar pyrotechnics and taking on a slightly harder-edged persona, [Beverley] was being pushed...I wouldn't say offstage, but she didn't have as clear an identity to present. Also, with children at home, suddenly one person takes on the role as caretaker. I think that happened very naturally, I don't even know that it was discussed. The sense I always had was that she just always assumed she would be with the kids and John would be with the guitar."

Joe Boyd largely concurred with that assessment, saying "I think John wanted Bev to stay at home, not perform with him, and Island, who had signed him originally as a solo artist, naturally wanted the LP to reflect the touring situation."

Chris Blackwell, the head of Island, doesn't remember exactly, but he was willing to speculate that "knowing how I think and how I am, I wouldn't have said to John that we didn't want another record with Beverley. So I don't know what went on."

However it actually happened, the final result was that John would be making a solo album. And, he said, Island wasn't especially generous in its budget, giving him only £6000 for the project.

Unlike record labels these days, in the '60s and '70s companies were willing to invest in their artists and allow them the time to grow and develop their music. Of course, if there was no financial return in the long-term, then performers would be dropped, but there was definitely a longer shelf life. That didn't mean they received big budgets for every LP, but £6000 was a reasonable investment in John, given his track record. At the very least, they wouldn't be losing money.

"He was very good, and his records didn't cost a lot," observed Blackwell. "My approach to the record business came from being a fan of jazz, of jazz music, jazz artists, and jazz record labels. If you make something good, it's not too expensive and it sells reasonably well, that's fine. It's never been about hits."

It wasn't a time when an artist could live off the advance for a record, certainly not someone on John's level. Labels weren't lining up to throw money at him. His bread and butter, the way he supported his family, was by gigging, which meant endless travel up and down the country. John was just graduating to the more lucrative university circuit, which paid far better than the folk clubs – but was also more limited. You could only tour so much before a saturation point was reached, and that happened quite quickly.

One of those tours was with a new Island act, Claire Hamill, a teenager from Middlesborough who'd just released her debut, *One House Left Standing*. John had played guitar on the two opening tracks, "Baseball Blues" and "The Man Who Cannot See Tomorrow's Sunshine."

He'd guested, Hamill said, "because Chris Blackwell was producing the album, along with John McCoy, my manager, and Chris thought it would be good to get John on the album. Not just from a musical point of view, but John was up-and-coming, and Chris thought it would be good to have young up-and-coming stars on to draw attention to me, I think. So it was a record company/producer decision. I didn't know John's work at the time. I'd heard of him, and I might have heard something, but I didn't know him. He plays marvellously on the album, and I'm thrilled he did."

Hamill was present when John overdubbed his guitar parts.

"I was there at all the sessions, because it was such a thrill for me to be there. It was very quick to record; I think it took about three weeks. Everything was done very much live, onto tape, and you had to play it and get it right. It wasn't the norm to spend a long time recording albums. In the studio I got along fine with John, but I was very wet behind the ears, I was very naïve. I think John was being kindly to me, he was very sweet and nice, but we were both a bit distant."

Hamill supported John on his tour in 1971, his first time through the colleges. They were both openers for another Island act, Jess Roden's Bronco (later in the year John would be the third act on a bill with Bronco and Mott the Hoople). He'd yet to record *Bless the Weather*, but he'd developed his new style, and was giving the Echoplex its full debut after learning how to utilise it properly. He was away from home and family for the first time in a couple of years and possibly feeling the freedom, especially as his gigs were receiving widespread praise and a buzz was beginning to circulate about him.

"When I toured with him he was starting to be wild," Hamill recalled. "He was starting to wow everybody, and everybody was talking about him. He was certainly smoking a lot of dope by then. All that scene was for artists and people in the rock scene, not the general public. Maybe a few students were doing it, but it wasn't as common as it is now."

Hamill retains fond memories of the tour, and the way the two acts complemented each other.

"It was a wonderful pairing when I toured with him. My songs were very saccharine sweet in a way, a young girl's look at love, and the songs were very innocent. John's were much more punchy and raw and masculine. So you had these very feminine and masculine acts. He didn't have Danny Thompson on the first tour we did, but we did another tour later, and there were the two of them. I didn't hang out with him and Danny too much!"

One of the dates on that first tour was Glasgow. As an indication of the lack of luxury for performers, Hamill recalled "the dressing room – the dressing room? Blimey! It was a room with paint pots. No chairs, just paint pots. It was a state, nothing to sit on, nothing to hang anything on."

Enjoying life on the road, John had already begun to enter into the party spirit that would be his guide for the next several years, and was starting to indulge more heavily in alcohol.

"The amount that man used to drink...he's a legend," Hamill said. "Doubles, trebles – in the pub he'd order treble vodkas. I couldn't keep up with him – I tried! He was always a party animal. Wherever you were with him, it was a party. And so generous. He'd buy drinks for everybody. Of course, being a woman I never had to buy a drink – he'd never let a woman buy a drink; he was always very gentlemanly in that respect. The wine flowed around him; you always had a good time around John, no doubt about it."

"It had more of a personal stamp on it," John said later of *Bless the Weather*. "The ones that came before were folky albums. I think it was ahead of its time. I think *Bless the Weather*, despite being basically acoustic, was nowhere near as folky. It was very innocent in retrospect."

It was the album of a man who'd changed in many ways. It brought together all the things he'd been experimenting with, from a radically altered singing style, the use of drums with acoustic guitar, and his improved, adventurous technique with the Echoplex.

But one of the biggest influences on the sound was the foil he chose for his new recording.

Danny Thompson had become known in the late '60s as the bassist in Pentangle, a quintet who freely trampled over the barriers between traditional folk and jazz. Pentangle was blessed with two of the greatest guitar talents in folk, John Renbourn and Bert Jansch, who weren't afraid to nibble away at any kind of boundary. Thompson was able to match them every step of the way.

Born in Devon on April 4, 1939, he was the son of a miner. During World War II, his father volunteered for submarine duty and was lost at sea. When he was six, his mother settled in the Battersea area of London, a better place to find work than rural Devon. Danny was a gifted footballer and swimmer, but it was music that captured his heart, especially the blues he heard on the Voice of America.

By the time he was 14 he'd formed a band with a friend, making his own tea chest bass. A year later he moved from home, renting a room in a house. The tea chest was replaced by a real double bass when he heard of one for sale in Battersea.

"I went running round and sure enough there was a bass, a great big black thing. The owner was an old boy, he must have been about eighty-five years old. I asked him how much he wanted and he said five pounds, which was a lot of money to me. So I asked him whether I could pay it off at five shillings a week and he agreed. I took it away with me and that night I was working with a jazz group and I tied the bass on the top of the car with no cover. It then started to rain and when I got to the gig I had to wipe off the water. The black paint also came off to reveal a beautiful varnish underneath." It turned out that the instrument had been made in 1865, and was actually worth £150. "I went back to the old boy and told him it was worth much more than a fiver. He said, 'I know that son, but if you want it and you're really going to do it then just give me the five bob a week like we said.'"

For the next couple of years he played in clubs and bands all over London, practicing for up to 10 hours a day. Then, called up for National Service just after marrying his wife Daphne, he was sent to Malaya, becoming lead trombone in the regimental band (he also held the title of regimental boxing champion).

At home, the music scene having changed in his absence, he became a lorry driver for a while to support his family, before briefly picking up the electric bass to tour with Roy Orbison. Once that was over, he joined Alexis Korner's Blues Incorporated (as the replacement for Jack Bruce), while working with a host of other names in jazz and blues. And there was also the recording of the theme for Gerry Anderson's *Thunderbirds*, possibly his most timeless – and most widely-known – recording.

Pentangle began to come together after Danny met Renbourn. Danny had never been exposed to folk music and he began going to the sessions Renbourn and Jansch held at the Three Horseshoes pub in Tottenham Court Road, sitting in and learning more. It proved to be a serendipitous collaboration. Danny's jazz and blues background meshed unexpectedly well with the two guitars, and sparks were quickly flying. Singer Jacqui McShee joined, then Danny recommended percussionist Terry Cox, his former Blues Incorporated colleague.

Although generally thought of as a folk band, Pentangle handily defied easy categorisation. They were equally at home in folk, blues, and jazz, or anywhere in between. They could also handle pop - the single "Light Flight" (taken from their live *Basket of Light* album), which became the theme for the TV comedy *Take Three Girls*, proved to be a hit, landing the band on *Top of the Pops* in 1969.

Danny was also becoming known as a larger-than-life figure, with a quick sense of humour that was as big as his bass, who could also be a wild practical joker.

He and John had first met at the Newport Folk Festival in 1969 and, after his work on *Road to Ruin*, he was a natural to pair with John. Danny's background meant he knew more about jazz, but John had come up through folk and was feeling his way around outside it.

John wanted to create something new and different with *Bless the Weather*. In part, it was because of his dissatisfaction with the singer-songwriter label; he'd outgrown the hippie sensibilities it implied. "People expect some Donovanesque performer sitting on the edge of a toadstool playing the acoustic guitar," he said.

But there was also the desire to bring in the new techniques he'd been mastering, the Echoplex and the unusual singing style. The instant bond between John and Danny created the trust and freedom for improvisation – more live than on record – that thrust the music more in the direction of jazz, but without landing completely in the middle of the genre.

More than ever, John was beginning to trust his instincts. As he noted, there was "a bit less importance stuck on the lyrics. I sort of gave up trying to be poetic...I decided to make the voice a bit more like an instrument, if possible." And that instrument was the tenor sax.

The other factor that set *Bless the Weather* apart from its predecessors was its spontaneity. The material came quickly and naturally, some of it on the day it was recorded. Whereas *Stormbringer* and *Road to Ruin* were both heavily arranged and rehearsed, and his first two albums consisted of material that had been largely concert-tested, this was a plunge into unknown waters.

It probably wouldn't have been possible without Danny Thompson, whose bass was far more foil than underpinning for John's voice and guitar work. They could lead, follow and play off each other as if they'd been together for years, the kind of rare empathetic musical communication that's almost magical. It was most apparent on the title track, but moments of it spring up all over the disc.

After the drawn-out, tortuous process that had been the recording of *Road to Ruin*, this seemed like an absurdly easy time in the studio; John would call it "very innocent, very beautiful and a pleasure to make."

It remains a very fresh-sounding record. For many, it marks the beginning of the "classic" John Martyn period that stretched from 1971 to the end of the decade and it's certainly a quantum leap from what went before. With it, John found his voice, metaphorically and literally.

The slurred vocals that became his signature appear here fully developed, letting the voice wander over and around the lyric like a sax solo, using the words as a device, as much as an end in themselves.

Also apparent was his new acoustic guitar technique, tapping the strings with the back of the fingers to keep a rhythm going, while changing the fingerpicking style itself, making it sparer, but more effective – the right hand actually became more important than the left. John claimed to have been the first to have done this and certainly it doesn't seem to be evident on any record before *Bless the Weather* (although it's since become fairly widely imitated).

For the first time, too, John produced himself (along with engineer John Wood), using the now-familiar Sound Techniques studio. Although credited to Witchseason Productions, by that time Joe Boyd was back in the US - and he said "there was no further involvement. *Bless the Weather* isn't bad, but I was never a huge John Martyn fan."

Call it the first album of John's maturity. The voice was deeper, more assured (and with a deliberately stoned edge), the guitar playing more individual. The songs themselves mined untried territory. They weren't folk, they weren't jazz; they simply were. They existed in their own little limbo somewhere between, but with enough appeal to reach outside both. As John noted, "People kind of sat up and took notice of me after that album, I don't know why..."

To contrast with the laid-back, acoustic sensibility of most of the album, John cut loose electrically on 'Glistening Glyndebourne,' a six-and-a-half minute odyssey that seemed to take some of its inspiration from Miles Davis's recent *Bitches Brew*. Over a backing by what was essentially Mighty Baby plus Danny Thompson, John manipulated the Echoplex to create shifting sheets and waves of notes and rhythm that attacked and decayed majestically. A largely improvised piece, it's the sound of a man who still hadn't absolutely mastered and tamed the effect (although he seemed by now to understand when to kick in the fuzz pedal) - and he needed a band behind him for comfort when heading into unexplored territory. But in the way it managed to pull together strands of psychedelia, modern jazz, and (perhaps unknowingly) the avant-garde, it was a success, both startling and reflective.

Perhaps the key to *Bless the Weather*, and indeed to John's entire oeuvre until 1975, isn't in that track, or even in "Go Easy" or "Bless The Weather." Instead it's in "Head And Heart," which reflects the tricky balancing act he pulled off for several years. As he stated in several interviews through the period, both head and heart were equally important to him, not just in music, but in life.

"Initial reactions, to me, are heart reactions. I wouldn't trust head, or heart, finally though. The closest I can get is that I use my head to temper the judgments of my heart."

And with the record he proved to be a very effective self-editor, with the grace to take away the tension of "Glistening Glyndebourne" by adding an abbreviated, light-hearted cover of the standard "Singin' In The Rain" (and establishing an occasional tradition of recording standards, long before it became fashionable; at the time, it seemed merrily kitsch).

It was the start of John being taken seriously as an artist. His first two albums had been fine, but lacking in any real distinction; pleasant enough, but with little to enable anyone to pick him out from a crowd of similar singer-songwriters. Even the formative jazzy touches of *The Tumbler* didn't help it stand out. Both *Stormbringer* and *Road to Ruin* stood apart, largely because they were duo – or possibly group - albums. John's compositions for them, at least for the most part, were utterly different from what he'd done before. He was writing for a band setting, not for himself.

Bless the Weather not only synthesised all those previous experiences, but also moved several steps ahead. It should be remembered that John was still only twenty-two when he recorded the album. He still had a lot of growth and exploration ahead of him.

The album also reflected his contentment with his domestic situation. Songs like "Head And Heart," "Let The Good Things Come," "Walk On The Water," and "Bless The Weather" were all essentially love songs to his wife, even where they might be wrapped up in allegory. Without deliberately trying, he'd developed a talent for writing a serious love song that worked well above the emotional lowest common denominator. His new, more minimal lyrical style was the perfect framework for that, in partnership with a singing style that seemed to be better at communicating emotion.

In other words, for the first time all the elements came together, and *Bless the Weather* became greater than the sum of its parts. It towered above his previous work, so different, really, that it could have been the work of a new artist. About the only mundane track was 'Sugar Lump,' a bluesy little jam that seemed more like letting off steam than a real song. But even then, the enjoyment of the players was so palpable that it could be excused.

John also seemed to have developed his own style of songwriting. The genesis of it had been there on the two albums he recorded with Beverley, something more stripped-down lyrically, and not as obviously "pretty" as many of his contemporaries. He wasn't afraid to rely on his instrumental chops, as the title cut showed, and there was a slightly harder musical edge, the sign of someone pushing himself.

"Go Easy" and "Bless The Weather" kicked it off in high fashion, firm illustrations of the new direction, eminently memorable – especially the latter, with its insistent refrain – but still very daring for the time, moving gingerly away from anything that could be defined as folk, while keeping an acoustic feel.

John obviously had a very strong idea of how he wanted everything to sound and a clear vision of its presentation. His voice had developed into a far more individual instrument with this record and lyrically he'd become far more adept, managing the neat trick of seemingly opening himself up in tried-and-true singer/songwriter fashion, yet using words like veils to hide emotions, so the listener actually knew little more than when he began, but thought he'd been let in on the secrets; the lyrics meant many things to many people.

"Bless The Weather" - undoubtedly one of John's classic songs, perhaps the first of them, to a large number of fans – became magical because of the empathy between John and Danny Thompson. Thompson's bass provided the urgency that worked against the relaxed guitar playing and matched John note for note on the musical coda. It was the way everything worked together that transformed it into something remarkable that required several listenings to appreciate fully.

Two cuts that have rarely been singled out, but deserve praise, are "Walk On The Water" and "Just Now." The former, with simmering steel drums giving the feel of the baking Caribbean sun (a place John had yet to see), is masterfully sensual, an ode to a woman that's rawer than anything from the Romantic poets, but still as loving, with woman as goddess. On the LP, "Just Now" closed out the first side, a piece that seems impossibly knowing for someone who was just twenty-two. Very simple musically, it's straightforward to the point that it wouldn't have sounded out of place on an Elton John album of the period. It's a man leaving his past life behind and finding joy where he is now, a true happiness. But at the same time, for all the "better friend now than I've ever known," there was a darker note under the pretty guitar and piano arpeggios, with its hints of "always" a way to get happy, and friends on the road. With hindsight, it could be seen as John issuing a warning to himself, as if he perfectly understood what the future held, but embraced it anyway in order to be able to grasp the total joy of the present. If *Bless the Weather* signalled the start of paradise, "Just Now" cast the first faint shadow on the horizon.

"Head And Heart" was the most succinct statement of the philosophy that ruled his life. It's a request for total love, and in that love is the place he wants to be, strives to be, a "place that's clean." In its own way, it's almost religious, suffused with a rich but simple joy. We're all sinners, but in total love there can be salvation. Musically it's the twin of "Bless The Weather," with the same rhythmic and melodic impulses and even the same improvisational ideas and tension between bass and guitar.

With "Let The Good Things Come," there's almost a return to the feel of *Stormbringer*, but with the strong lyrical whiff of nostalgia. Sparingly used electric guitar helps the atmosphere, while Beverley's backing vocals take on an ethereal cast. Like so much of this album, it was looking back and letting go of the past in order to step into the present and the future. But it's also a love song, wanting his wife to be able to see his past and understand him as he is now, all the things that shaped and changed him growing up.

As pleasant a piece of fingerpicking as it was, "Back Down The River" was a relatively lightweight song in comparison to some of the other material on the album. There wasn't the same sense of emotional investment behind it; instead it seemed like a vaguely hippie-fied love song.

Released in November 1971, it received glowing reviews ("quite definitely one of the very best of 1971" raved *ZigZag*) and helped push John firmly onto the more lucrative university and college circuit. He and Beverley had played prestige gigs before, at places like the Queen Elizabeth Hall, and for the last couple of years he'd been slowly shifting from the folk clubs to more rock-orientated venues. But while the Town Hall circuit was the Holy Grail for British performers, the college circuit was only slightly below it. The money was much better than the clubs and the audiences far more appreciative and attentive, making it an enjoyable experience for both the ego and the wallet.

John's operating costs were relatively low. When playing solo, he could travel easily by car, with just his amplifier, effects, and one or two guitars; it was streamlined and efficient. When paired with Danny Thompson, as he frequently would be for the next few years, there was the addition of a double bass. Compared to the equipment of a full band, they travelled very light indeed.

Their accommodations weren't plush hotels. They both had families to feed. With Witchseason, John had received a salary during recording periods, but that era was over - and Island wasn't as generous. So keeping expenses down was paramount and that meant the type of bed and breakfast or dingy hotels that still existed as grim leftovers from the music hall era. There were no Holiday Inns in Bolton at the time, simply small, residential places.

Danny Thompson was still with Pentangle, and would be until 1972, when he quit, ostensibly to spend more time with his family. He had no shortage of session work, but toured Britain regularly with John for a few years. But there were also plenty of times John went on the road alone from 1971 onward.

He was one of several performers in folk clubs who'd graduated to the colleges. Along with Michael Chapman, Al Stewart, Bridget St. John and others, he'd never been a folk singer per se, but a singer-songwriter who happened to work without a band. However, while he might have found the folk clubs constricting, the lessons he learned in them were invaluable. John knew how to communicate with an audience, to entertain with banter as much as with music.

He was, to all intents and purposes, the same age as his university audience. He dressed like them and his elfin looks (which actually belied his size, something that constantly amazed people), long hair and beard put him at the liberal end of the spectrum. It was a favourite trick to ask if anyone in the audience had a joint. Not only did John enjoy a smoke, the question also acted as an icebreaker and a bond – he's one of us! He was skilled at carrying the audience with him. The different outgoing personalities - both English and Scots - that he'd developed as a defence during childhood served him well up on the stage.

Above all, he put on a good show. With this new material, he finally seemed able to plumb the depths of a song, to explore instead of simply performing it. He could use the material as a jumping-off point to extemporise, and he often did, especially with the Echoplex. With Danny, the two of them could constantly push each other musically, and they frequently did.

Everything seemed to be going well for John. From being another singer-songwriter, he'd been elevated to a cult status, still unknown to most, but popular with those few in the know (a status that remained with him more than three decades later). By having music that was open-ended in its possibilities, he could stretch out his shows. And in an age when guitar heroes were firmly ensconced at the top of the rock tree, the sounds he could produce via the Echoplex helped win him a number of fans who might have been bemused at his acoustic work.

He embraced gadgets at a time when there weren't too many available, and used them to make himself into a guitar orchestra. As he explained it, "the note comes out of the pick-up on the guitar and goes into the fuzz box which I use now and again, and then it goes into a combination of volume and wah-wah pedal which I use a fair bit. It come out of that and goes into an Echoplex which repeats the note so you chop in between rhythms, and you can choose your own timings because it's completely elastic. And you can set the number of repeats."

Road work was both a pleasure and an evil - an evil, because it took him from home, where he definitely liked to be. But it was a pleasure for the same reason, bringing him in contact with new people and giving him the chance to play music and be appreciated as an artist. His star was rising and that brought more adulation. Like any artist, he needed the acclaim, the reassurance that he was doing something important, and the validation of his ideas.

There was also a lot of boredom, time spent waiting to go onstage, time coming down from the adrenalin buzz that followed performing. There was always drink around, to which John had always been partial. And he'd enjoyed a smoke for several years. Now he had the chance to indulge both to a greater extent - and he did. On the road he was young and free. The restraints of home life were a long way away.

It was perhaps at this point that the indulgence, which had been moderate before, seemed to edge beyond that to extended periods of excess. For the first time he was being feted, and he enjoyed it. To be fair, after several years of struggle, why shouldn't he? And he was young, able to handle the fun and being the life of the party. It was enjoyment, not a disease. He could function normally and the release was welcome. Indulgence wouldn't reach legendary proportions until he and Danny began to hit the road together regularly.

There was less contact with old friends now that John and Beverley were living in Hastings and had a growing family. Away from the social centre of London, there was no network of musicians around. Nick Drake was falling deeper and deeper into a crippling depression that worried both John and Beverley. He would occasionally visit and try writing with Beverley, whom he trusted. Island, through their agreement with Witchseason, paid Drake a stipend and kept his albums in print, but there was no longer anyone in his corner at the label. And, with Boyd no longer around, Beverley didn't have anyone to encourage her own musical ambitions. She'd been given the role of wife and mother, it appeared, and nothing more. And with John's career beginning to take off, she was somewhat stuck.

Bless the Weather had set John up well, and he toured throughout 1972 on the back of it, accompanied at times by Danny - and together they seemed to roar up and down the country like marauding Vikings. They played storming gigs, and led equally loud lives together, accompanied by lots of alcohol – one of their rituals was getting drunk before they appeared on the stage. Both funny and communicative, their inhibitions vanished as the alcohol content rose. There were occasions when the verbal jousts between them turned physical. The crowds lapped it up, seeing it all as entertainment – as did the two of them, really. It was a 24-hour party when they toured together.

CHAPTER FIVE –Solid Air

A truism of the music business is that an artist is only as good as his next album. To maintain his status, John had to come up with an album that was at least the equal of, if not better than, *Bless the Weather*. That created real pressure. *Bless the Weather* had largely defined his new style and his interplay with Danny Thompson had become more refined.

Solid Air, the follow-up to *Bless the Weather,* is generally viewed as the apex of John's work, which had to be frustrating for an artist who was still producing highly creative work more than 30 years later. For better or worse, it's the album that defined him as an artist, the one that's best-known. It's been widely lauded, with artists like Beth Orton citing it as a big influence, and in 1999 *Q* magazine named it one of the best chill-out albums of all-time (a term that had yet to be invented in 1973, when the LP was released). What is true is that *Solid Air* does contain some of the most memorable songs of his career, from the glorious title track to "May You Never" and the scary electrics of "I'd Rather Be The Devil" to the jaw-dropping fingerpicked work on "Easy Blues."

Perhaps because of its enduring popularity, it became something of a millstone around John's neck; he could never escape it. Indeed, late in his career he'd revisit it, building a tour around the disc. For much of his career, though, if he was to move ahead, he had to think of it as just another album.

"I have neither affection nor disaffection for it," he explained. "I tend to forget [albums] once I've done 'em. I know the songs are pretty good. I tend to get so involved in them when I'm doing them that I'm glad to walk away. I play the finished tapes for two or three days then forget them. I try to look forward."

In early 1973, when *Solid Air* was released, it was very much an album that looked forward. Although it caused endless comparisons with

American singer-songwriter Tim Buckley through the slightly jazzy vibe and the way John used his voice, modulating like a tenor saxophone, it was an album that stood decidedly alone. On the recorded evidence, John's new style of writing and playing had put him on a high, and the new disc easily outstripped its predecessor. It was quite unlike anything released in Britain before.

It was a more crafted work than its predecessor, the songs more structured and developed. Instead of the improvisational quality of *Bless the Weather*, this showed how much John had developed as a songwriter. He'd learned how to extract the best qualities of his new style and put them together. There was a minimalist feel to the lyrics, while his slurred voice took on a husky sexiness that was even more apparent than before.

Having reinvented himself on *Bless the Weather*, *Solid Air* saw John upping the stakes and pressing deeper into his new style. *Solid Air*, recorded as usual at Sound Techniques (and the Island studio at Basing Street) with John Wood – who also co-produced with John – during November and December 1972, proved to be a lucky synchronicity of style and performance. All the elements that make a good record came together perfectly here.

Fairport Convention drummer Dave Mattacks played on the album, as he did on so many others coming out in the early '70s and beyond.

"Within six months or a year of getting into Fairport, [bassist] Dave Pegg and I became the rhythm section of choice for all these singer-songwriters, and I remember John's sessions were a little bit different because the material had a different slant to it, a little bit more jazzy. It was apparent that John was a really great player, like Nick Drake, and a good singer."

While acknowledged as one of Britain's best drummers – he now makes his home in the US – at the time Mattacks had actually been affected by John's earlier work, as "I'd begun to realise how lacking my timekeeping was after hearing *Stormbringer* with the American rhythm section. I think the English rhythm sections had tended to focus a little bit too much on the lyrical side and less on the feel. I remember being brought up quite sharp by hearing those guys and how great they were, and started to get a little bit more aware of pocket and feel, and thinking of bringing that sensibility to John's record."

When Mattacks questioned Wood, who'd also engineered those *Stormbringer* sessions in the US, "he was very peremptory, and said, 'Well, he just sat down and played it, didn't he?' and I was utterly intrigued. Then I began to bring in more of a groove. It was very obvious that John Martyn was much more aware of it than I was, because that is reflected in his subsequent choice of drummers – they're much more time and groove-oriented than I was at the time. At that time my time was a little on the loose side, and the groove wasn't as good as it should be."

The groove that propelled American soul and blues pushed the music ahead, in sharp contrast to the English style, which seemed to decorate the music. In Mattacks – an easy and obvious choice, since Fairport Convention was part of the Witchseason and Island families – John had made an astute choice. His background wasn't in folk music, and he wasn't afraid of adding a kick to the music, or of trying new things.

Jazz had grown to become an important part of John's musical lexicon, but it wasn't the only American influence on the record. Both "Don't Want To Know" and "Dreams By The Sea" showed soul music and proto-funk rearing their heads, while "The Easy Blues" (a song John had been playing at gigs for a long time) and "I'd Rather Be The Devil" were just blues, an early love of his, but performed with a twist.

The shift in John's music was apparent in the choice of session players. "Folk" instruments were featured only on "Over The Hill," a delightfully simple romp about the joys of returning home. Danny Thompson was a prominent fixture, but the Mattacks/Pegg rhythm axis also gave a grounding to much of the proceedings. Conga player Speedy Acquaye added a worldly looseness and Rabbit Bundrick, who seemed to hover all over the British music scene (playing, at various times with Free, the Who and Bob Marley), added keys, which filled out the sound perfectly.

This was an album of fully-developed songs, rather than a framework on which to hang John's guitar work. The only exception was "The Easy Blues," which was largely a patchwork of blues clichés, and even that highlighted how quietly virtuosic he'd become; remarkably complex to play, it showed how far he'd travelled from the earlier party piece of "Seven Black Roses."

"May You Never," written for Wesley, Beverley's son whom he'd adopted, was possibly his most complete and commercial creation. The sentiments were clear, simple and positive, and it was easy to sing. It spawned a number of cover versions, the most famous that of Eric Clapton, who covered it on his 1977 *Slowhand* album, which sold well on both sides of the Atlantic, bringing John some well-deserved royalties. The song, he admitted later, "popped out, they pop out you know..."

There were, in fact, two John Martyn versions of the song. The one on *Solid Air* differed from the "May You Never" that appeared as a single. The latter added electric guitar from Paul Kossoff, the troubled lead guitarist of Free (one of John's favourite rock bands). At the time though, there was little chance of John having a hit single. "Poppish" was a relative term; what seemed like pop for John was well outside the musical mainstream.

While "May You Never" did serve to pull people in, the art of *Solid Air* really pivoted around two tracks – the title cut and "I'd Rather Be The Devil," which reflected the two opposite poles of John.

"Solid Air" was written for Nick Drake, who would die of an overdose of prescription medication in November 1974. Although no longer as close as they had been when John and Beverley lived in Hampstead, there was no denying that a bond of some kind existed between them. There was, perhaps, a sad irony that an album containing a song *for* Drake sold more than Drake himself ever managed in his lifetime. And John would remain a devoted friend of Drake's until the end and even later would rarely discuss the man. One rare instance came in the '90s, when John's then-soundman, Alex Boyesen, asked him about Drake.

"One time in Hamburg I was at the bar talking to John about stuff and I posed

the inevitable question about Nick Drake. He paused, sighed and shook his head, 'We tried everything, girls, drugs, drinks, money, nothing would get him out of it, he just had to go, nothing we could do.' That was the end of the subject, still a lot of stuff going on there even after all this time."

To those not in the know – which was most people at the time – the lyrics of "Solid Air" seemed obscure. But it was more about the feel, a slow, jazz-inflected groove that John's voice and Tony Coe's sax wove around the changes, with Tristam Fry's vibes coming in to offer subtle backing. The inclusion of Fry surprised Dave Mattacks.

"One of the things I remember in particular was Tristam, whom I knew as a percussionist more in the straight world, because at that point I was starting to do recording sessions for films and such, and I'd bump into Tristam."

The term "chill-out" was still years from invention, but musically that exactly described the song, something to be played late at night, when its dreamy, gauzy quality was most resonant. The arrangement, which must have been John's (he could neither read nor write music, but he could guide the other musicians), was the perfect marriage of song and sound, tailor-made for the slurred voice style he'd practically perfected by this point. It wasn't too busy or too packed with instruments. Neither was it stripped to the bone. Danny Thompson's bass part underscored everything, gently pushing it all along. In this recorded form it didn't offer much chance for improvisation, but it didn't need to; that would come in live performance.

Chris Nickson

"Solid Air" was the diametric opposite of "I'd Rather Be The Devil," in almost every sense. The latter was loud, electric, and a showcase for what John could do with guitar and Echoplex.

If "Glistening Glyndebourne" showed how far he'd come in developing a technique with the Echoplex, then a year later he'd advanced it much further. The group ethos behind the former track – essentially a sort of jam session with Mighty Baby – had been pared down to guitar, bass, and drums, a showpiece that could easily be replicated in concert. The sheets and shards of sound he managed to wring from his guitar, along with the ebbing waves of notes created by the Echoplex, ranged from the lush to the vicious, powering the track along.

"I remember thinking, 'Oh this is different, I haven't heard this before'," commented Mattacks. "I think I came up with that hi-hat thing because there was so much drive from John's guitar. There didn't need to be backbeats through it."

It was a track guaranteed to startle, although it didn't make a guitar hero out of John – possibly because he played an amplified acoustic, rather than a solid-body electric. But it still offered something new and distinctly different and even with its volume, it didn't affect the overall mood of the record (placing it at the end of side one on the LP probably helped with that).

In retrospect, good as *Bless the Weather* was – and it's held up remarkably well – it was really just a prelude for the magnificence of *Solid Air*, an enduring classic, generally cited as his best work. It was certainly a moment where everything came together exactly right, with every song powerful and memorable.

It was a record that helped redefine the whole idea of the British singer-songwriter. Before this, John had been someone with an acoustic guitar, possibly backed by an electric band, but whose music fell within the area covered by folk, blues, and rock. This expanded that into jazz and soul, and took the music deep into the night.

78

At the time, hardly anyone knew that the title cut was written for Nick Drake. It simply stood alone as an enigmatic, beautiful song, lauded and loved by a thousand joint smokers for its laid-back, midnight textures. Quite deliberately, John's vocal phrasing had a jazz feel and a raw, slurred enunciation. But putting the louder, overtly folky "Over The Hill" directly after it completely jarred the mood that had been set. The yearning of the lyrics might have fitted, but musically it was out of place (indeed, it could be argued that it didn't belong on the album at all; wherever it was placed, it would have shattered the feel).

But it was followed by the masterful "Don't Want To Know," which over the years proved to be one of John's best, most enduring and underrated songs. Low-key, with glistening electric piano from Rabbit Bundrick, it was simple song, building through the first two verses before going into the piano break. Was it a lyrical plea to mankind? Or was it the lament of a man trying to keep on the straight and narrow, but ultimately failing. With just three verses, and clocking in at under three minutes, it was short, almost a throwaway, but one with remarkable staying power.

"Go Down Easy" and "Dreams By The Sea" both seemed to presage the more free-form approach that would appear a little later on *Inside Out*. The former was an odd little piece that seemed to twist in on itself. It seemed awkward, made up of near dissonances, but together they worked; however, no one could claim it as one of his major works, more as filler. "Dreams By The Sea" put both feet into funk, John Martyn style, working more on a rhythm than a melody – the basis was a single guitar note, at least until the middle section. Lyrically, it was nightmare visions, although with no indication of what induced them. At heart it was a blues song, right down to its words, and a first foray into something that would be explored more fully on the next couple of albums.

"May You Never" remained John's main calling card for years, maybe even an albatross around his neck, the song he could never manage to completely jettison. But it was a perfect piece of songwriting: catchy, seeming simple, but actually a complex guitar figure to play. Along with "Solid Air," it became one of the justifiable bases of his reputation.

Yet it didn't stand head and shoulders above most of the other pieces on this disc. "Man In The Station" was cut from the same musical cloth as "Don't Want To Know," although with more of a kick in the chorus, while its sentiments echoed "Over The Hill," a curious amalgam, with John given the rare chance to play an electric guitar solo. The sentiments of travel and home, one a trial, the other a sanctuary, were recurring themes throughout the record – understandable from someone who spent so much time on the road. But they were also symbolic of the opposing sides of John's personality, the outgoing performer and drinker and the quieter family man, both existing within the man, but never quite reconcilable.

It all finished with "The Easy Blues," the piece that had been in his stage repertoire for so long, a chance to show off his guitar work in the guise of a blues. It offered a virtuosic performance on six strings, with a contemporary touch of synthesizer at the end.

Solid Air proved to be John's best-selling album to date, establishing him as a force on the university concert circuit and upping the fees he could command. A buzz about him was spreading and it seemed only a matter of time before he became a major figure. With all the praise, he began to believe the legend, rather than focusing on the gritty fact. As he admitted, "it all just went to my head."

The LP was released in America, where it found a small, sympathetic audience. As the FM radio format there had changed from the free form of the late '60s to something more rigid, it was hard for him to receive any airplay. But yet some did manage to discover his work, although information about John himself was almost impossible to come by. Following the release, he undertook his first American tour as the opening act for Free and Traffic (who were then enjoying their first comeback glory).

Opening for two bands was never going to be an easy task for a solo artist, even one who could plug in and turn up the volume. He was onstage as people were coming into the venue and fighting the odds to even be heard or noticed over the noise of the crowd – not exactly ideal for a singer-songwriter. From being feted at home to largely unknown in such a vast country brought a severe dislocation; he'd been cock o' the walk and suddenly he was nobody. Add to that the stress of travelling and an extended period on the road away from his family – the tour consisted of 35 dates in a mere 39 days, meaning little time to decompress - along with a predisposition to party, and there was a definite danger. Alcohol was prevalent, but John explained that "I had also discovered cocaine and heroin. I was doing dope and acid at the time and drinking as well...you can imagine the state I was in." It was perhaps just as well that he was limited to 30 minute sets, and forced to focus on his electric side because of the sheer size of the venues.

He did, however, win at least one convert, a man who'd go on to become the most influential figure in reggae.

"When I started working with Bob Marley, his exposure to the rock world had been through Johnny Nash," recalled Island head Chris Blackwell. "So his thing was to get on the R&B charts, and to get on black radio. That was the world of everyone he worked with. When I signed them, I saw them as much more of a black rock group. I saw that we had to build them. Bob was sort of unsure of it. I took him to see Traffic, Free, and John Martyn, a tour we had, and I wanted him to see my bands – Traffic never had a hit single in America. We arrived about ninety five per cent into John Martyn's set. We arrived at the side of the stage just as John Martyn was getting applause and coming off. Bob looked around the curtains and looked at me and said 'Where's the rest of the band?' He got it, because he had an innate intelligence."

The tour finished on February 12, 1973. There was just enough time to fly home and get over the jet lag before returning to the States for a second tour promoting the new album. Then, in March, he was on the road in Britain for most of the month.

For financial reasons, Danny Thompson didn't make the US trips. But at home he and John had become an inseparable touring combo, whenever circumstances allowed. They were in sync musically and personally, with Danny quite capable of matching John through any wild act or amount of alcohol, as he was in his own period of excess.

Stories of the two of them on the road together have become legendary; they created as much mayhem as any major rock band. A sympathetic view would be to see the laddish pranks as a relief from the stress of boredom of touring, but there was a darker side to them. Fuelled by drink and drugs – after all, they rarely went onstage sober, and both were men of staggering capacity – they were wild binges with some (admittedly excellent) music in between.

At a gig in Bolton they dared each other to take off a piece of clothing after each song – and both ended up stark naked in front of the audience, hidden by their instruments. And then there was the time John "got really drunk one night and woke up and [Danny] had nailed me under the carpet. I couldn't move my hands or feet. I was very dry and had a hangover and I said, 'Danny, please...get me, get me a drink.' So he stepped over my helpless body, went to the phone, and in a very loud voice said, 'Can I have a glass of orange juice for one, please. Breakfast for one, please.' I was screaming blue murder by this time. I was furious! He met the guy in the hall, so the guy couldn't get in the room and see what was happening. He sat in front of me and downed the orange juice and had the breakfast."

Fights, both verbal and physical, weren't uncommon between the pair, but there were no lasting recriminations. They had a very close bond and took great pleasure in loud, outrageous behaviour. It's possible that John thought his actions were acceptable simply because he had been lauded so much for his recent albums – he was going to be a star, so he could do what he liked. And there was also the "kids out of school" aspect of touring. While it had its own routines, it existed in a kind of vacuum where normal rules of life didn't seem to apply.

John could be absolutely, thoroughly charming, but in his cups the aggressive side emerged at times. While not normally given to violence, his size, coupled with a Glasgow accent, could be intimidating.

But he was out there for a reason and that was to earn money to support his family. Much as he revelled in the fact that he could bring home a good amount just from his musical talent, the Scots puritan inside was also outraged that he could earn so much, as opposed to the paltry amount his father had earned doing "real" work.

When he was at home, a responsible parent with yet another child on the way – son Spencer would be born in 1974 – John had to put all this aside, or at least as much as he could. It could be argued that his excesses came about in part because he missed home and hearth. That he loved Beverley is beyond doubt, judging from the song lyrics and interviews of the period. But he was on the verge of becoming a man torn between doing the right thing and falling into the addictions that were encouraged on tour.

On the road, drugs were available –and the John Martyn of the mid '70s wasn't about to turn anything down. As he freely admitted in 1975, "I'll do anything I can get my hands on...If you gave me eight grams of Charlie [cocaine] and eight grams of Horse [heroin], I'd get thru' it in a week. There again, I go months and months without anything other than dope. I've always got some dope to smoke."

While on tour, it provided a diversion from the boredom. Bridget St. John recalled, "We were in Wales. John and Danny had a contest. They were taking all kinds of drugs, pills, everything. The idea was to see who could ward off the effects longest."

John didn't seem to consider alcohol to be a problem, possibly because it was legal, and because drinking was a natural part of life for him, a family trait. Yet more than anything else, alcohol would prove to be the ongoing bane in his life. Many times during his career, John claimed to have given up drinking – and probably did, for a while.

Home was a refuge from the road, a place to come down and return to normal. It represented stability in a world where he was constantly on the move and under pressure. It was a place where he could work on ideas and feel grounded, attached to something, something important.

And yet for Beverley it had to be galling. She'd been working on her career before meeting John. Even as a parent, she'd been half of a duo with John, able to write, record, and tour. Now her world had largely become defined by her children and four walls. There would be talk of a solo record, due in 1976, although even then John remarked that "I wouldn't fancy her doin' a lot of touring." The album was never released, if recording was ever completed.

While Beverley's music was stalled and going nowhere, John's was on the up and up. *Solid Air* brought in new fans, mostly in the UK, but also in the US, thanks not only to the disc, but also to the three tours he'd undertaken there. Although his status was still low in the States, he had at least had the experience of being there, of seeing the place coast to coast and finding a small core of followers.

Island had been gratified by the response to *Solid Air*, both commercial and critical. After all, he'd been signed by Chris Blackwell himself, rather than anyone from the A & R (Artist and Repertoire) department, and he'd also been one of the label's earliest signings. The faith in him was finally justified, as he'd developed into a significant artist - one who could become much bigger if he held to the same course.

Undoubtedly, that was what the label thought he would do. He was still discovering the new terrain he'd found on *Bless the Weather* and, as *Solid Air* showed, there was still plenty to be explored. Island believed in him and had high hopes - which may have been why they offered him a completely free hand for his next album. He'd proved himself, on disc and on the road. They obviously trusted that he wanted to build on what he'd achieved and take it to the next level.

Unfortunately, they were wrong.

What he seemed to want to do in the studio and what his label had envisaged were two very different things. They almost certainly saw a *Solid Air II*, which would in all probability have taken him to the next level. What they received – and, to be fair, released and promoted – was *Inside Out*, something that could easily have been titled *The Love Album*. It was an exploration of the emotion: for friends, for life, but above all, for his wife. There was plenty of guilt in it, including virtual admissions of sleeping with other women, but it was a plea to love.

"It was more adventurous," John remembered, "not as poppy. I think I was expected to make another *Solid Air*, and it came as a bit of a shock to the record company that I didn't. But it didn't bother me. And it got the Golden Rose of Montreux, so I wasn't worried."

Yes, it did win that prize, and it certainly was more adventurous. It demanded a lot from the listener, taking him on a trip into the unknown on "Ain't No Saint" and "Outside In." The former seemed to take equal inspiration from Indian music, the tabla providing the beat while John tried to make his acoustic guitar imitate a sitar (as opposed to using a sitar itself, as he had on his debut; by now the guitar was John's sole instrument). The latter seemed to use John Coltrane's magnificent "A Love Supreme" as its jumping off point, but pointing it in a direction Coltrane himself had probably never envisioned.

It certainly seemed to start off in a mellow enough fashion with "Fine Lines," which had an intimacy that boded well – John's voice had never sounded so slurred; even to a fan it took a couple of hearings to be able to make out what he was singing. But then came the dislocation of a pipe lament played on electric guitar, the two previously mentioned tracks, and a cover of the perennial "The Glory Of Love," a song that largely set up the second side of the album. For while love was the overall theme, it was a record of two halves, the material not so easily pigeonholed coming first. Flipping the record over, it wasn't until the last three tracks ("Make No Mistake," "Ways To Cry," and "So Much In Love With You") that the sound seemed to stabilise into something familiar to lovers of the previous two discs.

Looking back, it could be seen as a kind of attempted career suicide. It wasn't a record that was going to convert people into John Martyn fans. It could easily even turn away those who'd recently joined the flock. That it was the record of his heart is beyond doubt (it remained his own favourite).

This was a disc that was spontaneous and unedited. It was the heart untempered by the head, as John might have said at the time. Recorded and mixed in July 1973 at Island Studios in Basing Street, mostly during late night sessions, it was an album that wasn't at all commercial, except by chance.

John would define the record as "a vision into my own half-finished self," which was probably true. He was still young and unsure exactly where he was going. At the same time, he admitted "I would have liked to have attacked it with more technical ability. I would have liked to have been more technically able at that point." However, he wasn't - so what emerged what largely a sketch of what might have been, which was, at its best, some very daring fusion music that owed far more to Miles Davis or later Coltrane than anything to do with folk music, which was perhaps what he needed right then.

For all that he'd developed a loathing of folk music, and being defined as a folkie because he played an acoustic guitar, John remained a singer-songwriter. He was an exceptional guitar player, whether working acoustically or electrically, with a mind and fingers that leapt ahead. But his real medium was the song - and that was what his audience loved above all else. For an adventurous artist, the framework of a song could seem constricting at times, and *Inside Out* – which he saw as bringing feelings and emotions into the open – was an attempt to capsize that, and be taken seriously as a jazz musician.

Upsetting the apple cart didn't exactly work, however. It perplexed a lot of people, but it didn't set John on a new musical career path. It didn't turn him into a jazzbo. He was still a singer-songwriter, however much he appeared to kick against the idea.

Danny Thompson was his most reliable support on the record. By now their communication was remarkable and he proved to be the ideal foil for John, adding melodically to 'Fine Lines,' or providing the bowed drone underpinning that held together "Eibhli Ghail Chiuin Ni Chearbhaill" (his attempt to subvert the Scots tradition by using a sustained electric guitar on a bagpipe tune). Steve Winwood offered a light touch on piano, while Bobby Keyes (aka Keys) took a turn away from the Rolling Stones to air out his jazz side.

For something so spontaneous, the arrangements were very trim and economical. The record didn't sprawl in the way it could have done, especially considering that the recording was done in just a few extended sessions, rather than spread out over a longer period. Indeed, everything was very concentrated, which was completely in tune with the emotion behind the album, covering the gamut of love, from its pure ideal, to lust and guilt. John's declaration of "It felt natural" in the disc's opening moments was perhaps the key to understanding it – something he obviously instinctively realised at the time.

Touring exhausted him, physically and mentally, as it does so many musicians, and the abuse he chose to put himself through when on the road certainly didn't help matters, even if it served as release. So *Inside Out* was as much as cry for home and an apology for continually leaving to go out on the road, as much as anything else. It was a loud, hoarse shout. Even if it did his career few favours commercially, it was an artistic success. In interviews, John has said that during this time he'd become disenchanted with a lot of popular song (and by refusing to be defined as a folkie, he had by default fallen into the rock camp) and also with the notion of and trappings involved with commercial success.

At least on some level, *Inside Out* kicks against both things. Most of the songs don't conform to anything in pop music, while some are doggedly uncommercial. And the mere act of releasing an album like this was a good way to sidestep commercial success.

John was lucky enough to have a devoted fan base by this time. It meant he could go out and tour and still get bums on seats – and touring was very much his bread and butter. He might loathe it, but it clothed and fed his family. He wasn't in the top tier of acts by any means, but he could make a living at it - and he could afford the luxury of a record that would garner excellent reviews, but not sell in any sterling quantities. It remains one of the touchstones of his career by its sheer perversity and is one of John's proudest achievements.

American Brian Cullman had remained in close touch with John and Beverley since meeting them in 1970 and he talked to John during this period.

"At that point I was starting to question him about songwriting, because he was one of my favourite songwriters. I looked forward to his songs, and I loved the songs on *Bless the Weather* and *Solid Air*. He was so proud of *Inside Out*. I remember him playing me acetates of it, and being really annoyed that I didn't jump up and down. I felt that as he was getting more and more involved in the texture, the songwriting was slipping away, and I remember asking him about that and he was really pissed at me for even bringing it up. Looking back, there are some great songs on there that I missed. It felt like what he was hearing had suddenly changed. Where he'd been moving in a parallel line to, say, Nick Drake, where they were trying to recreate a personal conversation or a mood, or really trying to capture a certain kind of energy that had to do with conversation, even an inner dialogue, suddenly he was tapping into something very different. I can't say if it was any better or any worse, but it didn't have anything to do with melody as I knew it, or with language as I knew it. His argument at the time was that I was ignorant of jazz, and he was really trying to access some of the same feelings as Miles Davis. When I'd question that, he'd always bring up Stevie Wonder, and I'd go, 'Yeah, but he writes melodies! There are songs there'."

The life of a musician was an endless cycle of record and tour - and with a new album out, John had to return to the road, with which he had a love-hate relationship.

Inside Out arrived remarkably quickly on the heels of *Solid Air*, with a nine-month gap in between. Given that Island wanted to capitalise on John's growing status and popularity, a fast follow-up made sense. With it came a relatively short jaunt around Britain in the company of Danny Thompson - an opportunity to wreak havoc.

However, that was light relief compared to what was to come early in 1974. John had spent a fair portion of 1973 touring, including three daunting trips through the US. He was heading back across the Atlantic again, this time for more than two months, opening for Yes, who were out in support of *Tales from Topographic Oceans* and who had already achieved superstar status, playing massive arenas. That meant John, all alone, was facing the biggest audiences of his career - and for the most part, they'd never heard of him and simply wanted him off so the act they'd paid to see could take the stage.

Jon Anderson, the singer and de facto leader of Yes, characterised John as "a brilliant guitar player. He had this amazing talent to sound like a full orchestra, it was unbelievable. We toured and had a great time with him. It worked. I didn't like the idea of a band opening. By the time they took all the equipment away the audience had lost the momentum. To have one guy create that kind of sound, then have Yes take over, was a great thing for me."

Unfortunately, it wasn't as successful for John.

"It was a long tour, three months, and towards the end he was spacing out a lot, I know that," Anderson remembered. "He and Steve [Howe] didn't see eye to eye for a couple of days. But I always felt he was a bit of a hard nut. I didn't speak to him that much, but I did like him. I remember walking through Notting Hill Gate one day and I heard this voice: 'Jon! You fucking cunt, how are you, mate?' It was John, with his head out of the car window. I said, 'What are you up to?' and he said, 'Nothing much, I'm just driving past.' He just had to recognise me, and it was good. He had that niceness to make that greeting."

John's recollection of the tour was that "I did very well with the audience, it was just Yes I didn't like! You go from 70,000 people to 70, it's very odd. I think there were just a couple of [my] albums available [in the US]."

The weight and length of the tour took a toll on John; that was apparent even to Anderson, who didn't have too much contact with him: "Towards the end of that tour he was becoming a little out of control. On the tour the P.A. started to distort. The guys would come to me, Steve would say, 'The P.A.'s distorting, man. We can't let him go on and distort the P.A.' So I went to Roy Clair, who ran the system, and asked him to turn John down a bit. After his set, somebody told him, and John came in screaming at me. I told him, 'Listen, it was distorting. I'm sorry, man, but it was *distorting*! He was freaking out on me, and Steve defended me. Then the two of them it was like two bulls in a china shop. Then Steve really resolved it, and they hugged each other at the end."

To say John hated the trek was putting it mildly. At one show he reportedly came onstage – his "set," such as it was, consisted of a bunch of large pillows – then walked off again without playing a note because he was so disgusted with everything. He felt he shouldn't be opening for Yes, and certainly not in such giant venues. His music could be electric and aggressive, but it demanded more intimacy than was possible before thousands and thousands.

John was depressed by the lack of appreciation from audiences and far from home on a tour that seemed endless as it criss-crossed America. He was drinking heavily, and doing whatever drugs came to hand. All in all, he was in a volatile state. Claire Hamill, on tour herself, met up with John in New York.

"John was staying at the Chelsea Hotel. I went over to visit him. We were chilling, as you'd say, watching TV, drinking, and smoking. He just up and threw the TV out of the window! It was one of those rock'n'roll stories. I thought, 'Oh my God, I've heard about this sort of thing happening.' It was amazing! Even though it was a cliché, I thought I'd never see it. But John went and did it."

It was uncharacteristic behaviour, the sign of a man rapidly falling out of control. But there would be little relief until the middle of the year. As soon as he was back in England, there were more gigs, although they were tempered by the sweet relief of time at home.

Unlike America - where he essentially remained an unknown quantity - in Britain, John was a headlining act at colleges and small theatres, and was quite capable of filling them. The question of whether he could move up to a higher level remained moot – he'd sidestepped the issue neatly with *Inside Out*. It hadn't lost him any fans, and possibly the guitar prowess it showed, along with its sense of broken barriers, had even attracted a few people in the long run. But ultimately, the record was a distraction and a dead end. Without being a trained and accomplished musician – on the lines of his jazz heroes – there was no way for John to properly pursue some of the trails he'd broken on the album.

He was, however, playing better than ever, thanks in large part to the continual touring, where he'd been forced to perform every night. And if the audiences in some places hadn't been listening, that gave him the chance to experiment even more.

John finished off the round of gigs in support of *Inside Out* with an appearance at the London Rock Proms on July 5th. The title was perhaps a misnomer. Along with John, the bill consisted of Fairport Convention, Roy Harper, and the Sutherland Brothers & Quiver, along with "special guest' Beverley Martyn," in what would be her one of her last major appearances for many years. In other words, there was very little real rock involved in the concert itself. But at a very cheap £2.60 it was good value (tickets for John's solo shows invariably cost more than that; it's worth remembering that at that time an income of £2500 p.a. was considered reasonable).

He'd spent an exhausting, draining five months on the road, a good portion of it in the States, where his confidence had been battered, along with his body and his mind. He needed a break and with the birth of his son, Spencer, it was the perfect time to enjoy the pleasures of home and family once more - and an excuse to put the guitar down for a while, something he liked to do when the chance occurred, noting "I've gone a month without picking a guitar up – which is bad, but I've done it – especially after a tour. I'll just sit and watch television. Don't care what's on. I'll just sit and stare at the interference to clear my head out." And after the lengthy ordeal that had been the first half of 1974, he needed it.

CHAPTER SIX – Confounding Expectations

The problem with being a musician is that you put yourself on a treadmill. No sooner does one cycle end, than the next begins. With a brief period to write some new material, John was expected to begin work on a new record – and once it was out, he'd have to be back on the road, supporting it with gigs.

He'd been there and done that and the pleasure of it was obviously palling on him. His intake of alcohol and drugs had increased (although John used heroin, there's never been any indication that he was a junkie) and with it, the mood swings. At home he could still be relatively stable and there's no doubt at all that he revelled in Beverley's love, which he truly needed, and the nearness of his family.

But the fact that he was gone so much, sometimes for extended periods, put strain on Beverley and their relationship. For a good part of each year she was a single parent, responsible for the day-to-day care of three young children and given the fact that there was no steady income on which to depend – it wasn't as if John was paid a salary – she had to be able to budget accordingly.

Also, her own career was on indefinite hold. There was talk of John producing an album for her and tracks were recorded, but nothing ever came of it. She'd have to wait more than twenty years before having product of her own in her hand.

John had no such delays in releasing a new album. In August he was back in Island Studios on Basing Street. By now his guitar techniques, both acoustic and electric, were firmly established, although he didn't use his electric (a Les Paul) for gigs. Instead he relied on his trusty Martin D-28, which utilized two separate pickups. A DeArmond ran through a Gibson Boomer pedal, a fuzz box, the Echoplex, an Electro-Harmonix Big Muff and a phase shifter into a Fender amplifier. For a straight acoustic sound, there was also a Barcus-Berry pickup that ran directly into the amp. With Darco light gauge wire-wound strings he could pick nimbly and be able to bend the strings well, yet they were thick enough not to go out of tune easily.

Although John used a lot of tunings, not merely standard or DADGAD, he was beginning to settle on one that had worked well for him, an odd C tuning of his own devising – DGCCFC (from bottom string to top).

The joys of family pervaded his next work, *Sunday's Child* - curiously, the most overlooked of his "classic period" albums, appearing between *Outside In* and *Live at Leeds*. According to John, it was "recorded in six days and it was all improvised, all of it."

Danny Thompson remained John's foil, their partnership now extremely close. Liam Genochey played drums, while Al Anderson (presumably the same Al Anderson whom Chris Blackwell had brought in to play guitar with Bob Marley and the Wailers) played bass on "One Day Without You." "Clutches" served to solidify the connection between John and former Free guitarist Paul Kossoff, as two member of Koss's nascent new band, Back Street Crawler, formed the rhythm section for the track. The extended Free family was rounded out by former Free keyboard player (who'd end up in Back Street Crawler) John "Rabbit" Bundrick on piano – he'd also guested on *Solid Air*. Beverley made an appearance, singing on (appropriately) "My Baby Girl," John's paean to daughter Mhairi, then three years old.

John had never taken a linear approach to albums. There was no steady arc to his work. But after the electric excess of *Inside Out*, which stood as almost a detour from what had gone before, this could easily have been the real follow-up to *Solid Air*. There were a couple of tracks that were heavy on funk ('Root Love' and 'Clutches'), but the rest was decidedly acoustic and informal. On what he called "the family album" he was even willing to put a traditional folk song ("Spencer the Rover," a Copper Family favourite, for his new son), although he'd publicly blasted folk music and denied any connection to it. And with "Satisfied Mind" he delved into the tradition of American song (it was not actually a traditional song, though it was listed that way).

It was a disc with a spring in its step. *Inside Out* had been a confessional; this was a man safe in the bosom of his family. All eleven tracks were love songs, whether to his wife, children, or just the sentiment of home, and a satisfying mix of electric and acoustic, with the extended Echoplex outings nowhere in evidence. This was nothing more than it claimed to be, an album of love songs of different kinds, from the ache of "One Day Without You" to the gentle slurred lilt of "Lay It All Down," where John's acoustic guitar and voice, along with Danny's bass, sounded as full as any orchestra.

As befitted its sentiments, simplicity was the key throughout. And when he did refer to his bad behaviour away from home (on the proto electro-funk of "Root Love," a restless tiger prowl of a track that could have happily sat on *Inside Out*), it was counted in drinks rather than infidelities, although the allusion to "cheap experience" was clear enough. Yet that murkiness was followed by the talcum powder freshness of "My Baby Girl" that managed to stop just short of cloying, with the unusual view of John as a shamelessly doting father. "Sunday's Child" itself was a jazzy workout that wouldn't have worked properly without Danny's towering bass as the engine behind John's layers of acoustic and electric guitars. As an exercise in funk, though, it was lukewarm rather than hot, a good idea that never translated properly onto disc.

Having done a song for his daughter, it was only fitting that John also recorded one for his new baby, Spencer. And the easy, arpeggioed simplicity of the traditional "Spencer The Rover" proved to be the record's surprise delight, with Danny's bowed bass the tide on which it floated. The emotion fitted perfectly with the rest of the record, a gorgeous exhale of breath before plunging into the rest of the album. And with "Clutches," that was quite a dive. Not even lasting two minutes, it was more a snatch than a full song. But it worked, a steaming little piece of white funk, where everyone sounded to be having fun in the studio.

"The Message," interpolated with the traditional Scots song "Mhairi's Wedding," was a plea to someone, although who isn't clear – possibly daughter Mhairi herself. But somehow it's the lost track, one that never seems to develop into anything, remaining an unformed ball of clay.

In feel, "Satisfied Mind" might not have sounded too far out of place on *Stormbringer* and not only because it was an American song. Restrained and (like "Spencer The Rover") more a workout for the voice than anything, it was John's ode to the joys of family.

It was on the two final cuts that the glimmerings of new ideas trickled in. "You Can Discover" seemed typical John Martyn, accompanied by Danny. But its more open, jazzy tone and subtle arrangement (like the twinkling piano in the right channel working against the electric guitar in the left behind the verse, with acoustic instruments, voice, and spacey electric in the centre) demonstrated a sophisticated subtlety that would come more to the fore in a few more years. This was even truer of "Call Me Crazy," which stood as the bridge between *Inside Out* and the yet-to-come *One World*. Its unusual intervals and tabla percussion, hypnotic patterns and mantra-like repetition of the lyrics harked back a year. The second section, with its slow cascade of notes and careful use of the volume pedal and the Echoplex being used for sustain, not momentum, was the seed of the ideas that came to full flower on "Small Hours."

There was a sense of contentment about the whole record that indicated he'd decompressed from the touring experience and had relaxed back into home life. As he noted, "I was a Sunday's child, I was born on a Sunday. I was very relaxed, it was a very peaceful time in my life. It was a very domestic album. I was very happy in those days."

While remembered as a tranquil time, unlike the period that would follow, the words were true. It was a happy record. The songs were open and real songs, unlike some of his last work.

But John was also upset at the workings of the music business and disheartened by the amount of time he had to spend on the road. In fact, he declared in one of the music papers that if the album didn't sell, he'd give up and become a social worker instead. Almost twenty years later he declared, "Well, this was almost true. I felt like I'd been working myself to death. I was almost sacrificing my marriage to the music industry and I was kind of pissed off at the whole lot."

Sunday's Child, unfortunately, seemed lost in the wake of the three records that had preceded it. To be fair, it didn't have anything quite as strong as "Solid Air" or "May You Never," nor anything as sonically arresting and daring as "Outside In." It could probably have used a little more time to develop the songs and performances, rather than being delivered in such an off-the-cuff fashion. But pieces like "Root Love," "One Day Without You" and "You Can Discover" did become regulars in his live set for a long time.

Inevitably, the record was to be supported with a tour and Island seemed to be willing to give some support in terms of advertising. Certainly it seemed like an easier record to market than the last one. One idea they couldn't find much enthusiasm for was the live album that John suggested.

That was odd, perhaps. John was a strong live performer. His rapport with audiences was immediate and he could entertain – he frequently spent as much time talking as he did singing. Live, his singing and playing took on another dimension, more powerful, immediate and improvisational than his records. And when he worked with Danny Thompson, musical sparks frequently flew (as well as conflicts of personality, mock and otherwise).

For this tour, in addition to Danny, John was adding drummer John Stevens. He may have been unknown to John's fans, but Stevens had an extensive reputation in British avant-garde jazz circles. Among other things, he led a small group called Jon Stevens' Away (with whom John would record the single "Anni," in March 1976), although he was best known for his work with the spontaneous Music Ensemble.

Adding a drummer to the touring equation would certainly alter things, although someone with the flexibility Stevens offered meant there was still freedom to improvise. But there's no doubt it was hard on Stevens, who was coming into what was a long-established unit.

However, in rehearsals the three of them gelled remarkably well and in January they hit the road together. By all accounts, Stevens also enjoyed a drink, which at least helped him fit in socially with the other two.

There was an additional factor entering the mix, too. John had invited guitarist Paul Kossoff to join them. The pair had played together before, when Koss added electric guitar to the single version of "May You Never," and the pair also recorded the jam that became "Time Away" on Koss's 1973 solo debut, *Back Street Crawler*. He wasn't going to be billed as part of the show and would only be on stage playing during the encores. Kossoff, who'd become a close friend, was struggling to break his drug dependency, and John wanted to help him. After all, with Nick Drake's death in November 1974, John had just lost one close friend; he had no desire to see another fall by the wayside. He had Kossoff stay with his family in Hastings and took him on the road, thinking gigging might help.

That didn't prove to be the case. It was impossible for John to babysit Kossoff when he had all the responsibility of the tour on his shoulders. So the guitarist would frequently vanish, often not even showing up to play. And like any junkie, he managed to find drugs – or they managed to find him. When he did play though, it could be joyous. But ultimately, although both John and Bev adored him, it proved to be a losing battle between Kossoff and addiction. He'd die in March 1976 of a drug-induced heart attack while flying from Los Angeles to New York.

It was, John would admit later, "a weird band, because upright bass and very heavy Les Paul very distorted is a strange combination. It didn't actually work that well for me."

Although Island had turned down the concept of a live album, John had managed to negotiate an interesting deal with the label. They would let him record and release one himself. That was a highly unusual move. Prior to the rise of punk in 1976, artists only tended to work through established labels, not independently - especially someone like John, who was established, with a track record.

It placed plenty of pressure on him, as he was bearing the costs himself – and it wasn't cheap, especially using a mobile studio. Then he had to pick the right show to record. It had to be after every musician had been worked in well, but not the final night of the trip, which always tended to be very loose. Instead he plumped for the next to last night, February 13 at the University of Leeds. By then they'd been going almost a month and any and all glitches had been resolved.

The hall was packed and, in typical '70s fashion, everyone was sitting on the floor. Interestingly, rather than focusing on his new release, the bulk of the set was taken from previous albums, with plenty of room to stretch out – which was of course one of the joys of his live playing, along with the banter. The original vinyl release of the album actually contained no material from *Sunday's Child*; it wasn't until the expanded CD version appeared in 1998 that three tracks from that record could finally be heard (along with the otherwise unreleased encore of "Mailman"), with Kossoff featured on the final three cuts.

In the mid-'90s, John insisted that he'd only ever heard the tracks from the original release, saying "I haven't heard the rest of it. It'll by lying somewhere in a dusty vault, as they say. I don't know, search me."

There was no animosity between him and Island over their refusal to completely sanction a live album (although it did come out with an Island number – ILPS 9343).

"I asked them and they didn't want to put it out, they just didn't feel like putting a live album out. There must have been a reason but I never enquired. I did it myself. It wasn't as if we fell out over it or anything."

John did manage to persuade Island to order 10,000 copies to be pressed by EMI. The record's working title was supposedly *Ring Side Seat* and was set to feature a picture of John and Danny in a boxing ring – and the photo shoot actually occurred, becoming the occasion for another Martyn/Thompson tale. The pair of them were set up in a London boxing gym, in shorts and wearing gloves, outfitted for sparring. It was all meant to be fake, a joking reference to their onstage personalities. But, as usual, John wanted to push it as far as he could. He hit Danny, who threatened him, then hit him again. That wasn't a wise move. John might well have been able to hold his own in youthful fights in Glasgow, but here he was up against a former regimental boxing champion, a man who knew his way around a ring. All it took was one punch, and John was on the floor, with the whole episode captured on film. That might have been why the plans were changed and it became simply *Live at Leeds*, an echo of the Who's seminal album, also recorded at Leeds University.

John's original plan, according to *Street Life*, was for "the cover and centre label to be just plain, unsullied white, with no info. This demand (a reaction on Martyn's part to having recently lost control of his albums' cover design) has not met with widespread approval."

Instead the front cover was given a rubber stamp design (again redolent of the Who) and the back cover was plain.

The album itself wasn't advertised until September 1975, when a full-page ad appeared in *Melody Maker*, including a coupon, so the willing could send their £3 (including postage) for a signed copy of the disc. The address was John's home and the assumption was that the albums would be sent back speedily.

"It would have been fantastic if it wasn't for EMI," John pointed out. "EMI fucked it all up simply by a seven-week delay on the pressing, and when I should have been at home sitting doin' albums, I was away on tour so Bev had to do them. Like we advertised it on EMI's word that it would be pressed by Tuesday. So that people were already writing' the day I got the albums; I was getting complaints like 'Where's my fuckin' album?' And of course I was away on tour."

At the same time, "the first of the record independents" (as John mistakenly characterized himself) did see a positive side to all of this. He sold all 10,000 copies of the record (the original pressing is now a very desirable collector's item, especially if autographed and numbered, as many of the original batch were) and "every morning for months I woke up and there was another couple of thousand quid lying on the floor." However, keeping track of everything demanded a high level of organization, while signing and personalizing several thousand record sleeves took a lot of time, with wear and tear on the hand. It was November 1975 before they were all sent out, when John was on the road for the entire month (including a return to Leeds University). By this point he was just grinding it out. He was weary, homesick, worn down by the problems with EMI and actually getting the live album out. Interviews from the time showed a man rapidly reaching the end of his tether and simply counting down the time until he could go home. For three straight years he'd spent several months on the road, logging a lot of miles and playing for a lot of people, and financially the rewards hadn't been overwhelming. Along the way, he'd managed to abuse his body a great deal with alcohol and drugs.

For a short time he flirted with the idea of quitting music altogether, at times resenting it, because without music he might have gone to university and become a doctor.

He was tired, he explained to a French publication, from "too much cocaine, heroin…but I have decided to go on because I love playing too much, and travelling. I have learned my lesson! I will never take the trip again of touring for eight months a year, for three years in a row. Not surprisingly you get sick…"

John needed a break. Not to simply stop touring for a little while, but a true sabbatical, going somewhere different, where he could relax properly, and where a change of scene could refresh his mind and spirit, and his body might have a chance to heal, since the toll was physical as well as mental.

It would be important, too, to spend time with Beverley and the kids, who'd also suffered from John's absences and his substance problems. By printing their address in the ad for *Live at Leeds,* they'd left themselves open for visits by fans, some of whom hoped to be able to stay for a night or two (they were politely but firmly refused). The cracks in the marital relationship were just beginning to show and both John and Bev hoped that time away might mend them.

The problems in taking an extended holiday of any kind were logistical. There had to be a place to go to, and renting a house somewhere would cost money, as they weren't about to completely abandon their place in Hastings. It was Island head Chris Blackwell who came to the rescue. Now a wealthy man in his own right, he had a house on Strawberry Hill in Jamaica that was sitting empty and he offered the Martyns the use of it. Sun and warmth and the laid-back island atmosphere (plus the availability of copious amounts of ganja) was exactly what the doctor ordered. So the couple took their savings, some £7,500, and used it to finance their break.

They were gone for about four months in the early part of 1976 and John fell in love with Jamaica, particularly Kingston, which he called "Glasgow transported to Paradise!" It's possible that John came home briefly during this period, since he did record with John Stevens' Away in March.

The intention had been for him to take a complete break from music, but that didn't happen. Island had strong musical connections with Jamaica – it remained the pre-eminent reggae label with the cream of the artists – and John inevitably hooked up with some of them. He played guitar on Burning Spear's *Man in the Hills*, although his contribution has never been credited, and most famously worked with Lee "Scratch" Perry, the eccentric (some would say mad) genius of dub and reggae, with whom he seemed to forge a deep bond, on some Max Romeo sessions. As John related, "I've never got credited for most of it. It's rather like (a) you don't get credit, and (b) you don't get *paid*! No, I got paid in two crates of Tia Maria, or was it Kahlua? Coffee liqueur, whatever it was. Better than a poke in the eye..."

Working in Jamaica, and especially working with Perry, had a big effect on John. He learned a great deal about the textures used in the music, and the detail of production. For all his apparent lunacy, Scratch could be a genius in the studio, and he knew how to make use of his effects and ideas to achieve the fullest possible sound; he came to it with a vision that would definitely rub off on John.

"He's his own person," John said of Perry, "and somewhat eccentric. We were both using double and triple echo around the same time."

To this point, John's records had been very straightforward in their sound, relying on the musicians and the notes they played, rather than making the studio into another instrument, as important as the players themselves. That was in part because he'd come from an acoustic angle, where it was the song and the performance that counted, and giving a true representation of that was vital. Even his electric material had been based around the performance. But Jamaica seemed to open his ears to the possibilities of the studio itself.

Was the sabbatical a success? That it was needed is beyond question, and it obviously erased the doubts John had about carrying on in the music business, since he resumed gigging after returning home, albeit at a less frantic pace.

More important, he was preparing material for his next album. Instead of creating songs in the studio, as he had with *Inside Out* and *Sunday's Child*, he was consciously writing well in advance of the deadline. Among the material were two pieces he was playing live in the latter half of 1976, "Black Man At Your Shoulder," his reaction to some of the racist ideas welling up in England at the time, and "Dead On Arrival," which he'd composed following the passing of Paul Kossoff. Both these pieces would be recorded and the former finally appeared on the *Another World* release.

On their return from the Caribbean, John, Beverley and the kids moved out of Hastings, twenty miles inland to Heathfield, a smaller town in the country. Whether the break from England had done more than put a sticking plaster over the marital problems remains moot, but they were still together and obviously attempting a fresh start.

John continued to gig sporadically in late 1976 and into early 1977, undertaking a 14-date tour in February and March. Meanwhile, the plans for his new album were well underway. In a surprising move, Chris Blackwell was going to have real hands-on involvement for the first time in the decade John had been recording for Island.

Phil Brown, who engineered, has said the disc was made in the summer of 1977.

In fact, that period saw John back in North America, playing on the East Coast in both Canada and the US, which culminated in a three-night stand at Kenny's Castaways in New York, alongside old friend Bridget St. John, so the actual recording must have taken place earlier.

"He came over in '77," she recalled. "He'd put me in touch with Island at the end of '76, and I left for Canada and got stuck there. I came back in [to New York] to do a gig at Kenny's with John. I met him up in Canada, too – when he came to play Toronto I was there. I went to a gig and spent time with him there."

By this time St. John was living in New York, established in Greenwich Village. She'd stayed in touch with John and Beverley after they'd moved to the coast, "the kind of friendship that's always been there and we come and go, depending on what we're doing. I've always had this big thing for John as a human being."

Legend has it that John was unhappy with the gigs at Kenny's because the owner charged admission. However, that didn't stop him delivering a strong set, and showing what one journalist called "an intense but engaging stage presence...it was enjoyable to witness his easy rapport with the large crowd which seemed ready to follow along on each of his musical excursions." St. John, playing her first US gigs, also came in for praise as "a fresh, exciting talent well worth watching for the future."

As John was getting ready to begin recording his new album, Island pulled a surprise on him by releasing the *So Far, So Good* compilation. With its none too flattering cover painting by Ray Winder, it was a small excursion into the world of John Martyn, although it only covered music from his most acclaimed (and most accessible) albums to date – *Bless the Weather*, *Solid Air* and *Sunday's Child*, but with the addition of a previously unreleased live version of "I'd Rather Be The Devil" (notably not the one from *Live at Leeds*). John wasn't happy with the choice of tracks, but it was out of his hands – as was the single from the disc, "Over The Hill," which was in a DJ format, with the words "dirty champagne" substituting for "sweet cocaine" in an attempt to make the track more radio friendly (not that it received any airplay, anyway).

For all that John disagreed with the songs included, it served as a good primer, and sold well enough to earn him his first-ever gold disc, which he supposedly attempted to smash in disgust.

CHAPTER SEVEN – One World

John called *One World* "more produced, not nearly as raw as the other stuff. Chris Blackwell produced that, so I can't take any credit for changing the lineup. I like it. In retrospect, it's a pretty good album. I recorded it in Blackwell's backyard. We brought the Island mobile up to his house and did it there. Lee [Perry] was there all the time."

As summaries go, there was some truth in that – and also a touch of exaggeration.

The album was recorded at Woolwich Green Farm, a property Blackwell owned in Theale, about half an hour from London, in the Berkshire countryside near Reading. Engineer Phil Brown had used it before, "to do the overdubs of *Pressure Drop* with Robert Palmer and a few other bits and pieces. It was Blackwell's idea to take the mobile and do John's album out there. Bearing in mind that you had John Martyn singing and playing, which could have been done at Basing Street or any studio, it seemed to make it a bit of an adventure."

Brown had been a staff engineer for Island from 1970-76, but he'd recently gone freelance. While working for the label, he'd known both John and Nick Drake, both of whom "would occasionally pop by the studio. [John]'s a very imposing figure, he's a big guy." When he'd first met John, at the start of the decade, Brown recalled that "he and Beverley were incredibly thin – Beverley was elfin-like, and they both ended up putting on a lot of weight." John certainly seemed larger than he had just a few years before, as if he was finally growing into his adult figure as he entered his late twenties.

Chris Blackwell had produced albums for his artists before. He'd heard John's original demos for the new disc "and he wanted John to do a great album. It was difficult getting John to just get albums out, or something commercially saleable," Brown recalled.

"I always liked John a lot. It may have been that I thought I could bring something out in him," Blackwell agreed.

The house where they'd be working was quite isolated. Blackwell "had bought a house there back in the '60s that was a derelict farmhouse on part of this gravel pit that was being dug," Brown said. "After five or six years they'd finished digging out all the gravel, and it was left as this amazing house. He refurbished the house and it was surrounded by water."

According to Brown's notes, he, along with assistant Ray Doyle, set up the mobile on July 16th.

"There was Chris Blackwell and myself in the mobile, and John Martyn basically in a room by himself that we were recording. So initially it was down to the four of us. We set John up in one of the flats there; they were basically stable blocks that had been converted into accommodation. John went through the songs on his own, singing and playing, maybe with a bit of rhythm box, and then brought in Steve Winwood and Danny Thompson to do overdubs and work on the album. But it was done in a low-key way."

In fact John spent the first ten days there working without other musicians around, "singing songs and running ideas." The arrangements for the material "just developed," Brown said. "John had a batch of tracks, and we were recording, running a reel for thirty minutes – we were recording at 15 inches per second – and letting him do take after take, or editing various takes together. 'Small Hours' was edited, and a couple of others were edited down from eight minutes to maybe four or five minutes, in order to keep it fairly free and let John do his stuff. Some of the songs did have very strict arrangements, but there were others that were much looser in our approach to recording them."

Brown brought a sense of experimentation to the proceedings, perhaps the wildest of which was recording outside for some of the work.

Having the mobile studio gave him the opportunity and he took full advantage of it. But it was something he'd tried before.

"I'd been into it since about '71. I did an album called *Nigel Lived* with a guy called Murray Head. We recorded it in St. Paul's Church in Covent Garden and at subway stations in London and in railway stations. That was my first real burst of recording with mobiles and out in the field."

With its lake and isolation, the house at Theale was perfect for outside recording. Setting it all up, however, required a great deal of work.

"We hired a P.A. system and set the monitor stack up on the far side of the stables pointing out across the lake," Brown explained. "I used two Neumann U87s [microphones] on the opposite side of the house, to mike up the outdoor P.A. sound coming back off the lake. A further two Neumann U87s were placed close to the water's edge, as far away as our leads would allow. These picked up the sound of the water lapping, and a distant 'strangled' sound on the guitar which was perfect for lead solos."

Much of the outdoor recording was done at night, which presented it own problems as dew formed.

"We tried to protect the microphones from the damp night air using polythene, with limited success. When they 'went down' on particularly wet nights or because of a heavy dew, we replaced them and then dried out the originals. Between three a.m. and six a.m. was the toughest times on the mikes, but these quiet hours before dawn created the most magical atmosphere for recording." For Blackwell, "that's one of my favorite tracks, not of John's, but ever. We recorded at about four in the morning, and I love that."

'Small Hours' and 'One World' were the two tracks that benefited most from the open air, which gave them a wonderful feel. It's quite possible, however, that much of the laid-back feel that pervaded the album was due to the session drug – opium.

On their second day in Theale, a friend of Brown's rang saying he had an ounce of opium, but didn't like it because it kept making him throw up, and offering it to Brown for the very reasonable sum of £25. Brown took him up on the offer.

"I informed John of our acquisition and he laughed, took the opium, rolled a joint and opened a bottle of whisky. His actions immediately stamped a particular attitude on the recording of the whole album. Soon the five of us (John, Chris, Ray, Barry Sage [another assistant], and myself), under John's guidance, were mellow and laid back. John played a cassette of some of the demos on a portable cassette machine, and it was not long before we had a good idea of the approach to the songs we were about to put down. Every two or three hours we would eat a small ball of opium and roll a joint. It was a very enjoyable state – although unfortunately within five days we were all addicted. This was addiction in the sense that on waking the fifth day, one felt slightly hung-over, tired, lacking in energy and not really on top of things. After eating a small ball, the body and brain returned to working order and all the wonders of life flooded back."

Unbeknownst to each other, both John and Brown had been secreting emergency stashes of small opium balls in the barn, although eventually these ran out, after which "we substituted large quantities of grass and hash joints and the occasional hit of brandy."

After seven days' recording, they all took a weekend off and Brown drove John back to Heathfield (where Brown also lived), returning on the Monday.

"Lee 'Scratch' Perry came out to the house to see Chris, loved what we were doing, and hung around for the day [not the entire session, as John had intimated]...He giggled a lot, reeked of grass and was rarely seen without a half-smoked joint – the old seven-inch baseball bat. Lee was fascinated by John's F/X pedals and found naming a fuzz box 'Big

Muff' hilarious. He could not grasp that it was the manufacturer's name and not some coarse in-joke of John's. I don't think we ever convinced him otherwise and he and John wrote and recorded the track 'Big Muff,' inspired by the effects box, in a day. Lee's lyrical ideas for the song all had sexual connotations, while John's appeared to be about [producer] Muff Winwood and the layout of Basing Street Studios. When working, Lee was wonderful to watch, dancing around the room triggering echoes and phasing effects. We recorded eighty per cent of the finished song during that day. After this whirlwind of activity Lee left and we resumed working with John on his own, or with the occasional guest."

Among those guests was drummer Andy Newmark. He stayed a day and provided drums for "Dealer," "Smiling Stranger," "Certain Surprise," and "Big Muff." In the end, though, only his part for 'Dealer' survived, replaced by Bruce Rowland on the other tracks. Both Danny Thompson and Steve Winwood stayed for a couple of days, laying down a number of parts, although Brown noted that "we only kept the Moog on 'Small Hours' and 'Dealer' and the acoustic bass on 'Couldn't Love You More' and 'Certain Surprise.'

"I had Andy Newmark come down to play, and Steve Winwood," said Blackwell, "but because of the way John plays, it was very difficult to get a track, especially as I had the drums in one little area and John was in another area, so they weren't in the same room. We had quite a lot of problems in editing and putting tracks together."

All in all, Martyn, Blackwell, and the crew spent three weeks at Theale, doing the basic recording. From there the plan was to complete overdubs and mixing at the Basing Street Studios.

Blackwell's role proved to be interesting. Phil Brown had worked with him before, "on the Bob Marley stuff, and a bit of Jimmy Cliff, and various things through the '70s. He's hands-on, but in the old-fashioned producer role in a sense. He'd set up the situation, bring in people he thought would be good for it and a situation he thought would be good, then let people do what they do. So Chris was pretty hands-on in the [mobile] truck as far as arrangements and editing and deciding where things should go. But the initial setting-up of tracks was down to John and I. Chris wouldn't be hands-on compared to a modern producer, who tends to do everything. He allowed things to happen, which is often the best thing in the world."

Dealing with John was generally good. Brown got along reasonably well with him, as they lived in the same town and both had young children, and they developed a relationship outside the studio. But John could be volatile and unpredictable.

"Every time you work with John you never quite know where he's going to go, which is the excitement of it all. But it follows through into everyday life; you don't know if he's going to be sweet and friendly or give you a hard time. Most of the time he was very cool. But he overheard Chris and I talking one day about how to structure the album and what we needed to do to finish it. He took great offence at the fact that we were talking about him, which wasn't really the case. But John's a tricky guy. I love him dearly, but he can turn on you if he's drunk. I think he's been aggressive and upset people without meaning to."

The mood swings and changeability, especially under the influence of alcohol, seemed to have become more pronounced.

"If he was sober and in a good mood he would be mellow and laid back, charming, inventive, verbally amusing and spiritually alive," Brown said. "When dark, drunk or angry, he managed to reverse all these attributes and could become difficult, aggressive, loud and obnoxious, or alternatively, very quiet and depressed."

Brown had anticipated working on the album to its conclusion, through the overdubs and the mixing. As the initial recording period ended, however, Blackwell asked him to go to New York, to work with Robert Palmer, who was having problems with his new album (1978's *Double Fun*). Brown and Palmer had worked well together before. It was a sign of how desperate Blackwell was that he offered Brown a $5000 advance and a one per cent royalty for co-production - an irresistible temptation for someone still establishing himself as a freelance engineer. Blackwell also gave Brown the chance to re-mix any of the tracks from John's album that he didn't like. What could Brown do but say yes?

"We finished as much work as we could with John and two days later, on August the sixth, the mobile was packed up and Ray and Barry drove back to London. I drove John home to Heathfield. Throughout the journey there was an awkward atmosphere. I was feeling guilty about leaving John's album, and he behaved as though he thought I had a choice in the matter, which of course I didn't."

In the end, more vocals and the remaining overdubs were completed in London, and Brown did eventually re-mix a few of the tracks after returning from America. *One World* arrived in the shops on November 4, 1977.

At the time, its sound was a surprise to fans who'd grown with his music from *Bless the Weather* onward. It was more electric, and certainly a great deal smoother and more sophisticated. In hindsight, it was very much a transitional record, moving John from his acoustic past into the fuller band sound that would be the future.

Of course, John wasn't playing with a band on the record, merely others who came in to flesh out his sound and his vision. And that vision had decidedly changed. Acoustic guitar had been relegated to a secondary role, replaced by the Les Paul. And John's electric style had altered, too. The days of relying on the Echoplex had vanished; instead, the guitar was an integral part of *songs*, and the soloing, though still inventive and exploratory, was more "normal" in its context and style.

Stylistically it was a very varied album, ranging from the mutated dub of "Big Muff" and the dark, shadowed funk of "Smiling Stranger" to the extroverted light energy of "Dancing" and the glorious stillness of the title track and "Small Hours" (where the outdoor recording included a flock of Canada geese, which can be heard on the disc).

If *Bless the Weather* had found John easing into his maturity, this set him on a new path. But there's no denying that he was writing songs of depth and craft. They sparkle, some of the very best, most accomplished work of his career, and they were also immediately accessible, which perhaps helped explained why the album rose to 54 on the charts – the first time John had even managed a chart placing.

"Dancing" was picked as a single, an obvious choice, although it went nowhere. For collectors, however, it's possibly more interesting for its b-side, an instrumental version of "Dealer."

The limited release (1000 copies) of the two-CD set *Another World* in 1999 offered greater insight into the process of recording the album. Put together from outtakes and demos (some using a primitive drum machine), they spotlight how the songs and arrangements developed through the three weeks of recording, along with notes by Phil Brown and Danny Thompson.

Thompson had suffered a heart attack after the sessions and John was among those taking part in a benefit for him. It marked the end (for several years, at least) of their musical partnership, as Thompson gave up alcohol and his old wild lifestyle in favour of something more sedate, that offered the possibility of a longer life.

Touring was in John's blood, though, and he took off for Australia for several dates, before returning to undertake a November trek around the UK in support of the record, including a date at the Rainbow where he was helped out by Winwood and the rhythm section from Gong. Mostly he was accompanied by a Rhythm Doctor for some of the songs on tour - an early drum machine.

"People thought it was so funny, that this geezer would walk onstage with a glorified metronome. They could not see that it was in fact a bass drum, with a kick drum (*sic*) at the top. A lot of the things I used to fiddle about with confused people at first."

The record was doing well, reviews had been glowing, and he stayed on the road, hitting Europe, recording an *Old Grey Whistle Test* and then returning to America, where he was set to be the opening act for Eric Clapton, who'd moved into the superstar bracket as a solo act. Once again John was going to be in the giant arenas, working alone, and warming up crowds who weren't especially interested in him as they waited for the headliner.

By this time Brian Cullman, who'd first met him in London in 1970, was a working music journalist in New York. When he learned that John would be touring, he "made some calls to Island, and realised that nobody in the entire Island office in New York knew who he was – and this was at a time when he was opening for Eric Clapton! I'd go, 'You could do something with this guy, there are people who'd write about him.' There was a sense of carelessness and inattention that I think he was really upset by. He was taken seriously by musicians, and I think when he came to the States and realized that nobody cared, including his record label, he was devastated and became really bitter."

To call the experience unhappy barely did it justice. With 16 dates in a little over three weeks, all in the eastern half of the US, there was plenty of travelling, but also plenty of opportunity for indulgence of all kinds – and John had rarely been one to walk away from temptation. And there were compensations.

"Clapton gave me half an hour and paid me extra if I got off stage on time...but in a way, touring like that frees you up something wicked. All the groupies are waiting for the superstar main band and you're done and ready..."

That aside, artistically it proved to be an empty, soul-destroying experience.

"Because [Clapton] runs a tight ship, you'd always have to go on at half past seven, at which point there'd be about four or five thousand people in the hall...I didn't like it very much. I got paid very well for it...Apart from four or five gigs that were very good, I mean I did about 30 and about 25 of them, if they'd been my own gigs, I'd probably have topped myself after the second one."

He was home for a break by the middle of April, but by then things must have been getting strained in the Martyn household, as the relationship between John and Beverley was rapidly crumbling. So perhaps it was with a little relief that he undertook his second Australian tour in July, including a Sydney show organized by the makers of the film *In Search of Anna*. John had written some of the incidental music for the movie, in addition to the theme tune 'Anna,' which was based on 'Small Hours.'

By late summer, back in Sussex, he was working on another project, although not one of his own this time. He contributed guitar to *Harmony of the Spheres* by the late composer Neil Ardley.

"The reason we got together was that we shared the same manager," Ardley recounted a few months before his death. "His name was Bruce May, and he's Ralph McTell's brother. Because Bruce managed Ralph, he had several other artists – Bert Jansch was one of them, and John Martyn. A friend of mine went to work for Bruce and introduced me, although I was quite different, and he took me on. I got to know all the other people Bruce managed, which was nice for me, because it extended me."

Ardley worked in more of an avant-garde and jazz framework, which fitted well with John's interests, if not the course his own music was taking. By 1978 Ardley had a strong reputation in British music circles and had been starting work on his next piece.

"I was already preparing the album. It had taken a long time, with a lot of initial work done at home on synthesizers and tape machines. It either occurred to me or was suggested to me that it should feature John. Because John doesn't read music, I was able to take the music I'd composed to him and ask him how he'd fit into it. It was a very unusual way to do things."

In fact Ardley visited John in Heathfield – a sign that his marriage hadn't completely collapsed yet.

"[The house] was out in the country, it was lovely. I spent two or three days down there with him and his wife, Beverley, and we spent the time going through it, teaching it to John, and trying out ideas. After that we went into the studio. His was a fairly late contribution [making it probably September '78], after almost everything else had been done. He was always very nice to me, quite charming. He has a tremendous native talent, almost more than anyone I've ever met. Music just oozed out of his fingers, he was very creative in a totally untutored way."

John ended up playing rhythm guitar on the album, and also lead on four of its seven tracks. After familiarising himself with the pieces, John largely improvised his parts in the studio.

"I'm used to improvisation in jazz, of course," Ardley said, "but usually they work from chord symbols or something like that. In John's case it was totally by ear, and he just had to get to know the pieces, which he did."

Although John was reputedly less than happy with his work, Ardley was extremely pleased, so much so that he asked John to take part in a television programme devoted to the work.

"When we finished [the album], a friend of mine who was a television producer was very keen on it. *The South Bank Show* on ITV ran a half-hour feature on it. We recorded most of the music in the studio, and John was there. He broke a string and we had to wait around about forty minutes while another one was produced. One of the musicians turned around and said to John, 'What's the next number?' and he said 'I don't know until he starts.' That tells you a lot about the way he works, completely reactive. He would fit in with a rhythm pattern, a solo, whatever he felt was appropriate. I think it worked very well. I'd always rather liked this idea of presenting a composed piece to an improvising musician to work over the top. It requires an extremely creative musician, and that's more or less what John was doing. He has a very rare talent."

Notably he was playing electric guitar on the album, the acoustic put back in its case as much as possible now – although he'd still need it for solo tours, which were a quick and relatively easy way to make money.

But music had to take a back seat for a while. At the forefront of his life was the implosion of his marriage to Beverley. With three children, any separation and divorce was going to be complicated, but this was extremely difficult. His bouts with alcohol and drugs had affected his moods – and he could be moody at the best of times – and his increasing dependence on substances exacerbated all kinds of problems.

On top of that, Beverley had been moved purely to the role of wife and mother. According to some, that was how John preferred her, but she'd been a performer who was starting to break out when she'd put her career on hold. The promised album of 1975/76 had never materialized. John was gone a great deal of the time – more than ever, as he'd become more popular, and by his own admission in song he'd been unfaithful more than once.

It had all finally become too much and she ended things, even going to the extent of reportedly getting an order that forced him to keep away from his family. In her own book, *Sweet Honesty* (published after John's death, so he can't refute the charges), she makes allegations of both mental and physical abuse during their marriage. Although rumours of this have long circulated, nothing had ever been proven.

He'd been far from a perfect husband, gone much of the time, indulging in all manner of substances, so he often wasn't there in spirit, either. On the road he had his groupies, as so many musicians did, so he wasn't faithful. But that he loved Beverley in his own way was beyond doubt.

They'd been together for nine years and he was closer to her than he'd been to anybody, but he also knew he'd behaved badly. Home had a been a centre to him, a place to think of when he was on the road, a welcoming place to return to, and now that had been taken away. It's no understatement to say that he was thrown into a tailspin, and he went, at least briefly, into a cycle of self-destruction where "you name it, I soaked myself in it...it was a dark period in my life."

An era had ended, both personally and professionally, and it affected him deeply.

"Beverley basically left him after years of grief," Phil Brown noted, "and he turned round to me a few years ago and basically said, 'I've never written a good song since Beverley left.' And it's a tricky area. If you listen to his stuff from the '70s, when he was with Beverley, it's some of his best stuff. Hopefully it isn't true that he hasn't got it together since she left. But it has been over twenty years, and he's tormented in that sense."

What he did have was music, and he began writing songs that documented his emotional ups and downs, gearing towards what would be his next album. As he said, it would be "probably the most specific piece of autobiography I've written. Some people keep diaries, I make records."

However, John had generally tended to hide the specificity of events behind other things in his lyrics in the past. Not so this time. Instead, he let everything pour out. There was regret, love, loss, and plenty of anger in the music he was creating now, and it definitely was a diary of a sort.

Curiously, he was joined by the least expected person – Phil Collins, the drummer with Genesis, who'd also become their singer following the departure of Peter Gabriel in 1975, and who moved in completely different musical circles from John. He wasn't yet a solo star, however (that would happen in 1981 with "In The Air Tonight," the first of a string of hits that would transform him into a superstar), and was still regarded more as a drummer who also happened to sing.

"He just turned up at gigs, then turned up to record," John remembered. Like John, Collins was going through a messy, painful divorce and they became a shoulder for each other to cry on, "a certain kind of kindred spirit between us" as John called it.

"We'd have a couple of drinks, go down to his house, have a couple of drinks, then go out for dinner with our respective girlfriends."

And those were the good days. There were also tearful times on the phone to almost ex-wives, recriminations and guilt, and plenty of hurt that was channelled into the music John was making.

"We were both going through emotional trauma, so there was vast amounts of going down to the potting shed together and weeping. We'd both have these horrendous phone calls. I'd phone Beverley and it would be 'Aargh!' and then it would be Phil's turn. We were both making ourselves terribly miserable and then playing and singing about it, sob!"

With no place to call home any more, towards the end of 1978 he was living with Collins, and working on the new record, which proved to be a challenge for Collins, who was used to the heavily arranged structures of Genesis.

"It's difficult to play songs with only two or three chords as you rely entirely on the atmosphere you create within them, but he manages it," Collins observed. "He's totally unique, and he makes an almost lazy sound while knowing exactly what is needed."

Unsurprisingly, John was drowning a lot of his sorrows, diving heavily into the bottle. Perhaps that's the reason that the album he made, *Grace and Danger*, is such unfiltered emotion. He could have used an editor, but either chose not to find one, or refused one.

A quarter of a century on it still stands as perhaps the ultimate breakup album, largely because of the way it runs the gamut of emotions, from hurt to anger to glee, including a cover of the reggae standard "Johnny Too Bad," possibly to portray John as the baddest man in town, not someone to be messed with. And it's certainly notable that the closer is a piece John and Beverley had written together, "Our Love," an older song that he resurrected for this release.

While forged in pain, it did contain at least one classic, the aching "Sweet Little Mystery," with its chiming melody, and "Lookin' On" would become a staple of his live set, making an excellent guitar and vocal workout.

Musically John took the next logical step from *One World*, which was to work in a proper band format. His guitar work took a bit of a back seat in this; he was content with a subordinate role and often let the keyboards of former Grease Band member Tommy Eyre (along with ex-Greenslade man Dave Lawson on a couple of tracks) dominate the proceedings. Collins provided the foundation and occasional back-up vocals, while John Giblin, who worked with Collins in his prog-jazz side group Brand X, played bass (the start of what would be an ongoing association between Giblin and John).

Although it was his first step to working with a band, he wasn't used to working so closely with so many and still had plenty of his individuality intact - a spikiness that showed itself throughout the disc. To all intents and purposes, it was a solo album given to a band.

The lush, slow "Some People Are Crazy" made an easy entry point, working slowly into the overall mood of bitterness that pervaded the record, but putting the iron fist in a velvet glove. But with the title track that glove had been removed and what started out lyrically gracious became a a curious mix of furious kiss-off and undiluted self-pity, and containing the first "normal" guitar solo John had ever recorded, over a deliberately aggressive backing.

The more amorphous "Lookin' On" was a welter of emotions, reflected in music that tried to make jazzy melodic sense, the fusion of Collins' and Giblin's Brand X transferred to a song. On the other hand, the cover of the reggae classic "Johnny Too Bad" made perfect sense. Nastily scraped fuzz guitar chords drove it, and Johnny was too bad, although he lived and died by the ratchet (Jamaican patois for a knife), an allegory of John's own marital situation. Musically, "Sweet Little Mystery" was classic '70s John Martyn, although wrapped a little too sweetly in the glistening confection of electric piano and Phil Collins' backing vocals (it's worth mentioning, however, that Collins was exemplary on drums throughout). It's a perfect lost-my-girl-I-miss-her-and-I-want her-back broken heart song, although by John's standards, where emotions were usually only obliquely referred to, it was a wallow in the more of self-pity, albeit an undeniably honest one that laid his soul bare.

Musically, "Hurt In Your Heart" stepped back to *One World* territory, but used it as a framework on which to hang words of a come-back-to-me-when-the-pain-has-gone flavour. If they couldn't be a couple, maybe they could at least be friends and remember the good times. But, in spite of the graceful music, it came across as nothing more than a desperate plea. Yet it wasn't as straightforward as "Baby Please Come Home," which was outright grovelling, a man crying on disc.

By "Save Some (For Me)," however, the mood had changed again. There was still the vestige of love, one that went deep, but now he was over her and she was in the wrong. He was going to live his life without her and if she wanted to come back, it would be on his terms.

The sound of "Our Love" was a good bookend with "Some People Are Crazy," but it was the sound of a heart – quite possibly Beverley's – breaking. It made an appropriate coda, a well of sadness of how they had grown apart.

Grace and Danger was the last of John's albums for a long time to contain very definite songs, as opposed to the grooves that would come to characterise his music for well over a decade. They signalled the end of an era and a complete change, where the jeans and waistcoats that had been his wardrobe would be replaced by more expensive suits. Although John defended the new gear by the claim he'd been a Mod back in the '60s, that had been a brief phase at best (if it ever truly existed). It certainly wouldn't have meshed with the down-to-earth, working-class ethos of his mentor Hamish Imlach, nor would it have gone over well in the Glasgow folk clubs.

The new album was produced by Martin Levan and John turned the master tapes in to Island in 1979, with all the pain still very fresh in his mind. There was only one small problem – the label didn't release it. According to John they kept "the celebration of a miserable divorce" on the shelf "for a year and a bit, because that's when the Sex Pistols were getting very big. They didn't think the climate was right for such a ballady album."

In fact, the Sex Pistols had imploded in 1978, although punk and New Wave had certainly had an effect on popular music. But John's audience had never been the type to follow trends and now, just in his thirties, he was appealing to a slightly older crowd.

The decision on when – or even whether – to release the record ultimately rested with Chris Blackwell, the head of Island, and he was in no rush to let it out. While he admired John, he also liked Beverley, and was torn between the two of them. In part, he hoped John might change his mind about the disc and discard it, but above all he was thought to be reluctant to put out a record of such raw emotion.

In fact, Blackwell said, the real reason was much simpler: "I wasn't keen on it. It was I love you on one track, I hate you on the next. I was disappointed with it, I suppose."

Meanwhile, as he waited to see what might happen about a release, John had no choice but to take to the road. He had maintenance to pay for his children, which meant that he simply *had* to be earning money regularly. The easiest way was to tour alone, which kept expenses to a minimum, even if it didn't reflect the course his music was taking. Under the order of the court, he had to give Beverley £280 a week – a princely sum at the end of the '70s.

"I don't see why it should have to be so acrimonious," he complained at the time. "I didn't even want the fuckin' divorce in the first place: unreasonable behaviour on my part, apparently…basically, what is being said is that not only have I got to support my former wife, but they're also going to cut off my fucking nuts!"

He was in a difficult situation. The divorce wasn't something he'd wanted and the fact that he needed to spend so much time on the road to pay his ex-wife meant that he didn't have time to see his children; there wasn't even the luxury of being a weekend father to them. That meant they grew apart, as he couldn't see them often, something that would affect the rest of their lives.

1979 saw him travelling all over Europe to play gigs. He did finally have a home base, however, in the small Scots village of Moscow, some seventeen miles southwest of Glasgow – far from the South coast where his children lived. He hadn't necessarily returned to his homeland by choice, though. While John was staying with Collins, his father was taken ill, and John had gone back north of the border to be close to him.

While compounding one tragedy with another, it did at least take him far away from Beverley, probably a good thing under the circumstances. And after so long away, he was happy to be home again.

"Glasgow's wonderful – if they're going to rip you off, they do it neat, sweet and petite. It's very straight like that, Glasgow."

He wasn't in Moscow a great deal, but at least it brought him closer to his father, who recovered from his illness and would live for a number of years more.

He was still pressing Island to release *Grace and Danger*, a record he continued to describe as his "favourite" and insisting that it only eventually appeared in 1980 because "I freaked: 'Please get it out! I don't give a damn about how sad it makes you feel – it's what I'm about: direct communication of emotion'."

It was certainly that. Perhaps the biggest surprise, given the subject matter of the songs, was that it actually charted, rising as high as *One World*, to number 54. But the record's relative success left him in a strange position. His music had altered and was still changing, so he needed a band to do it justice – but at the same time, under the conditions of his divorce settlement, there was no way he could afford to take a band on the road. It was a Catch-22 situation. Solo, at least he could earn enough money to pay Beverley and still keep a roof over his head and enjoy life a little.

If *Grace and Danger* chronicled the end of his marriage and the ensuing emotional see-saw, it also marked the end of his long relationship with Island Records. They'd stuck together for a long time – 13 years – and his albums, cheap to make, had proved profitable for the label, although they'd never sold in massive quantities. There was certainly no animosity in the split – a pleasant change for John, perhaps – and John and Chris Blackwell kept a strong respect for each other.

According to John the split came after Blackwell told him "that he considered I had a jazz niche which I had succeeded in manufacturing for myself, and that that was where my career lay." However, John didn't see himself in such a pigeonhole. He was quite content to stick with Island until "[Blackwell's] minion made me an offer of money with which to make my next record, the amount was so paltry and made in such a bad way that I put the phone down on him – I'm not exactly known for my rudeness. I'm not known for my avarice, either; I've always been something of an idealist, and I will maintain that position. But quite simply I was not offered enough money to make the record I wanted to. It's odd: I've always sold plenty of records, and I'm not in debt to Island at all. In fact, they owe me money."

For Blackwell, it was a case of realising that "[John] was really free form, he wasn't really equipped to play with a structured-type band. Danny Thompson would be standing with him and watching where his hands were going to move. John's music doesn't go in fours, it changes on the thirteenth bar, or the tenth. So that in itself made me feel he was free form. And we weren't getting anywhere, we weren't building. And if it's not going anywhere, you may be the wrong person for them. So maybe one should try being with somebody else. And maybe it was because of *Grace and Danger*, since I didn't want to put it out. I'm not entirely sure he didn't go to someone else and talk to them about putting it out."

Possibly it was just the right time for a parting of the ways. At Island, John would always be known as a singer-songwriter and whatever work he produced would be held up against his classic albums from the first half of the '70s, even as he changed into something different. Add to that the problems he'd had persuading the label to release *Grace and Danger* and a new home for his music might well have seemed desirable.

On top of that, everything else in his life had changed, so working with a fresh company completed the set. And when he was ready to go, he was quickly snapped up by Warner Brothers, who obviously saw potential in what he was doing – and having Phil Collins to produce his next record most probably didn't hurt the deal (in the US, John's next two albums were released on Warner Brothers, but via Duke, the label run by Genesis; connections always help move business along), even if it was Collins' first production job.

Recording at London's Townhouse Studios, John entrenched himself for the entire length of the sessions, living in a room on the first floor and often keeping irregular hours. It wasn't unusual for the other musicians to work on backing tracks until three a.m., only to have John arrive on the scene in his dressing gown, saying it was time for him to lay down some lead vocals. As he had on several occasions in the past, John relied on the spirit to move him, allowing spontaneity to take precedence over preparation, something he'd regret when interviewed a decade later.

"I kinda felt that I let [Phil] down on that album by just not doing enough preparatory work on it," he said later. "He's faultless in the studio."

The aptly titled *Glorious Fool* showed John's new commitment to working with a band. It was really the only format for the new music he was writing and the style he was perfecting, much more electric and groove-orientated. Collins was on drums (and piano on one track), while Alan Thomson began a long-standing partnership with John on this record. Max Middleton, who'd once been part of the Jeff Beck Group, provided keyboards, with Danny Cummings on drums. Eric Clapton played lead on a retread of "Couldn't Love You More," which could have been seen as either a bitter parting shot at Beverley, or possibly a warm hello to new girlfriend Annie Furlong, whom he would marry in 1983. However it was done, it seemed oddly rushed and passionless - more like a Collins pop tune than a Martyn plea, with Clapton's solo not one of his best.

For the first time, John took a political tack on the record. Far from being self-referential, the title cut was about US President Ronald Reagan, and not in complimentary terms, while the plaintive "Don't You Go" was blatantly anti-war. "Amsterdam" was written for a friend who went to that city against John's advice and ended up leaving "on the six-foot pine express, toes up, dreadful shame." It tries for anger and gravity, but sadly the track ends up as busy instead of bitter.

Indeed, much of the record sounds as if it wanted to be frantic, but somehow quite couldn't break through. There was the throwaway disco of "Perfect Hustler" (John Martyn on the Latinesque dancefloor), "Never Say Never" (a vamp that went on too long) and "Didn't Do That," which seemed to be a vehicle for percussion, more than anything. The weepy "Heart And Keys" was a cluttered ballad that didn't come anywhere close to the emotional rawness of the previous disc. "Please Fall In Love With Me" attempted to revisit *One World* territory in its music, but the drum-heavy production kept it all too firmly anchored to the ground.

Only "Pascanel (Get Back Home)" and "Don't You Go" seemed to have any depth and emotional resonance; the former would stay in John's live set for quite some time, while the latter worked because it was a beautiful song and was presented in a very stripped-down form.

There was still the vestige of real songs on the record, but John was moving inexorably towards vamp territory, playing over the pattern of just a few chords. And the way Phil Collins had produced John vocals left him sounding nasal rather than experienced – it might have made him more acceptable to the masses, but it did him few favours artistically.

Collins' drumming was to the fore throughout, admirably concise, pushing the songs along, but never overpowering, and even his backing vocals came from the less-is-more school. His production captured an intimacy in the music, but also the new, small majesty of a band sound. The sound was less personal than the John of old. This was a newer, sharper John who'd begun to climb out of the emotional abyss of his divorce. His hair and beard were neatly trimmed and presentable and he'd taken to dressing in suits.

The big hurdle was playing with a regular band.

"It took me a long time...because when you're playing solo you don't have to count – the eleven-and-a-half bar blues or something," he said in an echo of Blackwell's theory. "You can't take that kind of liberty when you're playing with other musicians. You can get away with it in a trio if the other people know how your head works, but mostly it's kind of dangerous. And it's interesting, because you have to deal with other personalities; I never had to before. So you have to become a little more social and sociable when you have a band."

John's timekeeping was kept in line on the disc by Collins, who had an almost metronomic sense of rhythm, plus a very deep pocket in his style that kept a strong groove in the music. Alan Thompson was a vastly different bassist to John Giblin, whose Jaco Pastorius-like work on *Grace and Danger* had fleshed out the work (and it's worth noting that the late

Pastorius, of Weather Report, was one of John's favourite bass players); instead of a counterpoint, he offered a very solid underpinning, melodic yet relatively unobtrusive.

On *Glorious Fool*, John seemed more comfortable in his role as an electric guitarist and more than willing to defer to Eric Clapton for the reworking of "Couldn't Love You More." There was a smoothness to the overall sound that was similar to the new spirit of jazz, from Weather Report outward, and John's voice had rarely sounded smoother, a fully developed instrument. He'd taken *One World* as something of a foundation and built on it, but the new edifice was a world away from *Solid Air* in its sound, although the vibe remained remarkably similar.

What he'd slipped into, although it didn't have a name yet, was the AAA (adult album alternative) format, music aimed at grown ups, without being too mainstream. He'd come to it with a core audience that seemed willing to follow him, and along the way he'd managed to pick up more fans. The inclusion of a pair of big names on the record probably didn't hurt either, as the record gave him his best-ever chart placing, climbing to 25 on the album charts (none of the singles from the disc made a dent, however).

Collins was unavailable to tour behind the record, so John used Jeff Allen on drums, with Danny Cummings providing percussion (as he had on the album). Middleton played keys, and Thompson was the bass player. There had been a few gigs early in 1981, but a proper tour began in October, following the disc's release in September. It ran through November, taking in a few dates in Europe in addition to the UK.

Being a band leader and band member gave John a new musical lease on life. As he explained it to Trevor Dann, it had become "frustrating" to play alone. By 1980, he'd reached the stage where "unless I got utterly loaded and put myself through all kinds of dreadful tortures and abuses, I could not play as if I meant it, you know what I mean. I really could not, you understand...That doesn't arise so much with a band, because if you are feeling a little listless or jaded or without some inspiration, there's always going to be one of you that has really got that little spark and can kick it into you, you know, just makes you play."

It was a logical step in the evolution of John's art. He'd taken the idea of being a solo artist about as far as he could. On record he'd filled out his sound with other musicians for a number of years. It was only on serendipitous occasions that he'd been able to use more than a trio for gigs. But as his music was moving into a more electric area, to try and reproduce the new songs as a solo act would have been virtually impossible – and, given what was involved in the songs, probably boring for the audience. He'd hung up his acoustic and marched down a new road. Now there could be no looking back for him. It wasn't simply a learning curve for the musicians joining John; he himself had to adapt to playing electric. While the electric guitar still has six strings and the same notes on the fretboard, it's a completely different beast. The touch required isn't the same, the rhythmic style is different; virtually every aspect is altered. He'd been developing his electric style more or less since 1977, but now he had to take a quantum leap with it.

"I'm not into this whole guitar hero thing and don't want people to see me like that. My approach to playing the electric guitar is based on the way I play the acoustic – I hardly ever use a pick (plectrum), even though I know how to use it. I don't play like Van Halen or people like that. I don't have the chops for it, anyway, but I've got the brain, I know about harmony, and jazz players like what I do, which is great. But it's not necessary to be the fastest man in the world. You can say as much with a few notes as with a whole stream."

It's quite probable that John would have taken a band on the road a year earlier, after *Grace and Danger*, had it not been for the immediate financial imperatives of his divorce settlement and the need for quick, ready cash to give to Beverley. At that stage taking other musicians with him was simply not feasible, and even now it was hard. To some who loved the old John Martyn, *Glorious Fool* was the start of a decline into blandness that would last for the next ten years (and beyond, in the opinion of a few). He seemed happy to subsume himself into the greater identity of a band and to concentrate more on his vocals than his playing, consigning himself largely to a rhythm guitar role with occasional solos that, while good, were lacking in personality. However, it wasn't the instrumental virtuosity that was at stake here; instead it was the way everything contributed to the overall sound of the track. And even those tracks were constructed in a different way to John's older material. Now it was the groove that took pre-eminence, with the chord changes frequently vamped. That would become more accentuated in the years to come, but John had created a template which would serve him well.

There are those who blame Phil Collins. His production did bring a blandness to John's work that hadn't been there before. It sounded crafted and meticulous, but much of the passion had vanished into an even soundscape.

As a drummer, both with Genesis and Brand X, he'd proved himself among Britain's best. And he'd handily stepped into Peter Gabriel's shoes when the singer quit Genesis in 1975. Since then, however, the band had turned away from its prog-rock roots to find more of a pop sound and, along with that, huge commercial success on both sides of the Atlantic.

Some people have speculated that John was in awe of Collins, and flattered by his attention and participation on *Grace and Danger*. So when Collins offered to produce John's next record, he eagerly said yes and acceded to all the requests Collins made, even though they brought a radical alteration to his sound, effectively eviscerating it.

However the change and the sleeker music did bring commercial success, and it was hard to argue with that. It seemed the more John's music moved towards the middle of the road, the better he did – which was more a sad comment on the public's taste than on John's desire to finally see some financial rewards for his work.

His voice, though, became even more distinctive. In any band situation, there usually has to be one element that stands out and makes the sound distinctive. John wasn't a flash lead guitar player in the conventional sense. The band wasn't jazz and wasn't rock and certainly wasn't folk. What they did have to set them apart was John's pipes, which had developed into an even more whisky-soaked, gravelly instrument over the course of the past decade. He didn't exactly sing a song, but rather used his voice to explore it, still in the manner of a tenor sax player, working around and inside the melody more than singing it straight. For those unfamiliar with his style, making out the lyrics could be a daunting task. Even for fans, it could prove to be a difficult job.

With *Glorious Fool*, John really began looking outside himself for lyrical inspiration. Since *Bless the Weather*, he'd lived in a fairly hermetic world with Beverley and the children as its centre, and his own life orbiting around them, sometimes close, sometimes farther away. *One World* had seen a small opening of the shutters, and with *Grace and Danger* he'd definitely dived back into the turbulent sea of his own emotions, voicing them straightforwardly, rather than in allegory.

But *Glorious Fool* was specifically political at times. It was, in part, perhaps a sign of maturity – he was, after all, now thirty-three – but also an indicator of artistic development that he felt confident enough in himself to pronounce on things like this. Of course, these were tempered by more personal songs, but it was the beginning of a breakout (although, it has to be said, John's best songs have always been personal, containing the most emotion and passion).

He'd also changed managers again. Now he was working with Sandy Robertson and Paul Brown. Throughout his career, John changed management with surprising frequency and even went through periods where he managed himself. In part, perhaps, it was an example of the adversarial relationship he always had with authority, and a personality that could be intractable, especially after a few drinks. But there also seemed to be an underlying resentment of anyone taking a percentage of the money he'd earned by his sweat and creation.

Much like John's dependence on alcohol, which never really vanished in spite of several pronouncements that he'd stopped drinking (he realised the problem, but was unable to conquer it and obviously had learned to live with it), his problem with the very idea of being managed never vanished. In fairness, some might not have done well by him, but others certainly did. In a number of instances, he seemed to have aligned himself with managers who – for one reason or another – were almost certain to fail him, leaving him free to fire them, thus confirming his initial judgement about the whole management process.

John had never worked well with managers, or with anyone in authority. It could be argued that at times throughout his career he managed to sabotage his own success by alienating people. With alcohol and abuse – of both substances and people – he wrecked several relationships, sometimes to the point where things could never be repaired. He also split from managers who seemed to be guiding him to bigger things (as in 1975), in order to show his independence and ability to control his own future. That sense of control had long been important - even though he also apparently enjoyed the lack of control brought on by the use of alcohol.

A question worth raising is whether John was afraid of real success on a large scale. That he built and kept a cult audience is beyond question. But there were several times he was poised to move up to the next level and establish himself as a major artist – but he always took a left turn at the crucial moment. From the acclaim of *Solid Air*, for example, he appeared set to become the most influential British singer-songwriter of his generation, blessed with abundant singing and playing skills. Instead of following that with something equally commercial, he made the experimental *Inside Out*. Both *Glorious Fool* and its successor, *Well-Kept Secret*, charted, leaving him poised for bigger things. Instead, the Warner Brothers deal ended and it was two years before he returned to the studio with *Sapphire*, having lost all commercial momentum. Even in the '90s, his reworking of older material on *No Little Boy* found an American audience that had finally caught up with him, and he enjoyed two very successful tours of the country, playing acoustically in clubs. Again, he didn't capitalize on that. His next album, *And…*, which saw him exploring trip-hop, among other things, was never released in the US.

By the early '80s he'd morphed yet again, into a man fronting a very capable band – albeit one which seemed unable to keep a keyboard player, probably because John largely used session men who'd abandoned life on the road. He let keyboards dominate the sound.

To be fair, that was, in part, the fashion of the time. Musically, it was the era of the New Romantics, post-punk and proto machine-driven dance music. A new generation of synthesizers had proven very easy to play, and beats were simple to program, meaning one didn't require the technical ability and years of learning that went into being, say, a good guitarist. All over the radio, the sound of synths was in the air.

John's musicians could play very well. That was a given. An exceptional (if untutored) instrumentalist himself, he needed to be surrounded by people who could keep up with him and who had the skill and wit to follow when he took a song off on a tangent, as he was wont to do live.

Just because the music had changed stylistically and John had shifted into the suited, more urbane electric artist, with hints of jazz and sophistication to the fore, didn't mean the excesses had vanished. He was still drinking heavily and smoking a lot and indulging in fun and games on tour.

The divorce had been hard on him, both financially and emotionally. What he'd thought of as the centre of his life had been ripped away (whether or not it was his fault) and that left a vacuum that even a new marriage couldn't fill. He'd broken away from the old in every possible manner, but was perhaps still not completely comfortable with the new.

Surrounding himself with a band meant he didn't have to be alone on the road, and as leader he was in charge, setting the tone (probably the only time he'd *really* enjoyed an equal tour partnership was with Danny Thompson, who could give as good as he got, and match John outrageous stunt for outrageous stunt).

The success of *Glorious Fool* was encouraging, a sign to the record company that John was on to something good, and there was plenty of encouragement to return to the studio quickly. The best way to follow up an album that climbed to twenty-five was to release one that went even higher.

Well-Kept Secret delivered that, albeit at a price. Produced by manager Sandy Robertson, it built on the framework of *Glorious Fool*, sticking more to the up-tempo numbers and finding John in quite a funky mood, although "Never Let Me Go" took him back to the '50s, (a cover of the Johnny Ace ballad), and featured the late, great British jazzman Ronnie Scott on tenor.

The sessions were interrupted when John managed to impale himself on a fence at his house in Moscow and he was forced to complete his vocal work filled to the eyeballs on drugs – prescription ones, for a change.

"It took me into a mode that didn't fit. And I dug it, I sung my best, despite my two punctured lungs. 'The fence that ruined my life' – I'm surprised I haven't smashed the fucking thing for kindling."

Considering that John was focusing more on his voice, the injury – which was more severe than his comments let on – put him at a disadvantage for the record. Singing had become his main instrument of expression and he was, if not robbed of it, then forced to use it well below the level of which he was capable. Curiously though, it didn't really show too much; there were some excellent vocals on the record, especially the acerbic 'Back With a Vengeance.'

Jeff Allen's drumming proved to be very Collins-influenced, never overly busy, but still pushing the beat along - although the style of guest

Andy Duncan was ideal for "Back With A Vengeance" and "Changes Her Mind."

For those who'd loved the old John Martyn, it was difficult to take this record seriously. Pieces like "Could've Been Me," "You Might Need A Man" and the highly discofied "Love Up" were fluff compared to his earlier work. There was plenty of gloss on the arrangements, but precious little in the way of resonance in the material. The use of a pair of backup singers possibly testified to John's injury-depleted vocal ability.

This was a complete abandonment of the past, moving from pushing the boundaries to the middle of the road stylistically. Every artist has the right to do that and the fact that it paid off in sales and chart placing couldn't be denied. But how much of it was really John, and how much of it was chasing commercial success and money – which he desperately needed? By his own standards, this was by-the-numbers songwriting; he probably wouldn't have let any of these songs out of the door even five years before.

But with change came financial rewards, as the album climbed to number twenty. Yet for longtime fans it was impossible to hear the LP and not feel he was pandering to what he thought an audience would want rather than anything he might, in his heart of hearts, want to release. If John had simply been a smart pop singer, everything would have been fine with this disc; on that level it was all it claimed to be. But as a John Martyn album it was compromised and flawed, even more so than *Glorious Fool*.

He was selling records in greater quantities than he ever had, and getting plenty of bums on seats when he toured. About the only thing John wasn't able to do was make money.

Taking a band on tour was expensive. The venues needed to be bigger, musicians had to be paid, as did a road crew, equipment maintained and transported. On top of that came the hotel and travelling costs for everyone – the bills kept mounting.

Gigs were sold out, up and down the country. John even sold out the Hammersmith Odeon, one of London's best and most prestigious venues, and still only walked away with a profit of £60. He was caught in a Catch-22 bind. On the strength of his record, people were coming to his shows. They expected to see him with a band; that was what they were paying for - so that was what he had to give them. But to do it wasn't financially viable.

Yet for him to return to being a solo act wouldn't really work, either. That wasn't what the new fans wanted to hear and it wasn't really what he wanted to give them. Nor was he especially eager to return to working alone.

The band tended to play long sets, ranging from two to three-and-a-half hours – good value, by anyone's standards. They had a repertoire of about 40-50 songs, which meant extensive time working out material before they hit the road to bring everything up to snuff. Even allowing for high professional standards of the players, that still required a full month of intense practice, and learning five new songs every three days.

John toured with the band as much as he could afford to, taping some of the gigs (fortuitously for the future). But once again, change was coming.

CHAPTER EIGHT – Strange Times

John's contract with Warner Brothers had been for two albums - and he'd delivered them. They'd both done very well for John and the label. So why didn't John stick with the company?

In part it could have stemmed from the fact that he'd decided to split with his manager, whom he accused of "sharp practice." Like many of John's partings, it wasn't amicable. There were injunctions against John, by his own reports, which meant "I couldn't work and that sort of stuff, it was a bit of a pain..."

Legal problems could scare labels away even from good-selling artists and, at the same time, prevent artists from being able to sign new contracts. That left John in a terrifying limbo. He couldn't go with a label that would be able to give him an advance and he didn't have the money to take a band on the road.

His choices were limited, to say the least. He did take the band on the road, but not on a full tour - that simply wasn't economically feasible. Since rehearsal time was necessarily limited, he injected a solo set into the middle of performances. That helped satisfy older fans, although it didn't sit well with John. For a brief foray to North America he did travel alone, playing New York's Bottom Line for the first time. Toward the end of the year, he was going out with Alan Thomson covering bass and synth and Jeff Allen on drums - a stripped-down version of the band sound that put more pressure on John himself.

By virtue of taping some of the full band shows in 1982, in addition to a London gig in 1983, he was at least able to cobble together material for an LP, his second live album - one drastically different from the first.

Philentropy (the word isn't to be found on dictionary.com) arrived in November 1983 on John's own Body Swerve label (the name comes from a Glaswegian expression meaning " to avoid an unpleasant situation"). This time, however, he wasn't marketing it from home, having learned the lessons of *Live at Leeds*; instead it was distributed and marketed in the normal way, although with virtually no publicity, for the plain fact that he couldn't afford it; he'd put all his money into the making of the record.

The tracks were recorded at gigs in Oxford and Brighton in October 1982, featuring ex-Stone the Crows member Ronnie Leahy on keyboards, and at a London gig in the spring of 1983, with an unnamed keyboard player. There have been claims that the London tracks were actually recorded in a studio and the audience added later, but John refuted this (and from the performances themselves, there's no reason to doubt him). On the other hand, studio overdubs were done – to what extent he never said, and the supposed London gig where the recordings were made isn't mentioned on the sleeve, unlike the other two shows.

For all John seemed to be moving toward a much more easily digestible sound with his albums for Warner Brothers, live he injected a great deal more energy in the music (interestingly, only one track on the live disc, "Hung Up," came from his brief time with Warner Brothers; all the rest of the material harked back to the Island years, although they weren't his most famous songs). It was fierce, to the point of being downright vicious at times, and all the band seemed to be in the same spirit, not so much playing as attacking the pieces, as if they wanted to subdue them. There was a lot of pain and anger in his singing. In essence it was the liveliest, most aggressive record John had ever made and one that no commercial company would have been likely to release, since its ferocity ran entirely against the image John had been projecting for the last couple of years. The album, which has worn better than the rest of his '80s output, kept his name in the public eye, but commercially it wasn't the best move. Its real audience was with the hardcore fans, those who'd stuck with John through his changes in direction and would eagerly buy whatever he released.

That wasn't a large group, however; even though he'd charted very well with his last two LPs, the people who'd bought them were newcomers, many of whom would be unlikely to follow blindly, much less seek out a record that appeared without any fanfare or press.

As a second live release, it stood in contrast to *Live at Leeds*. Instead of being stripped-down, this was very full, an indication of the transformation of both sound and attitude that had happened. Moreover, it was the only document of this particular band incarnation which utterly reinvented older material like "Don't Want To Know," "Make No Mistake," and "Sunday's Child," while giving a true kick to "Smiling Stranger" and "Root Love," and injecting them with the kind of electricity they'd always needed.

Live at Leeds summed up one era; *Philentropy* was the synopsis of two, but from a different perspective, with not an acoustic guitar in sight. Instead, John seemed happy in his venom, his guitar on fire during "Make No Mistake" - and even the soft soul of "Don't Want To Know" was pumped up. "Root Love" stormed around the theatre in finely polished Doc Martens, daring everyone to mess with it. Even the jazz fusion of "Lookin' On" took on clearer colours in this context, making for an epic, sometimes downright violent workout. Interestingly, the most recent song, "Hung Up," fared worst - a weak sherbet that tried to cleanse the palate after a heavy main course, but failed miserably. Then it was back to the meat and potatoes with a take on "Johnny Too Bad" that was more exorcism than performance. Even a snappy, extended version of "Sunday's Child" (certainly the best recording of the piece) couldn't hold a candle against that, in spite of some glorious guitar work from John. Closing out proceedings was "Smiling Stranger," with extra funk, like Sly Stone filtered through the Brixton Frontline.

Granted, the album was never meant to be more than a stop-gap, a way of at least minimising his losses and keeping some money rolling in. Having learned from his experience with *Live at Leeds*, John had no real desire to be a label head; the hats he already wore were enough for him.

Philentropy wasn't waving farewell to a time period, but it was showing the sharp contrast that existed between John in the studio and

John live. In the vocal booth or the control room he could be so smooth he went down like cream. Under the lights, however, the edges remained sharp and jagged. Yet they were both as real as the Scots accent or the middle class English which made up his speech - all just facets of his personality, the masks that he used to keep the world at bay. The live John was probably closest to reality. It was impossible to spend time on a stage, singing and playing, without revealing at least something honest. And the anger inside him, that he released from time to time, was very tangible. It was better to let it out on guitar strings than in other, less socially acceptable ways.

Philentropy served its purpose; it was a way of marking time in an era when he was releasing an album a year, and it meant he didn't have to write new material. But what he really needed was a new label, one where he could continue to let his music develop and grow. Although what he was doing wasn't to everyone's tastes, especially those who'd loved his more acoustic '70s songs, there was no denying that his art was growing and changing at a rapid pace, and he had the ambition to go with it. To do justice to the music he heard in his head, he needed the kind of recording budget he simply wasn't going to be able to afford on his own.

He'd already begun using permutations of his core band and would soon take it all the way down to working live with just a keyboard player, new boy Fos Patterson. That certainly made touring easier, not to mention cheaper, and Patterson was able to supply both bass and keyboard parts by playing with two hands (and using more than one keyboard) in addition to programmed rhythm tracks.

The label move that John made in 1983 was one that no one had probably expected. After being on his own for a short while, he re-signed with Island, where he'd been for so many years. It was familiar, and Chris Blackwell, who'd been a longtime fan and who'd originally signed him, was happy to have him back – perhaps even more so in light of the fact that his last two studio albums had done so well. There was a strong foundation on which to build.

"I liked him," Blackwell explained simply. "The very things that are a problem are also the very things that attract you, somebody who's very real, who's a musician and less of a businessman. I never had any unpleasant experience with John directly. But I know it did cause problems, and he's a very strong personality."

Perhaps the depth of the label's new commitment to John was illustrated by the fact that they gave him the budget he desired to travel to Nassau in the Bahamas to record at Compass Point Studios. Alan Thomson (when he didn't have the 'p' in his surname) was John's main cohort, playing bass, keyboards, and helping to programme the Linn Drums that were used instead of a live drummer.

Almost inevitably, this being John, it didn't start out smoothly - and there were personality problems. There were arguments among the people who were set to work the album, which came close to scuppering everything before it could get off the ground.

"The musicians did not come out together," John said. "It had nothing to do with me personally, but the three purported musicians who'd played already on a couple of other albums together. When those sessions were done, they swore to themselves never to go into the same studio together. They hated each other."

Another story had it that John argued with the unnamed person who'd been set to produce the record, someone who then left the project.

As it was, John was officially given the production credit, although he freely admitted that without the "steadying influence" of singer Robert Palmer, who spent a great deal of time in the Nassau studio with John, he might have given up completely and returned with no tracks at all. As John remembered it, "...the production team had all fallen out, no-one was taking responsibility for anything, too much rum was being consumed all over the place, so I got Robert Palmer in, who brought in some other excellent musicians, and that was it...it was all down to Robert in the end."

Palmer "attended to the rhythm tracks. That was very practical, because he lives in Nassau, close to the Compass Point studio. I've known Robert a long time. Very interesting type, good to work with!"

Palmer brought in his keyboard player, Jack Waldman, and from going nowhere, the pace of recording speeded up.

"Jack Waldman is a fantastic musician. He came from New York to Nassau and in two and a half days we had fifteen keyboard parts. Just like that! Incredible! We began at nine o'clock in the morning and around ten, the first track was done. 'Okay. what comes next?' Jack asked. Around eleven he was done with next one."

John travelled with his wife, Annie (or at least the assumption is that he went with her – certainly he was with a woman), and shared a house with Tina Weymouth and Chris Frantz of Tom Tom Club fame, who were also recording there. Unfortunately, the musicians John had been forced to fire only lived a couple of houses away, and in a such a small place, he ran into them every day, which created a lot of tension – actually one reason he decided to record the vocals and overdubs in Scotland.

With Palmer on board, the sessions seemed to go fairly smoothly. Bringing in the Linn Drums was an adventurous move and one that was well ahead of its time. As he pointed out in an interview, once they were programmed, that was it. There was no need for another take. And as long as they were well-programmed, the sound could be very full and barely distinguishable from a real drummer. But with four people, including John himself, working on the programming, plus percussion from reggae veteran Uzziah "Sticky" Thompson, there was no danger of the rhythm sound being thin.

What was certainly interesting was that John's guitar featured so little. For the first time in many years he was using a second guitarist, Barry Reynolds (who'd played with Marianne Faithfull on her comeback records), and he handled much of the fretwork. John's guitar was actually treated so it sounded like a synthesiser, making it hard to tell where keyboard ended and fretboard began – which, obviously, was the intention. Virtually the only "real" guitar solo occurred on 'Fisherman's Dream,' and even that was an odd, juddering thing, although it fitted well with the song.

"I had to listen to the original demos because it happens that a song changes completely along the way, what was sad at the start becomes rather cheerful! All that is a little confusing. Over [in Nassau], you always imagine what you could be doing instead of being confined in studio! "

Whether it was due to the location or not, there was a lightness about the music that hadn't been apparent in John's work before. While never completely frothy and insubstantial, it didn't have the intensity of, say, *Grace and Danger*. But then, it was also the work of a man who'd recently remarried, which would have brightened his worldview.

At least, in theory, it should have - but that might not have been the case. Chris Blackwell related that, "Chris [Frantz] and Tina [Weymouth] of Talking Heads were living in the top flat. I wasn't there, so this is hearsay. But apparently John was beating up his girlfriend, and they were scared he was going to kill her. There were loud screams coming from the flat. By the time I got to Nassau he'd already gone. I don't think I've seen him since then. If I have, it was very briefly."

That the album had a very contemporary sound was beyond debate. Between the synthesizers, Thompson's fretless bass and the Linn Drums, it was very definitely '80s, a product very much of its time. And as time has passed, that's actually become its main problem. Some of the songs are excellent, especially "Mad Dog Days" (which John would dedicate to Margaret Thatcher in some performances) and "Fisherman's Dream," which he jokingly called "Johnny's first hymn."

In many ways, he intended the track to be just that, and on an early version brought in the Scottish National Choir, which was "terrible because we had the track on and it sounded great and they were absolutely 'perfect' and then as soon as they opened their mouths I went aargh." They were simply too pure, where he needed a bit of grit in the song (which he eventually got, with some backing singers). The choir was eventually featured, albeit briefly, on "Climb The Walls."

After the Bahamas, the rest of the recording was done at a new Glasgow studio, Ca Va, which had recently opened in the old Kelvingrove church in the city's West End, not far from Sauchiehall Street. It would become John's centre of recording operations for the next few years, working with engineer (and eventual studio owner) Brian Young, who'd been a member of '70s prog band Northwind.

At that point the studio was a great deal smaller than it is today, with only one large room – converted from an old gym and once used by the Sea Scouts - and a cramped control room. That made it difficult to fit in the choir, but it became even worse when they built a vocal booth for John in the room.

"We made it specially," Young recalled, "and put a top on it. John was singing away and sweating, and after a little while we had to get him out of there, he was just running out of air!"

The album did employ people who were part of the Ca Va family, like sax player Colin Tully and arranger Dave Murricane. But John seemed perfectly happy with that and also with having a good studio practically on his doorstep. Indeed, Ca Va has since grown to become probably the best-known studio in Scotland, thanks - in part at least - to the work John did there in the late '80s.

With *Sapphire*, as the new record was called, John arrived at Ca Va with the basic work done and already recorded on two-inch tape. The concepts and sounds were very firm already and all that was needed was some more vocals and the overdubs.

It was also the scene of a very wonderful accident. In the studio, John came up with a short drum loop and began singing over it – the melody of "Over The Rainbow," best known from *The Wizard of Oz*, which, John noted, "always seemed to have thinly veiled drug references. You know, they go to sleep in a field of poppies and wake up covered in snow. We were running short of things to do one night and I put a drum loop down. It went dee-dee-dee-deep. I just started wandering around the studio singing the melody. It was a happy accident."

It was hardly the first time John had covered a standard, of course, but it had been more than 10 years earlier that he'd done "The Glory Of Love," where he'd played up the song's ragtime qualities. This time around he'd given "Over The Rainbow" a very modern sheen. Its familiarity, along with the unusual treatment, prompted Island to release the song as a single. And to everyone's amazement, it went to seventeen in the British charts (the first and only time John had managed that feat) and climbed to the number two spot in Sweden.

In many ways, *Sapphire* was as much of an aberration in John's canon as *Inside Out* from more than a decade earlier, although for completely different reasons. John had always followed his own path, and in this case, as with *Inside Out* in 1973, it led him on a detour, at least in terms of sound. In the '70s, that had taken him briefly on an experimental path; this tried to make him into a very contemporary artist. *Sapphire* boasted better production and consummately professional, meticulously practiced performances, as opposed to the spontaneity of *Inside Out*. For all that, parts of it didn't seem like John. Alan Thompson co-wrote two of the cuts, a highly unusual move for John, who obviously trusted his bass player a great deal.

It started strongly enough with the title cut, as profound a piece as John had come up with in the last few years, before going into "Over The Rainbow," which, because of its loop, came across as more novelty (at least musically) than heartfelt balladry. But while "Fisherman's Dream" and "Mad Dog Days," both of which saw John looking outside himself for inspiration, were successful, there was very little to distinguish the rest of the disc. In part that was due to the arrangements, where synthesizer – or possibly guitar synth at times – created a sound very much of its time over the same kind of vamps he'd used on his last two albums; in other words, pleasant - but hardly memorable. And in retrospect, it's all terribly, terribly dated. By relying so heavily on the tools of the time, the mix of Linn Drums and keyboards that sounded so adventurous then (the "orchestral hit" patch being a very specific example), it's held up far less well over time than most of John's records.

Perhaps that was only to be expected, given the circumstances. On his return to Island, which had now become a major global player rather than the small, maverick independent label it had been when John first signed with them in 1966, he'd been given a very reasonable budget, with the expectation this release would perform as well as his last two for Warner Brotherss. To be fair, that was what he tried to achieve, albeit with an updated sound that relied very heavily on keyboards. Instead of leading a group, or at least coming off as a member, on this outing John seemed to be subsumed by the sounds that surrounded him.

What was most impressive about the album was the way John's voice had filled out. It now possessed a richness that had never been there before, like a good single malt. Thirty-five years old when the album was recorded, he'd completely grown into his pipes and was finally able to use them fully (which he hadn't been able to do on *Well-Kept Secret* because of the lung puncture). The little tics, such as the elongated, very pronounced "r"s were still there, and the slurring (although it was far less evident than before), but they'd become just one part of a much larger picture. For this album, at least, he was much more of a singer than a guitarist. Within the context of the music, it worked, as keyboards and other sounds dominated the proceedings. It was a much more arranged album than anything he'd done in the past.

Although it spawned a hit single, the album rose no higher than fifty-seven, which was lower than everyone had hoped from such a commercial and modern-sounding piece of work. As a record, it hasn't lasted well – only "Mad Dog Days" stayed in John's live shows for any great length of time. Seen in retrospect, *Sapphire* was perhaps an album John had to make at the time, not one that stayed especially close to his heart. That it brought a hit single was luck more than anything. Too many of the songs were lightweight, frothy confections; in some respects, it's a triumph of style over substance, a rarity for one of John's records. It lacked depth. Perhaps that was, in part, due to the recording location of the Bahamas and the problems that happened early in the process there. Whatever the cause, it remains a minor work in his canon, even though it marked a grand return to being part of the Island roster.

However, the style of the music made it easier to tour in his new format, going out with only keyboard player Fos Patterson to accompany him.

The original plan, John explained, had been to use two keyboard players, but that had proved too unwieldy and unfeasible. It wasn't a lineup that offered more musical freedom, since the programmed rhythm tracks didn't have much elasticity. But it certainly made going on the road a cheaper proposition.

Due to problems with the cover art, *Sapphire* was delayed, which caused problems with the tour – it ended up being split into two parts. The first, in November and December 1984, covered Britain, while the first couple of months of 1985 took John into Europe. Although he was on the road several times during 1985, the touring seemed somewhat half-hearted – a few dates followed by a lengthy break - although there was a storming appearance at the Cambridge Folk Festival in July, accompanied by the full band, playing anything but folk music (the set was eventually released on CD and more than lived up to the reports of the time).

One very good reason there was no lengthy string of dates in 1985 was that John was already hard at work on his next album. Ca Va, which was in the process of expanding, was the perfect recording location for John – just a few miles from home, with facilities more or less the equal of anything in London.

"He liked us," Ca Va owner Brian Young said. "There was a pub almost across the street where he could go, and he didn't live too far away."

Also, being markedly cheaper than a London studio, it offered John more opportunity to experiment. That was something he'd done a great deal in the '70s, but not as much in the past few years. And with the change in his musical style, there had been less opportunity. But, as the next album *Piece by Piece* showed, he'd perfected his groove-based style to the point where he could really play about with it.

"I remember he had one song that was almost done," Young recalled. "He was listening to it in the control room and picked out one section and said 'that's it,' and instead built a whole new song around that."

"Basically it's a duo album," John explained, "myself and Foster Paterson, although it doesn't sound like one." And that was true. Alan Thomson contributed string and fretless bass to two tracks, with Danny Cummings playing percussion on six tracks and Colin Tully playing sax and flute. The join between programming and live musicians was seamless.

In other words, it was a band, but at the same time it wasn't. John was taking the duo format he was using live, and expanding it in places for a record with musicians whose work he knew and liked. In that regard, the whole record was an experiment. Using what was a small crew, all familiar with him and trusted, gave John relative freedom.

It was an album of moods as much as songs, with the moods established by the grooves themselves. Perhaps because it was recorded in Scotland, rather than the Bahamas, that mood was darker than on *Sapphire*. For John, that was a good thing; a little darkness had always helped color his work well, from "Solid Air" onward. It gave more texture to the material and allowed him to shade things more. That was quite apparent on the contrast between, say, the breezy "Lonely Love" whose smooth sax transported it almost to MOR territory, and the blistering, furious "John Wayne." Written when "I was really pissed off with an ex-manager of mine." It raged, although during the composition, John saw the humorous, self-righteous indulgence of his own anger and thought "you sound like Rooster Cogburn being John Wayne." That turned the song around into a satire of sorts, partly about America and its ideals – almost a follow-up to "Glorious Fool" in that it ravaged false ideas.

There was also one song not by John on the disc. But it wasn't a version of a standard, or even an oldie. Instead, the title track was credited to Foster Paterson. According to John, it was originally about a miner being brought out from underground piece by piece, but they changed those rather gruesome lyrics to focus instead on the breakup of a relationship, much more acceptable fodder for a song, and particularly for an album like this, which was about relationships of all kinds, and even contained two of the most obvious love songs of John's career: "Angeline" (written for his wife Annie) and "Who Believes In Angels?"

Lyrically, this was probably the most direct record John had ever written, with the exception of *Grace and Danger*. He'd usually hidden behind allusions and obscurity, but as he was growing older, he was facing and confronting issues and emotions head on. Nearly thirty-eight by the time the album was released, he was beginning to settle into his maturity.

That didn't mean he'd overcome all his problems. John still liked a smoke and several drinks, although the worst of the '70s drug excesses seemed to have become a thing of the past. And though his alcohol intake could be prodigious and he could still engage in some tricks on the road, for the most part he'd learned to handle his alcohol well and with a certain amount of grace – as befitted his age. He could even turn it to his advantage. On this new record, he laid down the gritty, lengthy vocal to "John Wayne" in a single take after a long pub session - no mean achievement, and the start of a new trend for his singing.

For all his assertions time and again that he'd stopped drinking, John never did – but drink didn't seem to send him into the kind of frenzies he'd experienced a decade before, possibly because he was no longer mixing it with other substances. No longer did it affect his performance the way it had at times in the '70s, perhaps because he no longer had a partner like Danny Thompson to egg him on (Thompson quit drinking in 1978). He seemed to find a balance, one that worked for him and kept him going. But the role alcohol played in John's life should never be underestimated, for better or worse.

The recording of *Piece by Piece* was a joy for Brian Young at Ca Va.

"We'd just had studio one built – it was just finished when John came in [actually on July 5th 1985] and we were all eager to try it out. We still have the tape machines he used then, although we're digital now."

It was an intimate studio, perfect for what John wanted, especially as there were really only two musicians involved on all the sessions. John could record takes, then go over to the pub, return and listen to what he'd done.

"He'd pick out ideas," Young said, "and take those."

The album was notable for the amount of guitar synthesizer John used, making it a good foil for Paterson's keyboards. Indeed, there was more guitar on *Piece by Piece* than John had used in several years, just used in a slightly different context – and still all electric guitar; there was as yet no return to the acoustic in the studio. He continued to tour as a duo with Paterson.

Piece by Piece was a major John Martyn release for Island. The ball had been dropped a bit on *Sapphire* in 1984, and it was understood that there would be no repetition of the same mistake this time around. There would be a full tour and plenty of promotion. "Angeline" and the otherwise unavailable Dylan cover "Tight Connection To My Heart" were issued as a 7" single. That was expanded by three tracks ("Glistening Glyndebourne," "May You Never" and "Solid Air" in their original album versions) for both a 12" and CD single release. The CD, reputedly the first CD single ever issued, came in an elaborate fold-out pack under the title

Classic John Martyn, ostensibly to celebrate his 20th anniversary as a performer.

In fact, the original CD version of *Piece by Piece* also included the four extra tracks. Given that the "true" nine-track version only ran about 40 minutes, the same length as an average LP (the disc was also issued in its nine-track form on LP), it acted as an incentive for people to spend more on the new format, which was then brand new.

While "Angeline" stood as the original single, it was actually followed a month later, in March 1986, by what was probably a better single choice, the more overtly pop "Lonely Love." It was backed, interestingly, by a live version of "Sweet Little Mystery" culled from a London gig the same month as the single's release (the 12" version also added a live version of "Fisherman's Dream" from the same show) to tempt collectors. However, this too failed to make any chart waves. The fact was, and always had been, that John just wasn't a singles artist; the success of "Over The Rainbow" was an aberration, not the start of a new normality. That had worked because it was a novelty, a quirky modern version of a piece familiar to generations from its Judy Garland movie version.

But in returning to the style that suited him best these days, after the detour that was *Sapphire*, John achieved with the album what he couldn't manage with singles – a strong chart placing, as *Piece by Piece* rose to twenty-eight, virtually returning him to the level he'd managed with his Warner Brothers albums. Considering the last of those had been four years earlier, that showed he'd managed to keep the fans – and when he came out with something to satisfy them, they'd go out and buy it. Island put money behind it, even releasing a promotional box set with a recorded interview and springing for a video for "Tight Connection To My Heart" (whether it was ever aired remains a matter of conjecture), but ultimately it was down to the buyers, who obviously liked it.

It was a harder disc than *Sapphire*, with more grit in the singing, the playing, and the arrangements. Keyboards were still prominent, but the sounds were less definitely of their time than on the last album - and at least some of the material was stronger. "Nightline" burned with a flame, and "John Wayne" dazzled with its anger, the record's undoubted centerpiece, running almost seven minutes. "Angeline" was a lovely plea, and even the lightweight "Lonely Love" wasn't offensive, simply a background ditty of the kind John could knock off in his sleep. Beyond those, "Serendipity" had some real substance to it, but the remaining tracks were relatively anonymous. They worked well enough, but they weren't prime John Martyn material by any means. Still, it was good material for the audience who'd discovered him earlier in the decade, then lost touch as he seemed to drop out of sight in 1982.

As he had during his brief tenure with Warner Brothers, John was enjoying another career renaissance. There was a full and lengthy tour with a band – Paterson, Alan Thomson and drummer Dave Cantwell - that lasted throughout March and April 1986. He'd also provided the soundtrack for a Tyne Tees series on the environment called *Turning the Tide*, which was aired in the autumn of that year. The series theme song was a loose variation on 1973's "I Don't Want To Know," but with new lyrics. However, plans to make that and the rest of the soundtrack commercially available on disc were scrapped when the series ended up over budget.

In addition to that, John had been commissioned by Blackie Publishing to write some children's songs, which was "very difficult to do if you're a bit hairy-arsed and rough round the edges as I am." However, at the time he said that, in February 1986, it seemed he hadn't yet started the project, although plans appeared fairly concrete, as John claimed it would appear in both book form and on cassette.

As if that weren't enough, "I'm also working with Charlie Haden this year, who's an out-and-out avant-garde bebop bass jazzer. He's about the best bass player I've ever heard. I'm also hoping to do an album with Ry Cooder and Jim Keltner, all of that's going to happen in America."

While he did go to the US to play some gigs, neither of those projects happened for John. Nor did the children's songs. If they were ever written and recorded, they don't appear to have been released. It was the story of his life, really. He had so many irons in the fire that came out cold from the coals.

But all of that was tempered by the way *Piece by Piece* sold and the way the gigs were attended. Following the extensive touring for the album and after a break in May, John returned to the stage in June, but in a markedly different context.

He'd started playing acoustic again, for his own pleasure, after barely touching the instrument for several years. There had been acoustic interludes in his shows and the 1983 solo performances in the US. But this was different. Now he was going back on the road for a few shows with his old sparring partner – and the person with whom he'd enjoyed the closest musical connection – Danny Thompson. Older, wiser, and more restrained, they'd abandoned the legendary wildness, concentrating instead on putting on great performances in small venues (one of which, at the Brewery Arts Centre in Kendal, would end up on CD years later). Along with them – basically taking on the John Stevens role from 1975 – was a young drummer and percussionist, Welshman Arran Ahmun.

"I got [the gig] through Alan Thomson, the bass player," Ahmun explained. "I was working with Alan on some other project, and he put me forward for it. [John's] drummer, who was Jeff Allen, was moving on, so I replaced him on the '86 British tour, and I've been with him ever since."

While the reputation John and Danny had cultivated a decade before had gone before them, Ahmun found the new reality to be different.

"Their rogue days, or Danny's rogue days, were over by then, and he was a different character. He wasn't so rock'n'roll, he was more into keeping healthy and fit. John's never changed, though, in his habits and social activities. By the time I was there it was a lot less than all the previous years – I missed out on all the fun! There were still a few ups and downs, it wasn't all rosy, but he was a lot easier going, and every year he gets more and more mellow."

However, after the more peaceful oasis of a short acoustic tour, John turned around to appear at the Glastonbury festival at the end of June fronting a full band of Peterson, Thomson, Ahmun, and Colin Tully on sax in a performance that contained even more fire than the *Philentropy* album.

Curiously, only two of the tracks he played that day came from the newest record, "Serendipity" and "John Wayne" (the latter would become a staple of his set list), with another pair from *Sapphire* (one of which was "Over The Rainbow"). For the rest, he looked further back, to his first tenure with Island, both "Dealer" and "Big Muff" dating from 1977, and a radically reworked "Outside In" going back well over a decade. The performance saw the light of day in 1992 as *BBC Radio 1 Live in Concert*, adding three other tracks, a 1971 performance and two from a 1977 concert, the highlight of which was a gloriously extended, freewheeling take on "Outside In" that stretched over fifteen minutes of noise and loops (and originally titled "Man Walks Inside" on the BBC tapes, for some reason).

Again, Ahmun was the new kid on the block in this line-up, as all the others had worked with John frequently over the past few years. But for him, the setting felt even more natural than the acoustic trio, because "it was more modern, and more the fusion type of thing, and I'm from that background, so it was natural for me to go in that direction."

Immediately, he and John had got along well.

"I couldn't say enough about him. And that's not just musical, that's personal. As a friend I just love him. I've never ever fallen out with him, not once. John doesn't suffer fools. I'm used to working with different artists, so I'm used to fitting in. Some people retain their own personality, where you can get along great or piss people off." Evidence of how well Ahmun and John got along was that after 1986 "you might get two years where I wasn't with him due to unavailability, but it was broken up. I might have missed a tour or an album or something," but in the main, Ahmun always occupied the drum stool in John's band.

As musicians have learned over the years, working with John required not only a high level of musical ability, but also flexibility of thinking.

"It's hard to put your finger on what John wants," Ahmun observed. "If you do come in with a set attitude, you discover it has to be spontaneous on the day. And you have to listen and go with the flow. That's socially as well as musically. You have to toe the line to a certain degree and not impose yourself. I've just always really responded to John. If he's wanted to be a rogue, I've never stood in his way, but at the same time he's respected that and never turned on me."

This would essentially be his core band for a while, although changes and additions did occur. In November 1986, for example, when John toured, Thomson wasn't on bass – he was replaced by David Ball, while Danny Cummings augmented the sound with percussion and Jeff Castle added a second keyboard.

John had been writing new material and premiered at least three new songs on the tour – "The Apprentice," "Deny This Love," and "Send Me One Line," all of which appeared on *Foundations*, a document of a November 13th show at London's Town and Country Club that was also filmed for a video release.

They were all songs for a projected new album, as was "Patterns In The Rain," which would feature in 1987 on the Island *Alright Now* video. But before any new studio album, there was another live disc to be released.

CHAPTER NINE – Changes

What was it about John and live albums? He seemed to regard them as the ideal holding action, a way of keeping his name and his music out there while he negotiated the twists and turns involved in putting a new studio record together.

Live at Leeds had probably been a psychological necessity, given the wall of burn-out he was starting to run into at the time. It meant he didn't have to even think of writing new material for a while. And it was a very valuable portrait of what he was doing on the stage, and how far he could take some of the electric material with the Echoplex.

Philentropy served a need, too, letting him release some product while between record contracts and showing his biting electric band side to those who hadn't seen his shows. It illustrated how many of the songs had changed within the band format, in virtually every instance for the better, and showcased his quite formidable work on electric guitar.

Foundations, however, was more problematic. It was his third live release in 12 years – pretty heavy going by any artist's standards. Given the choice of material, perhaps it was meant as a way to present his newer material – there was only one old song on it, his classic "May You Never" in a decidedly light band version that was never touched by an acoustic guitar. In fact, "light" described much of the record, especially when compared to *Philentropy*; it seemed to be going through the motions, rather than playing with any huge feeling or commitment.

In many ways, the new songs were the standouts, not so much because they were new, but because there was more passion in the playing – maybe due to their relative unfamiliarity. Like so much of John's writing in the '80s (which would be true up to the Millennium, with the exception of his covers album, *The Church with One Bell*), they were groove-based, rather than the more old-fashioned process of melody and lyric he'd employed in his younger days.

"You could say there's been a gradual demise in his songwriting from the early days," ventured Ahmun. "I don't know exactly what was going on in those days, but he was churning them out. I guess when he started mixing with more modern styles of music and different influences it altered his songwriting. He emphasizes on instrumentals a lot, instead of songwriting. So now he fits a lyric around a groove, a vibe, as opposed to writing a song and fitting the music to it. I guess there's more distraction for him, and an excuse not to have to sit down and write the next big song."

But that next big song was what all performers needed, and John had managed at least one on all his studio albums since 1971, whether it was the dawn glow of "Small Hours" or the novelty-item joy of "Over The Rainbow."

One thing the new band performances definitely did show was that John seemed quite happy to let things drift a little. Where *Philentropy* had an undercurrent of anger that gave it a real edge, *Foundations* seemed too complacent in the manner in which it was treading water. The arrangements had a smoothness and sweetness the younger John could never have tolerated. It wasn't folk, it wasn't rock and it wasn't jazz; it stood as some sticky, slightly self-satisfied hybrid in the middle of them all.

John's music might have changed – to quite a few people, *Foundations* marked the start of his easy listening period – but not all of him had altered. He still liked a drink and a smoke and the occasional piece of hellraising on the road. At times he could even reach the legendary heights of the '70s, if he was in the right mood.

"We were in a German hotel in 1987, his [twentieth] anniversary tour," Ahmun recalled. "We'd come back from a gig and John was on the rampage, looking for someone's room to occupy and have a party. The rest of us were pretty tired, and he knew we were hiding. We were in this bedroom. He banged on the door and there was no answer, so he went out on the roof at the back and started banging on the glass with his shoes. It split the whole double glazing and he had a £1000 bill in the morning!"

Maybe it wasn't as extreme as being nailed into a carpet, but it was a lot more expensive.

Much of 1987 was spent on the road, honing the band and making them tight, with a strong camaraderie developing between everyone. And more new songs were developing.

Putting three new songs on a live album – which was usually a consolidation of old material and greatest hits – was unusual, and obviously meant the material had been around a little while and had been given the chance to develop in the band incubator. At the same time, it was hardly revolutionary for an artist to road-test new songs and judge what kind of reaction they received from crowds before making studio recordings of them. Letting live versions slip out first, however, was different for John.

But he was ready to give them the studio treatment, along with plenty of other new pieces. By February of 1988, John and the band had ten tracks completed and ready for a new disc, recorded, as usual those days, at Ca Va in Glasgow.

The new music reflected the slightly different approach John had begun to fashion in his music with *Foundations*. A lot of the grit that had been in evidence on *Piece by Piece* was missing, in favour of a sound that was even smoother than it had been in the early '80s. It was more mellifluous, certainly, but it lacked the depth that had usually characterised his work. Yet it didn't have the island lightness of *Sapphire*, which was shot through with breeziness (ironically, given the personal disputes that had attended its recording).

One thing was certain: when Island heard the new tracks, they weren't happy with them, or, more accurately, with the direction John was taking. And John didn't have much of a reputation for compromise, especially when it came to music.

However, he seemed genuinely surprised by the reaction. He believed that the 10 tracks he'd recorded were as good, if not better, than anything he'd done.

"I believed in it; I even re-recorded it in Glasgow at my own expense."

But Island still rejected the disc.

"I remember thinking that it didn't have much life to it," was Chris Blackwell's opinion of the music he heard

It was the first time John had had any material rejected, and at the age of forty, a full adult with a proven musical history, it smarted. It didn't help that it came at a time when John was reportedly drinking more heavily than ever – he was living in an alcoholic daze, to the extent that a doctor told him he *had* to stop drinking, which he did, briefly.

The decision to reject the tapes hadn't been entirely down to John's old ally and mentor Chris Blackwell. It was another label executive, Clive Banks, who had made the decision.

Over the course of years, Island had changed. No longer was it an independent label, with Blackwell making completely free decisions. He'd sold out much of his interest to the multinational giant, Polygram - and others came in to make many of the decisions.

Still, although *Foundations* had failed to capitalise on the impact of *Piece by Piece* (and in spite of the video of the concert, it was unlikely ever to do so), John had enjoyed a good track record with the label. *Piece by Piece* had charted well, 'Over The Rainbow' had been a Top 20 single, and while never spectacular in sales, John's base was solid and his recording costs relatively inexpensive – enough to bring a profit, albeit usually a small one, to the label.

However, with the changing times, and the bean counters starting to take over operations in the music business, small profits were no longer enough. The Nights of the Long Knives which have typified record labels over the last decade – slashing artist and employee rosters in search of a bigger and bigger bottom line – were in their infancy.

What was also apparent was that John's music wasn't going to appeal to the young audience – the ones who bought the most LPs (and, of course, the quickly emerging CD). This helped consign John even more to the margins under the new regime.

The rejected version of the album has never circulated in bootleg form, so it's impossible to judge it properly. Yet, on the evidence of *Foundations* and the re-recorded version, which was eventually released as *The Apprentice*, it would seem that John was headed straight for the middle of the road. The songs were the kind of vamps he'd been writing for a decade, but there seemed to be a march towards blandness in the sound. It's probably fair to say that was also the case in the rejected tracks; in fact, they might have been even cleaner, with more grit added to the re-recordings.

In addition to the crew who were by now the usual suspects (Paterson, Ahmun, and Cummings), John did manage to lure acclaimed British jazz saxophonist Andy Sheppard into the studio with him. He featured on both the rejected and released recordings. John had used a different sax player, whose performances simply hadn't worked, "and I eventually tracked Andy down in Glasgow at three o'clock in the morning." He'd been playing with a Dutch jazz group in the city and John made a very reasonable request, asking him to be at Ca Va Studios at seven a.m. Sheppard showed up, and "ended up improvising solos for four tracks, and he'd finished by ten. It was amazing."

The rejection of the album meant a parting of the ways for John and Island Records, this time permanently. The business had changed a great deal since John had first signed with them in the '60s – and John had never been that keen on the business to begin with, be it managers or labels; he'd always just wanted to focus on his music and play gigs. But the very nature of things meant he had to be more involved in the business side of music, whether it was in appointing a procession of managers with whom he'd fall out, or dealing with labels.

He'd been lucky to arrive on the scene at a fairly innocent time, when record labels were willing to give an artist the space to develop. He'd needed that to find his own voice and true style. Obviously that style had changed over the years, and the first parting with Island had been relatively amicable, and his return welcomed on both sides. Now, though, everything was different. The whole nature and attitude of the big labels had altered irrevocably. As a mature performer, John was no longer quite as welcome and had to prove himself each time. And this time he hadn't been able to - at least not to the satisfaction of the executives who made the final decisions, even after recording everything again.

Whether he was dropped or left of his own accord is irrelevant. The connection had been severed and not in a pleasant manner. For the second time in less than a decade, John was a man without a record label. At least he had master studio tapes this time, which put him in an advantageous position.

And he could still tour, which he did assiduously during 1988 and 1989, in various permutations. There were gigs with the band, but he also reverted to the Martyn/Paterson duo for a while in 1989 and even toured solo, playing several of the songs from the new album, at the end of '88.

What he really needed was to get the new album out. For obvious reasons, the lure of the major labels had diminished. It wasn't that John's time had come and gone, by any means; he simply needed a different approach. And working with a smaller label that could focus more attention on him and offer him more creative freedom seemed to be the natural choice. Even in his forties, John remained the same creature of head and heart he'd been twenty years before. He could be the wild romantic, the drunken fool, and the raging businessman as the mood shifted.

Although he called Permanent Records "formed for me," it wasn't. It was a small label that saw potential in John. With far lower overheads than a major, they could make him a figurehead for the label, which was what he became for a short while. It was a good pairing.

Permanent certainly gave John the kind of push he needed, with a major tour – the biggest one he'd ever undertaken – in support of the new release. *The Apprentice*, as the record was titled, was John's first foray into the new decade, although it had been a long time coming – his last album of new material had been four years earlier, in 1986. Only one track, "Send Me One Line," hadn't been written specifically for the album; it was a commission for the soundtrack of the film *84 Charing Cross Road*.

"Joe Lustig rang me and asked me to write a song for the film, so I read the book and wrote the song, I think it's a nice little tune. I wrote the song and then forgot about it, so it was too late to be used in the film!"

John was ready for another comeback. He'd come out of the drinking spiral that had occupied him for the last few years; that was a necessity if he was going to spend an extended period on the road, especially as he seemed to have fallen very low this last time – his split with Island not helping the proceedings one bit. He'd been away too long, and had lots of ground to make up – and he was more than eager to get to it in the wake of an album he believed in.

Although he claimed that "Income Town," one of the new record's highlights, was recorded live at the Green Banana in Toronto, it was in fact a studio recording, just like the rest of the album (he'd used the reference before). The title track had its origins with a man John had met in a pub in Carlisle.

"He was a very sick man. He worked at the nuclear plant in Sellafield and he had cancer, and he was convinced that working at Sellafield was causing his illness... He died. A terrible way to die. It took personal experience of something like that to make it hit home."

That had been in his set list since 1986, along with "Deny This Love" and "Send Me One Line," while "Patterns In The Rain" had been around since 1987, a co-credit with Paterson, who "likes the track now, he wasn't too sure at first, now he likes it, I think. I think it's good."

By the time the album appeared, in early 1990, John had had enough of it: "We had so many false starts to the album, it's a little difficult to listen to it right now." But after living with it for so long, and recording the whole thing twice, that was hardly surprising.

The Apprentice served to highlight the difference between John in the studio and John live. Onstage his guitar was more prominent, taking a vital role in the performance, often subtly leading and nudging the band in a particular direction during a song. The lyrics essentially became a secondary thing to the music itself, as pieces were stretched out. In the studio, however, it was the guitar that took the back seat. For John, it appeared, the studio was about the singing and the song, letting the band frame his voice. Compare the tracks that overlapped *Foundations* and *The Apprentice* (or *Live*, recorded on *The Apprentice* tour) and the differences became very clear.

With *The Apprentice*, John was going for a smoother, jazzier sound than he'd ever achieved on disc before. The problem was that that was at odds with the inherent roughness in his voice. Even when he slurred his words (and at this point, given that he liked to do his vocals after a pub session, one had to wonder about the cause of that slurring – was it natural or partly alcohol-induced?), there was a gritty underpinning that he could never erase – and shouldn't have wanted to, since it was one of the defining characteristics of his style. Ultimately, John just couldn't be a smooth balladeer. And by trying to make himself one on this record, he was pushing a round peg into a square hole.

Musically, *The Apprentice* fully mastered the blandness just hinted at on *Foundations*. It was pleasant, but that was damning with faint praise. Next to *Piece by Piece*, it was lightweight fluff. Even "Look At That Girl," a celebration of daughter Mhairi, who was now nineteen, was little more than a confection. By his own admission, John had stopped writing autobiographically and it seemed as if his material had lost something by that.

Of course, much of it had come from what was often considered to be his period of deepest alcoholism, which wasn't going to leave him at his most inspired. And he didn't have a subject, like the lost, failed romance of *Grace and Danger*, to fuel him. Nonetheless, he stood by his work.

Listening to the album, it was apparent that much of it coasted on John's voice. With a few exceptions, like the lovely "Send Me One Line" and the gritty "Income Town," the songs weren't especially memorable. There was very little guitar – indeed, only "Income Town" has a recognisable guitar solo, although it is possible to hear a little acoustic guitar (for the first time in years) elsewhere. It seemed strange for a man who'd made much of his name as a player. But it was typical of the way John had gone – in the studio, at least.

Possibly the album's biggest failing was its sound. As music in general was changing, with dance and techno becoming the new standard, this record retained a very '80s sound. It was evident in the big drums and most especially in the synthesizer tones. While making it somewhat contemporary, they also dated it (a reprise of the *Sapphire* syndrome) – to hear it later is to realise that. At times it sounds positively clunky.

The arrangements were made to highlight the groove and the vocal, although Andy Sheppard (not Shepherd as stated in the sparse CD booklet) did bring some bite to his four solos. It swung well enough, although not with the jazzy feel John was perhaps aiming for.

According to John, the record eventually sold 35,000 copies in the UK (it wasn't released elsewhere, although a licensed version eventually appeared in the US through the Off-Beat label). That was a respectable amount, given his fan base, but nowhere near enough to put him back in the charts.

It showed that once again John hadn't been able to capitalise on and maintain the success of *Piece by Piece*, although this time that might well have been due to his acknowledged alcohol problems. While it had rarely affected his live performances any more, it could well have sapped his creativity. Certainly there was nothing of the stature of "John Wayne" on this album. Instead it seemed like another make-weight, treading water until the Muse returned to guide him.

It was also indicative of why Island had refused the tapes he'd delivered. By the general standards of John's own work, this simply wasn't up to snuff. Even the re-recording possessed a rather uninspired emptiness. John was still in good voice, but as noted, his style didn't fit easily with the material.

The fact that it continued the decline which seemed to have begun with *Foundations* caused more than one journalist to wonder if John still had any relevance in the changing musical world.

There was one major change coming, which was that Foster Paterson was preparing to bow out as the keyboard player in the band. He'd been John's right hand for the previous seven years, longer than any other musician apart from Danny Thompson, but also a trusted collaborator and friend – and one of the only people John had played with in a long, long time whose songs he'd allow on a record.

"I think he'd had enough of being on the road," offered Spencer Cozens, who was brought in as his replacement. "He was married, and he needed to be at home for a while. It was Alan Thomson who suggested me. We'd been playing together in Julia Fordham's band – I think John basically pinched her whole group!"

There was more than a grain of truth in that. Arran Ahmun had featured on Fordham's second album, *Porcelain*, in 1989, along with guitarist Taj Wyzgowski, who contributed guitar to two tracks of the final version of *The Apprentice*. Thomson and Cozens, though not on the record, played in her touring band. But the smoothness of her sound had its echoes in what John was doing, and he liked to employ very professional performers with a touch of jazz and improvisation in their souls. Unlike Fordham, who also aimed at the adult end of the record-buying market, John did more than sing onstage; he was a band *leader*, not merely a focal point.

And there were advantages in getting musicians who were already familiar with each other's styles; it made the adjustment time a great deal shorter.

"I listened to all his stuff before I went on the road with him," Cozens remembered. At that time he was still a student who hadn't sat his final exams, but he'd already proved himself professionally in the studio and on the road.

Cozen's baptism of fire with John came early in 1990, on the very lengthy tour for *The Apprentice*. He sat in when Paterson was unable to make some shows, including a ten-night stand at the Shaw Theatre in London (it spoke volumes about John's popularity as a live act that he was able to fill the place for so many nights), with the March 31st 1990 show (like *Foundations* a few years before) taped and videoed for future release. Arran Ahmun wasn't in the band that night either, his place taken by Miles Bould, who'd played with John before, part of the pool of musicians he could turn to.

The tour was certainly gruelling, running from mid-March to the middle of June, with few real breaks. Cozens wasn't with the band for long, only until Paterson was able to return, and he felt a little slighted.

"I'd learned everything, and I thought I'd done a good job," he said. "When he didn't call me for the rest of the tour, I was disappointed."

But it seemed he'd done too good a job. He'd prepared himself too well, not allowing for the kind of spontaneity John enjoyed in his musicians. But when Paterson decided he didn't want to do the German leg of the tour, John called Cozens, who'd had chance to think about what he was doing.

"I loosened up quite a bit. John demands a lot from you, you've got to be watching him the whole time, to be ready to react when he changes things. I think he'd liked my playing before, but he wasn't too sure about me and what I could do."

With keyboards such an important part of John's sound, that was the pivotal role within the band, at least for melody, which put a lot of pressure on the keyboard player.

"I had to learn to deal with him. You've got to be straight up with John, tell him what you think, and you have to have the energy to keep up with him. One of the big things is if he likes you. If he doesn't, you soon know about it. John doesn't suffer fools gladly at all."

It proved to be a fairly seamless transition as Cozens took over from Paterson. English-born, but trained at Berklee and Juilliard, Cozens was a more than competent player, and one already familiar with the general group of musicians John used, as well as the material he was performing. What would become interesting was the fact that he'd also take over Paterson's position at John's right hand, working with him not only on the stage, but also in the creation of new material for future albums.

There was also constant reworking of the older material which made up the bulk of the set. At its peak, this version of the band was playing for about two and a half hours a night, stretching out a lot of pieces like "John Wayne" and "Looking On," with "Johnny Too Bad" often the highlight, running some fifteen minutes at times. Those older pieces actually offered everyone more freedom.

"We still do lots of his old stuff, but we revamp it," Ahmun explained. "We might stick in a bit of a different tempo, slightly different style.

"That's the way John likes to do it. He doesn't like to sing the same old songs the same old way. You treat them differently. He's all about spontaneity, John, he gets bored really fast. That's great for us, because we can experiment; you're always on your toes."

Playing so much, it was what they needed to keep themselves interested on the stage, rather than regurgitating the same notes night after night. And John needed it more than anything. Some of the pieces had been in his repertoire for the better part of 20 years. How could he keep singing them and make them sound real and affecting, the way the audience wanted to hear them? How was it possible to put emotion into lyrics he'd sung literally thousands of times, rather than simply going through the motions? Mixing it up a bit and constantly changing things around was the only answer.

It was impossible for one of the old songs to mean as much to John as it had when it was new and the emotions behind the lyrics still fresh. But that was true for any artist. Part of his job was to be able to constantly invest those pieces with meaning, even if it wasn't the same meaning it had originally possessed.

Also signing on at the beginning of the German tour was Alex Boyesen, who'd go on to run sound for John for the next five years. A longtime fan, and once an aspiring singer-songwriter himself, he'd worked with "a lot of the big African, Cuban, Turkish, Kurdish and reggae bands," in addition to several rock bands, before coming to work for John.

Like so many things in John's life, knowing about Boyesen happened by a lucky accident.

"One day my brother Perry rang to say he was meeting up with John's daughter , Mhairi, and did I want to come and meet up with them," Boyesen recalled. "Turns out she was his upstairs neighbour. We met up and Mhairi mentioned that her dad was looking for an engineer for a live tour, was I interested? I was still a great fan and this would be a dream come true. Couple of weeks later I was at John's house getting smashed with his then manager Archie. A taxi had picked me up from the airport, the driver of which had insisted on talking for the whole journey about that there's nowhere bigger than Biggar – which is near where John lived at the time. John was pretty late coming back and stormed into the room like a whirlwind, drunk and disorderly talking to Archie about how he had found himself on the other girl the next morning then turned to me and announced in his lowland Scottish accent, 'Hi, I'm John'."

The alcohol was getting to everyone, it seemed, and Boyesen said, "I was very smashed by this time and being in the same room as John was overwhelming. Then the two girls came in, Daisy and the one whose name I cannot remember. We all just sat down and got even more smashed. I was very hungry, but as soon as I sobered up John got cooking. I cannot remember exactly what he got together in that kitchen but John knew what he was doing, in the time that I stayed with him he made some amazing meals, at the oddest of times."

Boyesen's interview was informal, at best. His CV spoke for itself, and it was more a matter of having the right personality.

"We all seemed to get on, so it was agreed I would work the live sound for the tour and generally help out. John was travelling in an American passion wagon with his girlfriend, me and Daisy, who turned out to be the tour-manager and general help in the van with the gear and the band travelled in their own car. So John and mystery girlfriend, myself, Daisy, Spencer Cozens on keyboards, guy from Cat Stevens on drums, someone on bass and Jerry on sax."

However, the tour got off to a stuttering start, according to Boyesen.

"The tour was a lot of fun. I had prepared well with the equipment I was using and carried my own reverbs and a drum trigger box to get me solid drums no matter what the equipment. We were touring Germany, France and Holland. First gig West Berlin at 11.00 p.m. We missed the ferry at Dover and had to go to Folkestone and travel to

Denmark if we had any chance of making the gig – we travelled overnight, I could have got into a fight over a very attractive girl wanting to show me her tattoo - never happened before or since. Her friends dragged her off me and I have always ever since regretted not fighting for her." With that incident out of the way, "we arrived in Denmark and rushed towards Germany, living off coffee and sandwiches, we made it with 10 minutes to go before we were meant to be onstage. John was not happy and can be intimidating at the best of times. We got set up, I plugged in, the band came onstage and without ever having even had a sound check started to play. Probably the best way to kick off a relationship with someone like John. No time to think. It worked. I just knew every song that he was playing and what they should sound like. This had been the first time I had worked with an artist I knew so well. And it was a pleasure to make it sound how it should. At this time I barely knew John, but I knew what his music needed to sound like; for the first time I started to be really creative with what I was doing with the sound. It wouldn't always work, sometimes John would come up and say 'don't put all that echo on there,' or something like that. He was worried about some of the things I was doing, but on the whole let me get on with it. I was playing one of the gig tapes with Jerry in the van one night and at the end of 'John Wayne' there was this enormous (on purpose) crash from the band as they made an explosion sound as they ended the song, which I extended with the help of a liberal dose of echo and reverb just as it was reaching its climax. John opened the door to the van and screamed what the fuck was I doing with his music? It didn't sound like this? A lot of diplomacy ensued, but it was definitely a near miss."

However, Boyesen not only endured, but became virtually a fixture with the band for several years.

At the beginning of the '90s, John had been releasing albums for twenty three years. *The Apprentice* was the eighteenth disc. He'd moved from being an unknown folkie, to an experimenter in guitar electronics and one of Britain's best acoustic songwriters. From there he'd gone electric, making classy adult pop music during his stay with Warner

Brothers, before refining that sound after returning to Island, eventually making it into something smoother. And now he was on a small independent label.

It was a career arc – inasmuch as it was an arc at all – that reflected John's growth as a person, as much as a musician. The boy who'd split his time between Glasgow and London, discovering his talent as a guitar player and writing songs that drew from traditional folk and Bob Dylan, had grown up. He'd discovered jazz and rock, absorbed a lot of blues – both musically and personally – and become a man, a parent, divorced and remarried; in other words, he'd gone through many of the personal changes that applied to most men of his generation.

As much as a present and a future, he'd had plenty of past. He carried around baggage, and his history was on display in his older songs, the ones that remained popular and which were already labelled "classic." Unlike most men, he couldn't put that behind him. When he reinvented himself – as an electric guitarist, a bandleader, a sharp dresser - the weight of the years gone by was always there and, because of his position, always visible.

More than anything, his musical past was the standard against which he was measured. The '70s, certainly from 1971-1977, had been a golden age for John's music, when he'd reeled off wonderful songs, almost effortlessly it seemed, in addition to breaking down all kinds of barriers with his playing. In that period he'd released six LPs; over the course of the thirteen years since, he'd managed ten. Granted, things had changed, and an artist was no longer obligated to put out an album (or more) a year. But it was apparent that during that six-year period John had been at a creative peak in both quality and quantity, one he'd been unable to recapture since.

To most critics, he'd devolved into someone whose artistry had become bland. Even John himself had wondered if he'd written a good song since splitting up with Beverley, although he'd been married to

Annie for a number of years now, and should have enjoyed similar marital contentment.

He'd certainly changed his style of writing, as Arran Ahmun had noted. Where he'd once written complete songs, now he preferred to work around a groove and let that dictate everything. But it has to be remembered that previously he'd written just for himself, as a solo artist, and now he was writing for himself as just one member of a band. There were the parts of other musicians to consider, so in this situation working around a groove was easier – and offered the kind of freedom and elasticity John needed in a band, something traditionally structured songs couldn't manage, for the most part.

Perhaps, too, that change in writing style gave a definitive break with the past. It had certainly brought more commercial success at a time John desperately needed it, in order to pay maintenance. And with chart placings and even a hit single – albeit a fluke one – it was a move that had paid off. So sticking with it made sense. After all, after so many years of scraping a living, he was perfectly justified in pursuing something more lucrative.

However, stability never seemed to last too long with John. In some regard, he almost thrived on a certain amount of controlled chaos – especially if he was the one controlling it. Although he complained about them, he seemed to relish the periods of his life that went into free fall, and in a strange way he seemed to need them every once in a while. He lived in a small village, his rural retreat, where he could focus on his music and indulge what had become his other great passion - fishing. The man who covered 'Fishing Blues' all those years ago had become an aficionado of the sport. Certainly it offered a respite from the intensity of creation and performing. He could spend a day by a stream, casting and catching, and letting the world slip away.

It was the diametric opposite of the times he loved to be roaring, drinking, and indulging on the road. In other words, the pendulum still veered from side to side - maybe not as much as it once had, but John still had to attain a happy medium in his life. Considering he was now firmly into his forties, it remained to be seen whether he'd ever be capable of that.

His drinking wasn't what it had once been, but by most standards he was still a heavy drinker. But spending most of 1990 on the road had pushed him; from February to the end of September he'd been gigging virtually non-stop. It had made its demands on his body and his mental health, the way touring always did, but he'd come through it and returned home to decompress.

The purpose of the tour had been to let everyone know he was back and to push *The Apprentice* to the heights of his best-selling albums. But even sixty-five shows in the UK and Ireland across the course of the year couldn't manage that. He remained a live draw, but the album didn't sell in the quantities needed to make it into a hit. The highest chart position it managed was ninety-two, which seemed to vindicate Island's decision, at least in commercial terms. But the only one who could fully judge its artistic success was John, and he seemed happy with it.

Perhaps the most important thing to come out of the lengthy touring was the fact that Spencer Cozens became John's musical confidant.

"After he'd dropped me for part of the tour, it hurt. But he invited me back, and I loosened up. That helped a lot. I seemed to fit in then. So when John was ready to begin work on his next album he invited me up to Scotland to work on ideas with him."

A couple of songs, notably "Annie Says" and "Hole In The Rain" had already been written, but much of the rest of the album came from the two of them collaborating.

"We jammed, really. I'd set up a groove and come up with a chord sequence, and we'd start from that, working during the day. I played keyboards and John played guitar, and we'd put it all on cassette. We'd keep going, coming up with lines and ideas, and shaping things. And I'd keep recording it all."

Cozens had more of a jazz background than his predecessor in the band, Fos Paterson, and that came out in his ideas. The material they developed, songs like "Jack The Lad," "Father Time," and "Cooltide" (which was originally titled "Running Up The Harbour" and had first been recorded by John in 1980 for *Grace and Danger*, although it was never used then) offered a different kind of texture. Over the course of a few weeks they hammered out the structure of the songs and the new album. In some cases the pieces developed beyond the demo stage.

"You can hear it over the cassettes we made," Cozens said. "There's the groove, then the bassline. Later John's singing some lyric ideas. Then I put in some chords and we played around with that. By the time it was done it was recognisable as the song on the album."

They worked in the shed in John's garden, away from the house and his wife, Annie. It offered them some privacy and a space in which to focus, which they did. While it sounded like fun – just sitting and jamming – there was plenty of work going on.

By the time the musicians arrived at Ca Va in Glasgow in May 1991, the songs were more or less ready. Along with John and Cozens, there were Alan Thomson, John Henderson on drums (Arran Ahmun was only available for one track, 'Number Nine'), and Miles Bould on percussion. Musically most things were in place, although Brian Young, who engineered and co-produced, had to be willing to work on the fly.

"John would listen to a playback, pick out a single idea, and they'd go and re-record based on that," he noted. The lyrics for three of the tracks – "Jack The Lad," "Father Time," and "Cooltide" – were improvised by John in the studio, in what had become his time-honoured fashion.

"John would go over to the pub and have a few drinks," Young remembered. "Then he'd come back, go into the vocal booth (by now Ca Va had built a real vocal booth) and just sing it through. He could be quite amazing, just go for it."

The whole disc was recorded and mixed in a total of eighteen days, spread across a couple of months. The timing proved serendipitous, coinciding with the Glasgow Jazz Festival, which brought a few friends into town, including Andy Sheppard and vibist Joe Locke. The pair happened to be appearing at The Lorne, a pub close to Ca Va, and both were persuaded to contribute. Locke's parts were laid down in just four hours, while Sheppard only took seven for his soprano sax work.

Even Fos Paterson returned, this time deputizing for a couple of days for Cozens who had to sit his final degree exams. Most of the music was played live in the studio, rather than having everything heavily sequenced, as it had been on *The Apprentice*. That made for a return to John's favoured way of working. Throughout, the original recordings featured bass guitar – either Thomson or Dave Ball – but in most cases John decided to replace the fretboard with a keyboard bass, just because "I found that we got a better feel by using keyboard bass."

John had actually originally suggested they record without a drummer, but Cozens managed to convince him otherwise, because "...with a serious drummer like John Henderson...that was really silly. I mean, we did six of the tracks live in just a day and a half."

Over the last several years John had experimented wildly with different guitar sounds and synthesizers (the most successful being a cheap Casio guitar that Annie had bought him), but had never found one with an accurate enough trigger to fit in with the band, especially for recording purposes. So for this album he kept everything very simple, playing his favourite 1954 Les Paul gold top either directly into the mixing board, or simply through a Fender Twin Reverb. The only effect he used on the entire disc was a fuzz pedal on "Hole In The Rain." By his standards, that was incredibly stripped down, certainly from a decade before, when he'd armed himself with a disconcerting array of pedals and effects.

He no longer even used his trusty Echoplex, although he still loved it dearly. But once again, its absence was dictated by the fact that he was playing in a band. On an analogue machine, the length of the delays couldn't be set exactly, and exact was what was needed. Instead he'd started using a digital SDE3000, which worked far better with sequences, as "you just measure things properly, so we're both playing at the same tempo and work things out mathematically."

Once again, it was apparent that John was playing very little lead guitar on the record, continuing the trend that had developed during the '80s. Live, where everyone stretched out, he could still turn out plenty of solos, but for the studio he was happier giving space to his singing and the other band members, rather than inserting a guitar solo for its own sake. It was a sign of how comfortable he'd become within a band format and how much he relied on and the trusted the other people he played with.

John was the first to admit that many of the developments in the studio had left him behind. Luckily, in Cozens he had someone who was very current with all the technology (far more necessary for a keyboardist than any other musician).

There was one guest whose work never made its way onto the finished album, although everyone wanted to include her. Bonnie Raitt was appearing in Glasgow, and John went to the gig. It transpired that she was a fan of his and she was easily persuaded to come to the studio and lay down a backing vocal for "Cooltide."

"That was amazing," said Young, who was present for the recording. "She came in, listened to the track, and then just nailed it. She's a complete pro, a pleasure to work with."

Unfortunately, because of contractual problems, John was unable to use her voice on the finished product. It was just one of those things. At least everyone had the memory of her being there.

The album was produced by John, Cozens, and Ca Va's Brian Young. John tended to be the hands-off one in that trio, simply because he quickly became bored with all the details of studio work. He was far more musician than techie. Instead, after offering suggestions as to the sound, "I tend to bugger off for a couple of hours and then come back in for half an hour and say, right, I like this, keep that bit, shift that, sample that, stick a bit on the chorus and I'll see you in half an hour."

He was certainly a believer in happy accidents and still liked to give spontaneity its head whenever he could. Many of the improvised passages stayed on the record, especially on "Cooltide" itself.

Interestingly, considering the facilities at the studio, John chose to begin recording on the same 24-track analogue machines he'd used for his last two studio discs, liking the warmth they'd given. It was only after a week that they switched everything over to digital. But for his tastes, that wasn't always successful, especially when they began to master the record. For that they started on digital audio tape (DAT), before finally dumping it back on to the analogue machines to achieve a completely satisfactory sound.

And there was a definite warmth to the record, tinged with jazziness. Cooltide continued along the path John had been taking. The songs bore little comparison to what he'd been writing two decades earlier, these days revolving around the groove instead of the changes. But there was a joy about them, whether the gleeful grittiness of his vocal on "Jack The Lad," his guitar on "Hole In The Rain," or "Number Nine," which offered what was probably the most slurred Martyn vocal to date - slurred to the point of incomprehensibility.

Much as Fos Paterson had been before him, the linchpin of the whole sound was Spencer Cozens. The record was very keyboard driven, whether in the rampant arpeggios or the keyboard bass that provided that main springboard. Everything else seemed subordinate, even the drums, which were frequently mixed down.

That said, the lightly funky "Father Time" was powered by drums and percussion, with Locke's vibes solo a bubbly joy over the top. It stood in contrast to "Call Me," whose lazy smoothness had the silkiness of modern R&B, even if John's style of vocal pyrotechnics were far removed from the divas generally associated with the style – in fact, his grittiness had more in common with an Otis Redding or James Carr.

Apart from "Jack The Lad," the real key to the album was its title track. As a song, it wasn't among John's greatest, but as a workout piece it was perfect, a showcase – on this disc, at least – for Sheppard's soprano sax and for John's rare, angular guitar work. It was a structure on which to hang a jam, which was how John and the band used it in concert. Even the studio version ran more than ten minutes, allowing the players to trade lines before resolving itself again with a vocal.

But like the whole album, it was relatively low key. There was nothing to match the anger of a "John Wayne" or the emotion of "Just Now" or "Head And Heart." All the raw feelings were comfortably shrouded and the corners carefully smoothed. If this was a diary, there was a great deal John wasn't saying, leaving it hidden between the lines. But obliqueness had always been his way, even if he sometimes seemed to let that mask slip.

As ever, he continued to be a man of many parts – or, more accurately, a man hiding himself behind many parts. As he'd done for so many years, he moved between the English and Scots accents, the bonhomie and charm and the glimpses of anger.

To get beyond all that was rare and a gift offered to very few. Certainly the journalists and the public-at-large didn't get a glimpse of the real John. He'd become very adept over the years at hiding his emotions. What he expressed in a song was controlled, some of it in a kind of personal code.

Age had mellowed him a little, but it had changed him too, certainly in a physical way. Still bearded, his hair had thinned, the lines on his face had deepened. But above all, he'd put on weight. The thin young man of 1970 was now decidedly heavyset. At times he seemed positively bloated - but after drinking heavily for so long, that was only to be expected. In some respects, he'd got off lightly for all his abuse of alcohol.

It didn't show much in his face and he seemed to have the constitution of an ox that enabled him to carry on through almost anything – witness the fact that he'd done all his vocals for an album after piercing his lungs with fencing in the '80s!

John continued to move ahead on his own path, even if it wasn't a roaring commercial success. But he couldn't deny his own musical past. Or ignore it. The songs from the '70s wouldn't disappear, even if John wished they would at times. "Solid Air" was still a staple, although now drastically rearranged to accommodate a band. He seemed happier with material from later in the decade, from *One World* onward, that had always been in a band format; they gave more freedom for live performance. That was quite apparent on *Live at Bristol 1991: Official Bootleg*, a record of a summer gig in the West Country. Interestingly, the only brand new song was "Cooltide," which John claimed they were currently recording. For almost everything else, he delved back more than a decade into his catalogue. Certainly he had a crack lineup behind him, with Alan Thomson on bass, Andy Sheppard on drums, and Spencer Cozens on bass, with John Henderson filling the drum stool this time.

It highlighted the contrast between studio and stage (and was a better album than *Live*, interestingly). Although the blazing fire of *Philentropy* had become more comfortably banked, there was still an energy to it, as shown on the opener, a version of "Big Muff" that featured an extended, scorching guitar solo. The sense of humour was apparent on the fake soul talking opening of "Couldn't Love You More," before turning serious with a gut-wrenching, emotional vocal and a tasteful, restrained guitar solo.

"Deny This Love" had been part of his live show for four years, an early entry into the "Martyn Lite" years. This was a more developed version than the one that had appeared on *Foundations*, with some strong bass work and more of John's guitar, something so crucially missing from his studio work. "Sweet Little Mystery," one of John's most heartfelt and vulnerable songs. wasn't quite as stripped down as it had been in its original form, with an incisive solo from Sheppard.

The next three pieces – "Looking On," "John Wayne," and "Johnny Too Bad," were staples of his live set and more or less the spine of it, where the band could really stretch out and let go. Most interesting was "Cooltide," which had moved beyond the embryonic, but which was still finding its final shape, however amorphous that might be. Its relative lack of form was evident, as was the fact that the band was still feeling its way through the piece; it never really seemed to go anywhere. And a downbeat, almost cabaret version of "Never Let Me Go" (or "Let Me Love You Tonight") rounded out the proceedings.

The album, which wasn't released until 1998 (and then only in a limited edition of 5000 copies), offered a snapshot of John at the time of recording *Cooltide*. And the overall impression was of a man trying hard to forge ahead, but still bound to his own past.

CHAPTER TEN – The Return of John Martyn

If it was impossible to escape the past, at least John could turn it to his advantage. On the tour for *Cooltide*, just as in so many tours before, he played plenty of older material, all heavily rearranged, and there were constant calls for more.

Given the relative commercial failures of *Cooltide* and *The Apprentice* it was possibly a good time to take another look at those old songs. They'd stood the test of time from the '70s, all this classic material, and showed no sign of aging or declining in popularity.

It precluded the need to write new material, which could be a drawn-out process, building up around the grooves. And since much of the material had been adapted to a group situation, the arrangements didn't need much work. The label was all in favour of the idea, especially as John could call on the services of some big name friends to help out on the tracks. Phil Collins had been a good mate for over a decade now and had become a superstar in his own right. And Pink Floyd's David Gilmour had taken the stage with John just a couple of years earlier, during John's extended run at the Shaw Theatre in London. Even though they weren't important to the songs themselves, the names offered marquee value, a sense of credibility (again, John hardly needed that), and the possibility of extra sales.

The idea certainly seemed like a winner. John was ahead of the curve of artists revisiting their earlier work, something that would later become a lucrative trend for other performers. He was still a critically admired performer, by now a grizzled veteran with a quarter of a century of recording under his belt. His older songs remained his most popular and enduring.

And there was another reason to put the songs on disc, because they "had changed so much from their original form. I like closing patterns in my life and starting again."

With this record, someone new came into John's professional and personal life, someone who'd work with him, on and off, for the rest of his life. Jim Tullio, a Chicagoan, had produced albums for a number of artists, ranging from Rick Danko of The Band to Steve Goodman, with whom he'd won two Grammy awards. Tullio had discovered John's music when he bought *London Conversation* in the '60s, one of the few Americans to find it. Since then he'd bought each of John's records as they appeared, while carving out his own career. As he said, "I became a fan, and it seemed like he had a new record every six months, although they were difficult to get in America."

He already knew John, too, having met him in the late '80s through a series of happy coincidences.

"In the 1980s I had a company with Jack Kelman and Dougie Thomson, who'd been the bass player in Supertramp. In 1988 Dougie and I went to Europe on business, and he wanted me to see Roberton, where he grew up. He took me to Ca Va Studios in Glasgow. John wasn't there, but Brian Young played me some outtakes from the recordings he'd made there. Brian came to Roberton with us. We went to get something to eat and pulled over by a church. Dougie knocked on the door. John was there, drunk and laughing – they'd set me up. I stayed for three days." A year later "John called me from New York. He wanted me to go there, but I was in the middle of producing a record. The disc just happened to include two of his songs. So I sent him a plane ticket, he came out and played on it, then stayed for two months."

It was ample time for the two to bond and John called Tullio – known to his friends as Tools – to try and find a US distributor for *Cooltide*. So when the tracks recorded for the new project weren't turning out well, John turned to Tullio.

"John had started the tracks for *No Little Boy* in London with Matt Butler. He wasn't thrilled and we made it better. We had the masters sent out, and there was very little of John's guitar on them, so I had him play. We re-did the backing vocals, added keyboards and we did a bunch of new songs. I taught him 'Rock Salt And Nails,' by Utah Bruce Phillips. Dylan had asked Utah at the 1971 Philadelphia Folk Festival if he could record it and Utah said no, as he didn't want anything to do with Columbia Records. I told John that story and he said I had to teach him the song. I asked Levon Helm to come in and sing as I'd been working with the Band, he sang on that and 'Just Now'."

Not everything was done in Chicago. Some of the record was made in LA.

"We went out to Los Angeles, where my ex-partner Patrick Leonard had built a new studio in Burbank. John wanted to record with Weather Report; he loved that group. Their drummer, Peter Erskine, was a friend of mine and a fan of John's. I set it up with him and [saxophonist] Wayne Shorter, but the keyboard player, Joe Zawinul, sent a fax turning us down a week before the session. Then, right before we were due to go, Wayne's family was killed in a plane crash, so that only left Peter."

For three whole months, Tullio was immersed in the making of the disc, working constantly with John. And John, having been willing to turn it all over to someone else, proved very tractable.

Even as they were busy in different studios in Chicago and Los Angeles, they received a shock. John had never imagined that his label, Permanent, would ever issue the tapes he'd decided weren't good enough. In fact, he'd refused them permission to do so. However, they went ahead and put the material out as out *Couldn't Love You More*, with production credited to Matt Butler. John was understandably furious.

"I had no idea they were going to release that," he said later. "They had the tapes and I was in America and when I came back the next thing I knew it was out."

183

In fact he'd learned about it while still in Chicago, Tullio recalled.

"While we were mixing, Permanent released a disc of the original British sessions. We were in the control room working on mixes and John was screaming in the phone to the label. They came out in several versions over the next few years."

Being so deep into it, he wasn't about to abandon the record and let an inferior product carry his name, not if he could do something to rectify the situation. And from this point, everything became extremely complicated. The finished version, under the name *No Little Boy*, appeared on the Mesa label in the US in July 1993, with production credited to Tullio and Butler – with the exception of the new recordings, which were credited solely to Tullio. That same month, *No Little Boy* also appeared in Britain – on the Permanent label! However, the UK CD version – which retailed alongside *Couldn't Love You More* - added three tracks, a cover of Utah Phillips's "Rock, Salt And Nails," "Pascanel," and "Hole In The Rain." The first two of those tracks had been recorded by Tullio in America, "but the British version of *No Little Boy* used everything. The US version was how John and I sequenced it, and they added the other tracks in rough mixes in England. That's when John severed ties with Permanent."

According to John, *No Little Boy* – the American version on Mesa – "is the legitimate album." With thirteen tracks, it was shorter than the British version, but it stood as he'd envisioned it and he was satisfied with the performances and the mixes.

The track listing was an intelligent mix of songs, mostly culled from the '70s, but just peeking into the '80s. *Bless the Weather* and *Solid Air* were the most heavily represented discs, the apex of John's songwriting to many people. Some of the choices might have seemed unlikely, such as "Ways To Cry," or "Just Now," a song that only a few years before John had said he could no longer sing, because he didn't feel the words any more. Here, alongside the harmony voice of Levon Helm – a connection that took him all the way back to Woodstock and *Stormbringer* in 1969 –

it sounded fresh and emotional. "Fine Lines," the opening track from *Inside Out* might also have seemed out of place, but back it 1973 it had been the only cut on the album that offered any kind of continuity from *Solid Air.*

The final version that surfaced on *No Little Boy* proved to be a fascinating, and generally convincing, exercise that connected John Martyn past and present. Some tracks worked better than others, to be sure: the rearranged "Solid Air" seemed tentative, lacking the soft airiness of the original, and "Could've Been Me" suffered by virtue of the fact that it simply wasn't on the same plane as the other songs. The biggest surprise, possibly, was "Just Now," which emerged as sophisticated roots rock, thanks to a clever arrangement and Levon Helm's excellent harmony work. But its directness kept it in contrast to the rest of the album, where the tone remained muted and late-night. "Fine Lines" hewed remarkably closely to the original version, while the mood of the original "One World" showed that it could easily have been a prototype for John's later band style as played here.

The most obvious change was in John's voice. The singing of the '70s seemed to have developed enormously in its sophistication. Over the course of a couple of decades, it had become a commanding instrument, while still keeping the same tone. There was far more confidence in it, but tempered with sensitivity. Considering how long he'd been singing these songs, he was still able to invest them with a great deal of emotion, and rarely had his vocals sounded better – as well they might, given the fact that in the studio he'd focused on them, rather than guitar, for a number of years.

Because he was playing with a band, there was naturally less of John's guitar. On several tracks he didn't even play the instrument – either there was none on the cut (as with "I Don't Wanna Know" and "One Day Without You," for example), or it was played by others and generally put into a rhythm role, rather than in the foreground. But John completely without guitar would have been heresy and some of these songs did demand acoustic guitar – "Bless The Weather" and "Fine Lines" would have been unthinkable without it. Tullio's insistence on John's playing gave the record the touch it needed.

Of course, all the material was familiar to longtime fans, but it was also apparent that these songs had a quality and structure that had largely been missing from John's output in recent years. Perhaps their construction was old-fashioned, as opposed to the way he worked now, but it was a framework that was very satisfactory, less amorphous than his more modern work, as the contrast between most of the songs and "Could've Been Me" proved.

The songs also proved beyond a shadow of a doubt that John had been an inspired craftsman in the '70s. Very few artists had been able to compose so many outstanding pieces over a similar period. For a while, the head and the heart had reached a conjunction that let it simply pour out of him.

No Little Boy wasn't perfect, by any means. Sometimes the arrangements seemed a little cluttered and lacking the spare grace of the originals. And sometimes the newer versions added nothing to what had gone before, as with 'Sweet Little Mystery,' whose simple quartet format was now filled out with female backing vocals that were largely unnecessary. But in a couple of instances, the newer versions cast the songs in a powerful new light. "Just Now" was one, taking a very simple piece and bring a much greater depth to it, or "Head And Heart," which in its new version sounded like a string quartet played by a band.

Overall it was a satisfying venture and easily John's best release since Piece by Piece in 1986. It might not have signalled the complete return of his Muse, but it was a good way to tread water while waiting for it to come back.

Yes, it was a holding action - but it was a strong one that was well-received in the press. It was a reminder not only of the talent John had once been, but of that talent that he still was - a sign that he was alive, kicking, and creative.

While John and Tullio were working on the record, a surprising offer came in. The London Contemporary Dance Theatre commissioned John to write the music for a new work called *The Monsoon*. Presented with the topic, John looked to his own past for the composition – a natural move, given that he was currently immersed in his own history. Working with Tullio, he created a piece in three parts, where "part one is a new version of 'Go Down Easy,' part two is a percussion piece, very wild and free, rain and chaos," Tullio said. "Part three is a version of 'Call Me Crazy'." The version of "Go Down Easy" would be the reworking of the song that appeared on 2004's *On the Cobbles*. The other two parts have never been released.

It might have interrupted the process of working on the album, but it also enhanced it, forcing John to look at his back catalogue from a new perspective and transform the two songs.

Recorded in Chicago, *The Monsoon* featured John on guitar, vocal, and synthesizer, and Tullio on fretless bass, percussion and synthesizer, along with a tenor sax player and six percussionists.

At twenty-seven minutes long, it was no minor work, but a full-blown dance piece (choreographed by Darshan Singh Bhuller) that received a performance in London during 1992, while John was still in the US working on *No Little Boy*, so unfortunately he was never able to see it performed.

All this work seemed to bring out a deep creativity in John, not just for writing and reworking songs, but also for arranging and adding to them.

"I was mixing the 'Call Me Crazy' piece in the studio in my house," Tullio said. "John was there and came stumbling downstairs, drunk, and said 'Tools, turn on the keyboard.' He was a keyboard dabbler. I gave him the keyboard and he started playing. Upfront it sounded like nonsense. After one take he went back upstairs. I took the track, put the keyboard low in the mix and you know what? It was perfect. So I learned to shut my mouth when John wanted to try something."

No Little Boy served a purpose beyond being the next John Martyn album. It was the first of his records to receive an American release since he'd left Island, albeit on a small independent label. But John had long been a quiet favourite of music journalists and they wrote extensively about the album on their home turf. It wasn't likely to turn the album into a hit, but it was enough to get it noticed by those familiar with John's canon and to get him some airplay on the kind of AAA (adult album alternative) radio stations these versions suited.

It was also enough to get John back to America for his first real tour in a long time. It was a solo tour and John played mostly acoustic guitar. Given his stature – or lack of it – in America, he was relegated to relatively small clubs. The surprising thing was that he sold them all out. Many in the audience had never had the opportunity to see him play live before. He stuck to the oldies but goodies, proving to be as entertaining verbally as he was musically. Finishing up on the West Coast, he decided to end the jaunt with a holiday in Hawaii.

"I got a call from an operator in Hawaii, would I take reverse call charges from a John Martyn," recalled soundman Alex Boyesen. "I said yes and John came on the line. He wanted to know how everything was over in the UK, had I heard from Archie (the

manager), was there any work being set up? I told him what I knew and then he went on to tell me he had just been stabbed in some kind of street brawl. Apparently he had been drinking in some bar, God knows what he was doing out there, and had had some kind of argument with someone, which then escalated out into the street. Apparently the other guy tried to hide under a car so John just pushed it over him which is when he jumped up and stabbed him."

But perhaps it wouldn't have been John without some kind of incident. Certainly he was drinking quite heavily on the tour, although - ever the professional - it didn't affect his performances.

Drugs could wreak havoc on a show, though. Alex Boyesen recalled that when John and the band were playing in Europe in 1993, "at the gig in Brussels we parked outside the venue Suede were due to play the following day and their people were down there scoping it out. When they got back to their car the wheels had gone. It was a very rough neighbourhood; we ended up having to leave someone with the vehicles all the time we were there. John met up with a friend of his who was obviously some kind of dealer who then proceeded to hand out lines of good coke. John confided to me later that this was 'Big Muff'. About a week later I heard he had fallen out of a window and killed himself. John was really upset; they had known each other for a very long time and this seemed to have been one in a long line of people going. John was never demonstrative in the time I worked with him, more resigned to the facts of life."

But there could also be some magical moments, Boyesen noted, such as "at a gig in Paris, I had a good setup and during an acoustic spot with John I had some echo spreading the sound of John around the room; it sounded amazing. John could obviously hear it on stage, as he soon latched onto the rhythm of his voice and in the same way he played with an Echoplex and guitar he had this whole thing going with his voice, harmonies and rhythm; he improvised for about 3 or four minutes. During this tour he used the Alesis solid state effects box - he loved the convenience of it, but was never too keen on the sound it made."

People, including John himself, noticed the reception he'd been given in the US, the way his performances had been well-received and how journalists were eager to talk to him. *No Little Boy* had received glowing reviews on both sides of the Atlantic (as compared to *Couldn't Love You More*, which was generally treated with disdain).

By reworking some of his older material, John not only satisfied audiences – although the album never charted – and bought a respite from having to write new material, he also inadvertently forced a reappraisal of those old songs - and of himself and his career.

If not overdue, it was certainly about time. John had been recording for twenty-six years and was respected by his peers as one of the greatest singer-songwriters of his generation, frequently cited as a highly influential acoustic guitar player. In commercial terms, he'd never created the kind of splash that some of his peers had managed and his personal life had been a shambles – he'd recently split up with his second wife, Annie, after a decade of marriage, and his drinking and substance abuse were legendary.

But in John's case it was sometimes necessary to separate the man from the artist - and in artistic terms many people revered him, especially journalists, who tended to be the tastemakers. Now, given the opportunity to praise his old songs and look at John once more, they took it.

Nor was Island Records oblivious to the groundswell of interest in John. After all, they owned the rights to the vast majority of his catalogue and a number of years had passed since there'd been any type of retrospective. Indeed, only two existed, 1977's *So Far So Good* and the 1982 rarities collection *The Electric John Martyn*. But there had been no real career overview of John's work. In the light of all this new interest, it was time to rectify that omission.

Sweet Little Mystery: The Island Anthology was a good summation of much of John's career, although far from complete. Ostensibly celebrating a quarter of a century of recording, it focused very heavily on the '70s material. There was nothing pre-*Bless the Weather* and only four of the thirty-four tracks were from John's second go-round with the label (curiously, the hit "Over The Rainbow" wasn't among them).

Most of the favourites were there, but even across the spread of two CDs, there was no attempt to go below the surface, to dig through the vaults and unearth any rarities. For instance, they could have included "Time Away," the track he recorded with former Free guitarist Paul Kossoff for Kossoff's solo album (which would eventually surface a few years later, in its entirety as "Time Spent," on the Free five-CD box set). There was nothing from *Live at Leeds*, possibly because Island no longer had the rights to that recording. Everything was taken from previously issued Island albums. While that made for a strong primer (actually bettered four years later by the single CD *Serendipity*, which only had seventeen tracks, but cast its net a little wider) which garnered plenty of press, it could hardly be called definitive..

However, with its glowing reviews, and coming on the heels of *No Little Boy*, it really raised John's profile. Suddenly he was being featured in music magazines again and even being described as a legend. It was stature that perhaps fit after all this time and some of his larger than life exploits. Add to that his expansive charm – when in the right mood – his ability to be a more than able raconteur, and he was an excellent interviewee. And with the release of the compilation, he was available to the press – who were truly interested for the first time in years.

John was more than happy to talk at length on any number of topics, including his own past, but he was quick to shrug off the new collection.

"Hrrrmmmph, well I'm glad they didn't wait until I was dead to do it," he told *Mojo*. "It's a compliment that Island have done this anthology thing, but I don't wanna hear it. I don't listen to the old stuff."

He might not have listened to it, but it still provided a big part of his income. Those were the songs that took him back to America at the beginning of 1994 and looked as if they might finally offer him a chance to establish himself there. Yet, in spite of spending much of March and April 1994 in the US and making a beachhead on the coasts, he never followed through conscientiously to progress further.

The fact that he had no new album to promote didn't help matters. The anthology, which was released in America, kept his name forward, but it was the past, not the present. Nor was there money available for him to take the band with him and show his true current style.

John was in a state of flux, both personally and professionally. Having split up with Annie, he had no emotional centre in his life. And following disagreements with Permanent over the release of *Couldn't Love You More* and *No Little Boy*, he was without a UK record label again.

That didn't stop him going on the road. It was a good way to raise money and keep his name in front of people. During June and part of July, he was criss-crossing Britain with the band, then for two more months, between mid-October and Christmas, he went out and did it all over again, this time as a solo act.

In spite of all the road work, John hadn't been creatively idle. He'd been working in the studio, inspired by music he was hearing, as all around him the musical climate in Britain had been changing, with the new idea of trip-hop suddenly hip.

It was a Bristol-based sound, a chilled-out mixing of hip-hop beats, soul, and jazz, personified by bands like Massive Attack and Portishead. It became the new musical buzzword, a laid-back style that fitted perfectly into the chill-out rooms of the club scene, made for late night listening.

Interestingly, it was remarkably close to the furrow John had been ploughing for over twenty years. Some of the new generation recognised that, giving John credit and pointing out that *Solid Air* was one of the classic chill-out albums, decades ahead of its time. But all his material in the years since fitted handily into the style, even if much of what he'd done in recent years had been lightweight. So it was just a short step for John to be making his own brand of trip-hop, borrowing a few ideas from those who'd come after him, while keeping the heart, and more particularly the soul, of his sound intact.

He'd been writing and experimenting with new material that was looser than anything he'd done in the past several years. At least four tracks had been arranged and demoed in the studio – "She's A Lover," "All In Your Favour," "Step It Up" and "A Little Strange." These would appear later as the *Snoo!* EP, the name coming (as anyone who saw John in the '90s would recall) from a favourite cry of his, one he'd picked up from a drunken Arsenal fan – "Snoo" being an abbreviated form of Arsenal (football club).

In the wake of the anthology, John had become a roundly lauded figure, and the new tracks seemed to find him cresting a new creative peak, some of the best work he'd done since the end of the '70s.

He was still without a label to release any of this new material, though, and that was something that needed to be rectified. It was perhaps good fortune that Permanent chose 1995 to release the double *Live* set. Although out of date – it was a document of one concert from his long stand at London's Shaw Theatre in 1990 – it kept his name out there.

Ultimately, though, the bottom line was that John hadn't put out a disc of new material since *Cooltide* in 1991. *No Little Boy* and the anthology had shored up his reputation, but hadn't moved it ahead. And musical stasis was anathema to John.

Trip-hop made him hip again. Time had caught up with his music, and he needed to take advantage of it. His era with the major labels had come and gone. He was well over forty, a cult figure at best, not someone who fitted into their youthful or big-selling demographic at all. Most recently he'd parted company with a small independent. What were the prospects?

Quite good, as it turned out, thanks to the adventurous Go! Discs label, a label with "the same attitude that Island had when I was starting out." It was a good match-up. John had a small but solid base of fans who'd buy anything he released. He'd received plenty of press and name checks in the last couple of years, enough to draw the curious to a new record. And the material he'd been writing was contemporary enough to possibly get some radio airplay.

As before, he worked closely with Spencer Cozens on the record.

"We sketch ideas, a groove or a phrase, and build from that," Cozens explained. "Or we'll get a rhythm and work from there. I think John was taken with bands like Portishead and Massive Attack; he saw it as an extension of what he'd been doing. I was doing a lot more programming this time around, and I was more involved in all the aspects of the record."

Cozens had become indispensable to John and when they went back into the studio with producer Stefon Taylor, whose studio resume ranged from working with former Guns N'Roses man Izzy Stradlin to blues harmonica player James Cotton, in addition to being a member of the band Ken Oak, they were firing on all cylinders. Taylor was able to bring a freshness to the sound, much as Jim Tullio had done with *No Little Boy*.

Many of the usual suspects were on board – Alan Thompson (now spelt with a p), John Giblin and Jerry Underwood, with Fos Paterson returning for a little keyboard work and Phil Collins taking the drum stool and contributing some backing vocals (all via digital audio tape – Collins was never in the same studio).

And., released in the middle of 1996, was the result of all the work John and Cozens had put into the demos they'd recorded in 1995. If Massive Attack was the rude, youthful face of trip-hop and Portishead its voice in the middle of a bleak night, this was what it looked like all grown up and fighting through middle age. There was an edge to it, but also a sultry, restless sophistication.

Perhaps because his most recent focus had been on his older material, with its more concrete structures, these songs were among his most memorable in years, from the irresistible pull of 'Suzanne' (which could almost have come off *Grace and Danger*, but had actually been recorded, without vocals, as a new track for *No Little Boy*) to 'A Little

Strange, which had been hewn into a solid form from its rather amorphous demo version.   In contrast to the past decade and a half, John seemed to be consciously pushing toward the edge with this release, stretching himself in a way he hadn't for a long time. There was a real emotional content to his singing, the kind he'd rediscovered going over his old work, and his voice was lovingly recorded, the centrepiece of the disc. Over the years, his soulful qualities had come more to the fore. He was as mannered as any blues or jazz great, with little tics that made him easy to spot, but it worked.

The disc seemed to look back over John's career, choose the best parts and put them all together. It had the intimate feel and quality songwriting of the '70s, meshed perfectly with the best sinewy grooves of the '80s. Collins was the ideal drummer, always in the pocket without being overbearing, yet propelling the tracks with a steady certainty. The jazzy touches were considered, but always subordinate to the song. And when the ensemble turned funky, it wasn't the whitebread, watered-down sound that had plagued John's previous studio attempts. "Step It Up," while never being mistaken for Motown or Stax, had some real muscle to it, down to its spare but biting guitar work. It was "Root Love" twenty years on.

It seemed like the first time in far too long that John had been willing to take real chances with his music. "Carmine" subverted the blues with plenty of modern touches, while keeping a dark underside. Even "Suzanne," while hardly the best track on the disc, revealed a raw emotional honesty that scraped at the wound of rejection. "She's A Lover" could almost have been the successor to "Solid Air" with its soft, breathy groove (indeed, the two would often be paired in concert). It might not have had quite the resonance of its predecessor, but it still worked on its own terms.

This was a reinvigorated John, one who showed he could still release an artistically satisfying album (although, at just over 48 minutes, it was short, by modern standards). It should have helped re-establish him as an important figure, one who could still push the limits, even though he was no longer young. The reviews were uniformly glowing and he looked set to become an elder statesman to the chill-out scene.

But that never happened.

In a twist of fate that seemed so typical of John's career, whether self-inflicted or otherwise, something came along to stop him taking advantage of the situation. In this case, his past caught up with him.

For years John had abused his body. During his years as a musician there'd been a constant, sometimes heavy, flow of dope, not to mention pills, cocaine, and even heroin on occasion. Far more importantly, there'd been alcohol, so much a part of his life since his early teens. The booze defined John almost as much as music did. Many times he'd announced that he'd stopped drinking, but he never had. John was an alcoholic - but, like many alcoholics, he was able to function. Over the years his body had developed a high tolerance, and need, for alcohol. On tour, drummer Arran Ahmun noted, "when he wasn't with me (sharing a joint), he was probably out drinking. In the past, I've loaded up John's spliffs so he wouldn't end up drinking too much."

As a young man in good health, he'd been able to slough off the heaviest binges in a short time. Even now, according to Ahmun, he seemed to have "the constitution of an ox." But he wasn't young any more and his body was reaching its limits. Finally it rebelled, with what John would later refer to in black humour as his "exploding pancreas."

It was the timing that was unfortunate. The album had just been released, and with some serious promotion and touring, John could possibly have made the leap beyond the cult figure status that had dogged him throughout his career. Instead, he ended up seriously ill, lying on his back in a hospital bed.

And though he made light of it, he *was* extremely ill. It began with severe abdominal pain that became worse as he ate, accompanied by violent nausea and vomiting. And it wouldn't go away.

He was admitted to hospital, where doctors were able to diagnose the cause, a burst pancreas. He spent several weeks in hospital on intravenous fluids. He could easily have died – quite probably only that ox-like constitution had saved him.

Sadly, while in hospital he received depressing news that did nothing to help him back onto his feet: his wife, Annie Furlong, had died in a car accident. She and John had been separated since 1993, but had never divorced. Her passing was a stark reminder of his own mortality – especially as he was seeing life from a prone position, still in considerable physical pain and with the prospect of a lengthy recovery ahead.

Apart from daily medication, patients who survive a burst pancreas receive two pieces of advice from their doctors: to eat a diet high in carbohydrates and low in fat and, more importantly, to stop drinking alcohol.

For much of the time, the first half was no problem for John. He loved to cook and was an accomplished chef, as much at home in the kitchen as he was in the recording studio or on stage. On tour, and at the mercy of promoter's pasta or whatever meals the band could find, a good diet became more problematic, although not impossible.

It was the second step that was the tricky one. Knowing what it could do to him and what the future might hold, could John stop drinking after all these years? He should have; he was certainly smart enough to understand the reasons and the possibilities. And several doctors had already told him that he had to lay off the booze if he wanted to keep on living. But, said Ahmun, "when he started recovering from that, he didn't stay off the drink, so that didn't help."

John was a slave to the drink, or - as future producer Garry Pollitt put it - "he drank just the way we Scots do." The people around him knew it and accepted it. Many, like Ahmun, did what they could to temper his excesses. On the road, though, it was impossible to watch him the whole time.

"In Ireland he came on stage really pissed, and there was a backdrop curtain," Ahmun remembered. "His guitar machine heads got caught on the curtain. He kept trying to get out and ended up completely wrapped in the curtain."

There were also times when John's dark side could spill out, encouraged by drink. Producer Jim Tullio recalled, "something I didn't know was that Eric Clapton's manager had a restraining order against John – he couldn't go within 100 feet of Eric – this was since Eric had been in rehab. On one of John's Chicago visits, Eric was playing at Legends, Buddy Guy's club, and John wanted to go down. He demanded to see Eric, but they wouldn't let him down to the dressing room, and that pissed John off. He was wearing one of those long rider coats, but it only had half pockets, not very deep. He also had about £7,000 in the coat pocket. He took off the coat and put it over a chair, then went to the bar to get a drink. The place was packed. When he got back someone had taken the money from the pocket. John just went berserk, going up to people, accusing them, threatening them. It took three bouncers to get him out of the club and we never got to watch Eric."

Overall, though, John remained vital and upbeat. Illness had robbed him of the chance to capitalize on *And.* and kept him off the road for an extended period of time, cutting heavily into his income. His life, physically and emotionally, had altered irrevocably. Still, playing music and creating music was what he knew how to do, the only thing he'd ever really done for a living. And nothing short of the grave was going to stop him continuing.

1997 saw him back on the road with the usual crew, at the normal demanding pace on what had become their annual trek through the British Isles. And he followed it up later in the year with what was billed as a solo tour, although he was in fact accompanied by bassist John Giblin.

Both were hard, gruelling slogs for a man who'd been seriously ill and who wasn't doing his health any favours by continuing to drink as much as he had before.

On top of that, he'd spent part of the year working on a new album. For various business reasons, Go! Discs became Independiente. John was still very much on the books, following the critical success of *And*. They wanted more material from him - but it seemed his songwriting well had run dry.

CHAPTER ELEVEN – The Church with One Bell

Even if John had been temporarily deserted by his songwriting Muse, he wasn't short of ideas for a new record. He made a proposition to Independiente; the deconsecrated church next door to his cottage in Roberton, Lanarkshire, was for sale. It was a building he'd coveted for over a decade (he'd first mentioned it in an interview in 1985), and now "it was going to be bought by these idiots. I did not fancy idiots living in the church next door." So John suggested giving the label an album, in exchange for which they'd buy him the church.

"They...said 'Give us a record of covers and we will buy the church.' So they sent us (John and the band) lots of songs and we sat around and waited 'til we all smiled at the same time and we thought, OK, we'll do that one... Every time we smiled simultaneously, that seemed like a good idea."

It made sense; for more than two decades John had been including other writers' material sparingly on his records. With the right song, he was a skilled interpreter, showing new facets of something old as he held it up to the light. His voice had developed too, almost beyond recognition. The early slurring attempts at imitating the growls and swoops of a tenor sax had become a style matured in oak. There was a depth of expression in it now, a way to cut to the heart of a line – even something utterly clichéd – and draw the emotion from it. That was a quality the great singers possessed and something John had grown into. Whether it was because he'd spent much of the '80s and early '90s focusing on his singing, or the weight of life experiences, he'd become a world-class vocalist.

Just a few years before, he'd very successfully reinterpreted his older songs - and given the dearth of new material, since John's Muse no longer seemed to visit as often, a record of covers seemed to be the obvious choice. It was time for him to return to the studio and this offered him the opportunity to show not only his range, but his influences.

The one caveat by the record company was to bring in an outside producer - and he was an unusual and unlikely choice. Norman Dayron had made his reputation by producing several blues greats, especially Howlin' Wolf. He'd been a chronicler of the Chicago blues scene in its heyday, whether in the studios like Chess, in the clubs, or out on Maxwell Street, recording the players at the open air market.

John knew the blues – possibly more intimately, on an emotional level, than many people. He knew the work of the people Dayron had produced and he was willing to work with him. The sessions themselves would be quick, just a week in the studio at Ca Va, to keep costs down. Everything was agreed, a cheque was cut, and suddenly John was the owner of the church with one bell in Roberton.

Using Cozens on keyboards, Ahmun on drums and Giblin on bass, all people with whom he'd worked a long time and who were familiar with him and his ways, meant that things could progress quickly. John hadn't used Ca Va since *Cooltide*, but its facilities – "the best in Scotland," he called them - were ideal for working quickly.

There's been speculation that John rejected the first set of tapes they made, which was the reason behind the hurried second recording (almost *No Little Boy* revisited). But that wasn't the case.

"It was all very professional," asserted Ca Va's Brian Young. "They worked quickly. John knew what he wanted, and they had it all very clearly worked out."

From a tape of thirty-five songs the label had sent, the list had been whittled down to sixteen, and these were the ones recorded in Glasgow. It was John the interpreter, sinking his teeth into the words and music of other people. It was at heart a blues album, as was to be expected with

Dayron at the controls. Whether it was something obvious, like Elmore James' "The Sky Is Crying," the difficult standard "Strange Fruit," Randy Newman's "God's Song," or material by Dead Can Dance and Portishead, it all worked within the larger framework of the blues.

Much of the credit for the album went to Dayron. He teased some excellent performances out of John that stretched him in a way he'd never been stretched before, wringing new emotion from lines that had been around for years. He'd played blues before, although there'd really been none on disc since his "Easy Blues" pastiche in the early '70s. One song John wanted to do, but which didn't make it onto the disc – probably because it just didn't fit - was Bruce Chane's "Hey Baby," a fluffy piece of '60s pop that he'd planned on slowing way down.

The whole record was understated, propelled most heavily by Arran Ahmun's drums. There wasn't a great deal of John's guitar work, but in this case any playing was the icing on the cake. This, probably more than anything he'd ever recorded, was an album about his voice. As John said, "there's a place between words and music and my voice lived there." In this case, he inhabited the space very comfortably and made it completely his own. Even something as amiable as "Small Town Talk" (a piece co-written by R&B great Bobby Charles and former Band member Rick Danko) contained an indigo undertone that John captured. It was a matter of nuance and degree, never giving away too much and letting the line and the emotion do the work. Interestingly, his enunciation had improved – he was no longer relying on the slur alone; it had become one tool in his arsenal – and he'd come to realize the importance of communicating the words.

Like the material on his last album, *The Church with One Bell* stepped back from making the groove the heart of the song, and put melody front and centre. That had always been one of John's long suits, one he'd discarded for too long, and rediscovered only with *No Little Boy*. It demanded more of him as a singer, but he'd reached the stature where he could deliver what was needed. Ben Harper's "Excuse Me Mister," a very political song, pushed him hard, but it all came together with a wonderful deep growl halfway thought the tune that lifted it to another plane.

The biggest test, without doubt, was "Strange Fruit." It was so associated with Billie Holiday, that few had dared attempt it – and fewer still had managed credible versions of the song. Stripping it down to the basics meant the full horror of the images could emerge, and there was no question of John over-singing on this. There was no catharsis in the song. It simply catalogued gruesome and horrible wrongs.

"The Sky Is Crying," on the other hand, brought relief. Taken at an almost funeral pace, with plenty of echo on the vocals, it became what blues should be, a complete cry from the heart, a soul finding renewal in heartbreak.

John even made the bleakly emotional "Glory Box" seem like a burst of sunshine. With its descending melody, it was open and inviting, with some restrained but tasty guitar work from John to complement his singing.

From the tortured centre, the lightness of "Feel So Bad" from Lightnin' Hopkins was pure playfulness, a shuffle that echoed the "Sugarcube" of years past – albeit much more subtly. And John took that reflection into the guitar solo, the only one on the whole disc.

The Reverend Gary Davis had been an influence on John during his adolescence and he was able to repay that by covering "Death Don't Have No Mercy" – "not exactly a thigh-slapper," as he described it, but highlighted by an unusual bowed double bass solo from John Giblin.

It was a sombre note on which to end the record, except it wasn't the closer; after several seconds' of silence there was another track, a vastly different take on "How Fortunate The Man With None," with a rhythm lifted directly from "Big Muff," an instance of John pillaging his past in a very creative way and a nod to those long-serving fans who'd recognise what he was doing.

It was a completely different facet of John. With three days of rehearsal, five days of recording, and another three days to mix everything, there was plenty of spontaneity about the project. It was vital and live, not mired in the world of overdubs and endlessly repeated takes.

"I think this record is very plain and simple," John noted to *Mojo*. "Therein would lie its charm...The lyrics were still being faxed through on the first day."

And it was as simple a record as John had done since *Outside In*, suffused with a spirit that kept it completely in the present. John admitted he'd made changes to all the songs (he wrote a note of apology to Ben Harper), but he'd made one of the most thoughtful and contemplative records of a long career.

It was quite a feat, connecting the dots between slide blues, jazz, R&B, trip-hop and a kind of world music. But he'd made it into a single piece and found the kernel of truth at the centre of each song, the way a true artist should. There was a spirituality to the work that made it almost luminous.

It was solid confirmation of the renaissance in John's work that had enjoyed its first stirring with *No Little Boy* and found its feet with *And*. He'd managed to lose the blandness of his '80s musical output with a renewed burst of considered creativity. In fact, when interviewed about *The Church with One Bell* he claimed to be making a blues/hip-hop record, in addition to preparing a new album to be released in February 1999. But John was a past master of the hopeful boast and in all likelihood no one took him at his word. There had been so many plans in the past that had never come to fruition and this, more than most, sounded unlikely.

Still, the hardcore fans would live in hope and anticipation. They'd become used to living with disappointment over the years, tempered with occasional bouts of relief when an album trickled out.

These days the wait between albums was longer, but the quality was becoming far more satisfying. He was on a creative roll, even if this last batch of songs hadn't been his, and the band was sounding more unified than ever before.

"Musically it's telepathic now," Ahmun stated. "We know even down to if he wants to change a movement in the song onstage. Spence will be watching his hands, the bass player will be watching his hands if he goes somewhere different, depending on John's mood. We're aware of changes, and we've got it down. Musically it's a real pleasure." And, maybe even more importantly, "it's everything. It's the sheer lack of formality, it's the spontaneity. It's like jumping in the van with a bunch of your mates and going on tour."

For the first time in five years, John also had an American label for this release. *The Church with One Bell* came out on the independent Thirsty Ear label, as Mesa, his last US label, had been bought by Atlantic.

With John long a critic's favourite, the album was as warmly received in the US as it had been in Britain and it was backed up with a relatively extensive tour that worked its way from the East Coast to the West during June.

That all came after what should have been a major English showcase gig for John. The Verve, at that point one of the top bands in the country, asked John to open a show in their hometown of Wigan. He was set to be the first act, just before Beck.

John was set to play with the band, even though it was certain to be a difficult gig. His brand of music wasn't likely to go over well with a crowd primed for much hipper things. That was compounded when it was discovered that, because of Beck's equipment, there was no room for John's band to set up, and he was forced to perform an on-the-fly solo show before a hostile(and very young) crowd of more than 30,000 people.

"Good Lord, they hated me," John said. "And I struggled through it...but that was somewhat disheartening."

It wasn't the best send off. John was pelted with bottles and all manner of things, but he kept going, like a real trouper. After that, America seemed like a breeze, and he was in good spirits on June 30 when he performed a session for the famous *Morning Becomes Eclectic* radio show in Los Angeles on KCRW, prior to playing at the Troubadour that night.

The album hadn't been officially released in the US at that point (that would come a week later), but the fans knew and were used to buying John's work on import, expensive as it was.

John was in a light, expansive mood as he talked to host Nic Harcourt, and the band (Cozens, Ahmun, and Jim Lampi on Chapman stick) aired "She's A Lover," which segued into "Solid Air," "Excuse Me Mister," and "Glory Box."

The session stood in sharp contrast to one earlier on the tour with WFUV in New York. There, although still funny, John sounded outrageously drunk (although manager Joe Hennessey claimed he was sober) and the music – the same as the KCRW session, with "Couldn't Love You More" instead of "Glory Box" – was, at best, tepid. John claimed the quality of playing was due to the band being crammed into a tiny studio. *The New York Session*, as it was called, was released on CD in November 2000 and deleted in 2002. It was for very serious fans only - and even then, only for those with a high tolerance for John at his most mainstream. The biggest question was why it was released at all. With lacklustre sound and a poor performance, it wasn't a credit to anyone, while John's ramblings were funny, but nonsensical. In fact, according to some sources, John was desperately out of it for the interview and session.

Thankfully, that mood didn't spill over into the tour itself, which went well. But in spite of that, John had every reason to be cheerful. After being on his own for several years, he'd met someone months earlier, in 1998, in Ireland.

John always classed himself as a romantic - and for all his roistering ways, he seemed happiest with a stable domestic situation and a woman to come home to and to love, who'd love him in return. It was an odd dichotomy of the wandering minstrel and the homebody. But it typified the contradiction of head and heart, which had always tugged him in conflicting directions.

His heart needed a centre, a real home with a woman in it, to love with a passion. His head kept him on the road. His heart had him following his desires and temptations, drinking when he shouldn't, even as his head knew he was doing himself no favours.

Achieving a balance between head and heart, a place where he could exist, had never been easy for him - but it was easier when he was in a relationship, at least as he aged. With Beverley he was still finding himself, as a musician and as a person. For the first time he was achieving some success, and he indulged as much as he could, too young to refuse.

With Annie there were good times, more settled times, even if despondency in the latter half of the 1980s brought a prolonged heavy bout with the bottle (excessive even by John's standards).

And then there was Teresa Walsh, or "Mama T-razor" as she'd become in the song of that name on John's next album. They'd met in Ireland - in a bar, of course - and she'd followed him to Scotland, to the church which was being made into a recording studio, a place where he could work out ideas and rehearse with the band.

He was in his fifties now, a time when some people start to slow down a little. But John had never been one to do things by halves.

During the decade, he'd found some spiritual comfort in Buddhism. Like so many of his generation, he'd first discovered it when young, reading books like Herman Hesse's *Siddhartha*. But, also like many others, he drifted away from religion, Western and Eastern, far too caught up in life and the business of living.

Getting older, and with a burst pancreas, he was far more aware of his mortality. Buddhism, which made few demands upon its adherents, still appealed. He even took a retreat at the Kagyu Samye-Ling Tibetan Centre in Eskdalemuir in the west Scottish lowlands, known to the locals as Sammy Ling. It was the biggest Buddhist centre in Europe, decorated with 1000 golden Buddhas, gold-encrusted pillars and silk-screen prints of dragons and birds. John found a beauty and peace there.

It was no surprise that the more enigmatic form of Buddhism – Zen – was what appealed to him. With its more mystic quality and enlightenment revealed through the riddles called "koans," it fitted well with John's personality, a way of removing the masks to get to the truth. But if John ever took off all his masks, it was going to be in private, never in public.

On the outside, in his public life, John was back on top of his game musically, even though he wasn't selling records in the same kinds of quantities he had at the start of the '80s. There was a sense of real pleasure in the music he was making, as if he'd rediscovered a part of himself and was taking the time to explore it fully. He wasn't as prolific as he had been when younger, but the material was of a high, even quality; these days the albums were all meat and no filler.

He'd become an established, lauded live attraction, whether with the band or alone, a man who could easily undertake a one-month tour of Britain and know he'd walk away with money, having put bums on seats. Yes, he still had to play the old songs, and that didn't always sit well with the big man, but part of being an entertainer was giving the public what they wanted, especially when being on the road was such a vital part of his income.

He'd make a lot of money, then spend it - and have to go touring again, "two years of money and five years of pain," as he characterised it. But by now it was a part of his life's rhythm, something he probably couldn't alter if he tried. There was precious little security in music, at least down at the sharp end where John lived. It wasn't always easy, though it did add zest and an edge to life.

He finally seemed to have a toehold in America, the country he'd been trying – on and off – to conquer for well over two decades. He played well on the coasts and had become a regular on the Guinness Fleadh circuit, both in the UK and the US, which offered him a chance to show his stuff in front of large crowds – sometimes with spectacular results, such as one Fleadh in Glasgow.

"We were based in the same encampment as Van Morrison, who we never got to talk to," said Alex Boyesen. "Some friends of mine who were playing with the band Aztec Camera came round to say hello and we then went off to the tent where John was playing. John was in a funny mood that day; he was playing on his home ground and he had a mission. The Aztec crew and myself set up at the front of house mixing desk and from the very first note it just worked. No one could do any wrong, the gig just escalated, the audience went wild and it made John go that extra bit and we all caught glimpses of what it should be like to see John without any compromises."

He still had the ability, and sometimes the desire, to let it rip and take it over the edge, even if those occasions were less frequent. But John still had things to prove. Too many times there had been opportunities for bigger things that had fallen through. Sometimes there had been outside factors, sometimes John had handily sabotaged his own career, as if the idea of superstardom scared him too much. Yet there was still a need to show what might have been, to make people aware that he was as good as any of their idols and that he could have been a contender.

At the same time, now he'd found his niche, with its cult status and comfortable stature, he appeared less inclined to try to break out of it. Like water, he'd found his own level. It might go up and down a little, but for the most part it remained the same. He knew what he could rely on and worked from that.

To be perfectly fair, as a live attraction, John gave strong value for money. With the band, he could be counted on to play a couple of hours, a good show in anyone's book. Much of his more recent work was harder to adapt to solo acoustic, but there were ways, if he did things imaginatively. There was a crossover of audiences between the two styles, but as a general rule it was those who'd come to John after 1980 who attended band gigs, while the older, folkier crowd plumped for the solo shows. And many knew of his reputation for hard living and excess. So when he fell over at a show, no one thought too much about the implications.

"We were at Cambridge," Cozens related, "and he just fell over. He couldn't stand up. Most people probably assumed he'd had too much to drink. But we knew it wasn't that, it was unlike John."

Once he could stand again, and his right leg seemed firm, John just shrugged the incident off and carried on – at least outwardly – as if nothing untoward had ever happened. It was easier than thinking about the possible causes and having to deal with them.

The tour continued and there was no repeat of the incident, but it was lucky that John had the rest of the year clear from touring. Whether he discussed it in public or not, it had to be worrying. But there were no other symptoms and so he let it go.

This was his job. He was making a living doing something he loved, something few people manage. And even if he cursed the guitar sometimes for setting him on this course, it was far too late to turn back now.

Yet John pointedly didn't think "there are [no] more risks I can take." Musically he'd tried so much: the Echoplex electricity of the '70s, the jazz trio, the smooth songster, the electric guitarist, forcing himself to improvise lyrics in the studio, exploring trip-hop and blues.

What was left to keep his interest?

The answer was simple - and it was the same thing that had brought him into the business in the first place: the songs. He'd marked his whole adult life off in songs, those he'd written himself, and those by others that he'd sung. They were, as he'd said many times, his "diary."

Ask any songwriter, and they'll describe the satisfaction and joy of a song that "works." It has its own logic, its own magic; it's more than the sum of its parts. And having achieved that once, there's always the need to do it again, to recreate that feeling. Having found her again in recent years, it was impossible for John to refuse his Muse.

She'd brought him new material and he was ready to go back into the studio. In spite of the new record being titled *Glasgow Walker*, it wasn't recorded there. Instead it was made at the church – what was the point in having your own studio if you didn't use it? – and in Kilkenny, where Teresa kept a house.

John had spent a great deal of time and money on the church, making it into a proper studio where he could work – his studio, where he wasn't constrained by time and expense. He imported Macintosh computers and other equipment, and Alex Boyesen came up from London to help him get everything in order.

"[The church] was where I got to sleep during one of the periods I was working with him in Scotland. It was pretty scary at night in that old chapel on your own, but a great space, at least it was out of earshot when John decided to play a record at full pelt at three in the morning. John needed that kind of space to spread himself out in. The whole room was filled with an extraordinary range of items collected over the years from all over the world. He loved to get things that made him laugh, that were bad taste or a reminder of an incident. He had a fan of fishing rods on one of the walls, almost got them out one day! There was a fire[place] at one end where we would hang out and play. John would sometimes pick up the guitar and play some tune we had never heard before, something traditional, sometimes the most beautiful thing you had ever heard him play."

It was his sanctuary, a place he could be at peace, a place to work with other musicians or on his own. It had taken a while and had depleted what savings he had, to make it fully functional, but the result was more than worth the effort and expense. So many others who'd made their start at the same time as John had their own studios; finally he had a place to hang his hat.

The new album had taken a long time to write, mostly because John had tried a new method of composition. Phil Collins had recommended that he try writing on a keyboard as an experiment - specifically, a Korg Trinity. John had spent the money on one, then had to learn how to use it: "He told me I should buy this computer that makes rabbits disappear up its whatsit...after eighteen months of going 'plink plonk' on this machine I lose half the tracks!'

All his life he'd written on guitar - and by his own admission, he was no keyboard player. Although untrained in music, he knew the guitar and understood instinctively how to make chords and sounds. This was different.

"I was completely enchanted by it, but I'm not a keyboard player; my hands don't fit. So it was a whole new adventure for me. I just did that for a time. It was a very slow process, the album from hell."

Spencer Cozens was on board, virtually a given those days. To all intents and purposes, he'd become John's musical director - and in many ways, he was as responsible for the new work as John himself.

"John had spent a couple of years working on the keyboard. He had phrases and ideas, and we worked to put them together and expand them and make them into songs. John was really just a two-finger player, so it would be short snatches. I'd sit with him then add things, link them up and see what he liked."

It was a trial and error process, although Cozens was used to John's style and way of working by now, and was able to second guess and make suggestions that fit in with John's way of thinking.

By now trip-hop had become passé, a style whose time had come and gone. But it had become one more weapon in John's arsenal, to be used sparingly. Programming had become a standard part of music making and John incorporated it into his work. Spencer worked on that with Stefon Taylor, who'd done such a sterling job on *And.*, while the pair known as Glasgow Gangster Funk contributed to several tracks, and sound man Alex Boyesen worked on "Cry Me A River."

Having his own studio gave John the luxury of time when it came to building the tracks with the band. This time out, he went for a wider breadth of sound, both on the tracks themselves, and also in the people playing on them. The usual suspects were around – Cozens, Ahmun, Alan Thomson, Jim Lampi - but others were included, such as Reggie Hastings playing slide guitar, along with musicians on bass flute, violin, and accordion (courtesy of Scots folk master Phil Cunningham).

John was hardly reinventing himself with this record, but it did reflect the fact that he'd tried something different in the writing. There was no real rush about things; after all, *The Church with One Bell* had only appeared in 1998, and it was now normal for artists to take a couple of years between albums.

He was helped by already having one track in the can. At the request of film director and writer Anthony Minghella, best known for *The English Patient*, John had covered the standard "You Don't Know What Love Is," by Dan Raye and Gene De Paul, for the soundtrack of *The Talented Mr. Ripley*. Working with the London-based Guy Barker International Quintet, it gave John the opportunity to become a full-on jazz singer for once, and he took to it perfectly. A late-night blues with piano and muted trumpet, opening into strings and vibes, it was an arrangement straight from the '50s. As in the film, it made an ideal coda to the album: breathy, soothing yet disturbing - and completely different.

It wasn't the only non-Martyn piece on the record. There was also a version of the standard "Cry Me A River," best known as a torch song, but given a complete makeover by John and the band. In place of the familiar big, brassy approach, this was low key and shadowy. It was a message of pain, rather than revenge.

It was one of the most varied and surprising albums John had released in a long career. "So Sweet" opened like something off a Peter Gabriel album, with African rhythms and keyboard marimbas, never settling into the "standard" John Martyn framework. The closest the album came to familiar territory was "Feel So Good" - and even that ratcheted up the funk factor.

Overall it was a complete return to the art of songwriting, even if it had been constructed as a thing of shreds and patches from John's small keyboard ideas (and he was even credited with keys on "Wildflower"). The grooves were still definitely there, but they weren't the basis of the material – or if they were, they'd been more completely clothed than ever before.

One surprise was bringing in Reggie Hastings to play slide guitar on a few tracks. John handled guitar on everything except "You Don't Know What Love Is," but was willing to relinquish some of the lead role to Hastings.

Musically, it was a very textured album, happy to step outside the normal boundaries. Even *And.* had stayed largely within the John Martyn formula, except for its rhythms. This added flute and violin, neither of which had been heard on one of John's records in almost two decades, and accordion, which had never been featured before. The ideas were expanded and given the chance to be fully realized. It could have been the result of writing on keyboard, but more likely it was due to John and Cozens having to put their heads together to piece together John's ideas and flesh them out.   And John was also willing to challenge himself in ways he hadn't before. Surrounded by a core crew that had been with him for over a decade, he was in a good position to take chances. He could rely on those around him, and he was flush with the confidence of two strong albums over the last four years.

He'd also found a kind of peace with Teresa.

"She's a good foil for him," Cozens said. "She'll take him up to a point, but no more, and he knows it."

John loved to cook, or to supervise Teresa in the kitchen, and he was happy to sit at home working his way through a bottle of wine or some spirits if she was around to keep him company. Above all, with her he was comfortable enough to take off all the masks he used to keep the world away. He didn't need to be "on," the way he seemed to be with most people. He could be himself.

Touring had gradually become one of the evils of a musical life that had to be endured. Everywhere he went, he was almost certain to have been before. The travelling and the hotels were all humdrum; the only excitement was in the playing itself, being onstage and letting the music happen, with feedback from the crowd, and the adulation, a reminder of who John Martyn was, or at least whoever tonight's John Martyn was. It was an affirmation; it helped make him solid.

And he'd developed a love of fishing – a vocation, not a hobby, as he termed it - after moving back to Scotland in the early '80s. Like anything he immersed himself in, he dove into it fully, becoming an expert on the different kinds of rods and even learning how to tie his own angling flies. It was an isolated pastime, one that absorbed quiet hours, and an indication that John had become more introspective as he'd grown older. He didn't need to be constantly surrounded by people and sound.

But for John, even something as peaceful as fishing had its misadventures. When he and Danny Thompson toured together in 1986, John had stopped in Southwest England to fish for a little while between gigs, with a reluctant Thompson in tow. But when Thompson tried his hand at fly fishing, he ended up casting and sticking the hook through his cheek – a feat managed while completely sober, as Danny had stopped drinking eight years earlier.

Without tools, removing a barbed hook was virtually impossible, but Danny asked John to try. Instead, all he could do was break the line "and the top of the hook off. Then he said, 'You'll be alright, it'll just get into your blood stream, go round your body, get to your heart and you'll die in about two years and you won't know anything about it.' The hook's still in there, when it gets cold you can see a blue hook in my cheek!"

Of course, there was an extensive tour planned for *Glasgow Walker*, and John and the boys – Cozens, Ahum, John Giblin, and Jim Lampi on Chapman Stick, whom John had discovered playing in a club in Soho – warmed up with some dates in Italy.

Rehearsal footage of the band sorting out arrangements in John's Scottish church was on the home video *Tell Them I'm Not Here*, both on the serious and light side (such as the band improvisation around a sample of someone saying "Jump, you fucker, jump").

The British tour was going to be lengthy, taking in the whole of June. The band was tight, but still with plenty of room for jamming, and John had his acoustic set slotted in the middle to please the punters who yearned for the old '70s sound. Only one thing gummed up the works – John managed to dislocate his shoulder, leaving him unable to play guitar. Reggie Hastings, who'd played slide on the album, was quickly drafted in for some of the dates. For the rest, the band simply managed without guitar.

He was still the joker, the man of the masks who could make the audience laugh with his patter one minute, then move them to tears with his singing the next. He'd become a big man in every way, the angelic face now with the more grizzled features of a Glasgow bouncer, with bulk to match. He sweated profusely under the lights; it wasn't uncommon for him to sweat out eleven pounds during a show. And, of course, he was still a drinker. Perhaps not to the extent he had been, but it was still part of what defined him, his everyday routine. That put the pounds right back on and didn't do his pancreas or heart – or the rest of him – any good.

Still, at least he had the remainder of the year off to spend lazing in Scotland with Teresa.

John was still being managed by Joe Hennessy, who'd handled his business affairs for a few years. No manager seemed to last long with John, however. Since his days with Blackhill in the '70s, he'd steered clear of major management, tending to deal with smaller figures, none of whom had ever met with his long-term approval. It was as if he picked them to fail him, to confirm in his mind that they were simply out to take his money, and that the music business was every bit as crooked as he imagined it to be (or wanted it to be). In fairness, he wasn't perhaps the easiest client, and could demand a lot from those around him. He'd said himself that when something went wrong, he wasn't usually one to shoulder the blame; instead, his inclination was to pass it off to someone around him, and a manager always made a good and convenient scapegoat for John's anger.

In spite of good reviews, *Glasgow Walker* wasn't a big seller. The era when critical acclaim could translate into big sales had passed. He was a cult figure, and it was his fate to remain that way. It was the young artists who could break through into bigger things - and at fifty-two, John's youth was long past.

That didn't mean he couldn't have young fans, especially among musicians. Singer/songwriter Beth Orton often referred to John as "the guv'nor" and had covered 'I Don't Want To Know' early in her career, on her 1993 debut, *Superpinkymandy*. While at college, she'd been heavily influenced by *Solid Air*, which was acknowledged as one of the classic chill-out albums (and was voted so in a *Q* magazine poll).

Another artist who was an admirer was vocalist Claire Martin, who'd been voted British Jazz Singer of the Year in 1995. After that, her career turned more towards sophisticated pop music and on her album *Perfect Alibi* she recorded a version of "Man In The Station," at "the beginning of 2000, or the arse end of '99. I did it with the band, and I just said, 'It'd be great if I could get him to sing it with me.' I got the record company to

217

phone his management and we got him to do it. The whole day was a cult event. I wanted to do a song, and that had a nice groove. I'm a jazz singer, but that album was more poppy."

The John who arrived in the studio wasn't on his best guest artist behaviour.

"The first thing he said when he came in was, 'You've been around for ages, haven't you?' and I said, 'Well, yeah, I have a bit,' like he was expecting some young girl. Also, he was pissed. Everyone said, 'Are you sure you want to do this, he's a loose cannon.' I said, 'He'll be fine, I'll take full responsibility, I'll nanny him all day. Just ask him, and let me deal with it'."

A very down-to-earth person, Claire wasn't about to let John get away with anything. She might have been a longtime fan, but she was also a professional, and expected the same from those she was working with.

"When he turned up, it was a Saturday morning session, and he had this bleeding hand, he'd put his thumb in the door the night before. He walks into the sound booth, sits on one of those big comfy chairs and just goes straight over backwards. Everyone, instead of looking at him, looks at me – it's your call, you booked this guy. So I just went in: 'Oh, come on, you stupid bastard, get up.' He loved all that. He's such a wonderful man. He's a very sensitive, deep, lovely kind guy. He sauntered around a bit, but when he went into the booth to actually sing, something clicked and he was just totally on it. He did about twelve takes. He knew where he'd messed up, and he was very, very focused. He listened to every take, he was very pedantic and very caring. He produced about six or seven definite tracks we could have used. He was there about three or four hours, and then off he went. He's a handful. He cracks jokes all the time. In the studio, over the track, he'd suddenly start whistling and tell a joke. And funny, not just stupid, Just a funny, very warm, warm bloke. Since then I've sat in with him on gigs where he has a broken arm and had the guitar around his neck (most probably when he had the dislocated shoulder). He's fearless, and I really love that."

It was a mark of his longevity and stature that younger artists were coming to him, valuing his name and reputation. One other project presented itself in 2000, singing on a new version of "Deliver Me," by Sister Bliss of Faithless – a cover of the 1996 song by the Beloved.

The track was produced by Phill Brown, who'd engineered *One World* back in the '70s. He became involved in the track after meeting Rollo, also from Faithless, in the '90s. Rollo was a fan of the work Brown had done with the band Talk Talk. "In the conversations it came out who I'd worked with, and he was a big fan of John Martyn," Brown explained. "We talked about that, and this track came up. He asked me if I thought John would come in and do it. I said, 'Your guess is as good as mine. The best bet is to phone the guy up and see if he's interested.' Which they did, and he was up for it."

The session took place on August 17, 2000 at Swan Yard Studios in London. John was already familiar with Faithless, although "I didn't know Sister Bliss was a DJ on her own. But I knew Faithless, simply because I'd been trying to get a friend of mine into jungle...Anyway, he wasn't too hot on it, but he'd listened to a Faithless single, which featured something like jungle, I don't know what it was..."

Regardless of the lack of depth of his knowledge of the new styles of music, John showed up. "He had a couple of bevvies, a little smoke, went out and did the vocals," Brown recounted. "To me he hadn't changed that much. He'd put on a little weight, but his approach was basically the same. He's very dedicated at what he does."

For Sister Bliss herself, "it was the most pain in the arse session ever, because we had 48 tracks of brilliant vocals. Which one do you choose? And for me, house music is at its best with a real yearning male vocal over beautiful music, and we really captured it on this track. When you play it in a club it's the most affecting thing, watching thousands of people being moved by music."

And so John was introduced to the clubbing generation, - with a reasonable amount of success, as the disc reached number thirty-one on the singles chart. His presence on the disc by Martyn and Sister Bliss became a kind of imprimatur, a signal that he'd moved into the elder statesman class; he'd become a hero of sorts to a select, hip few in a younger generation. And if he couldn't chart with his own material any more, at least he could sneak in through the back door.

All in all, everything seemed to be moving his way again, the pendulum swinging
back in his favour. It could never be the way it had been twenty years earlier, with hit albums. But there was at least his cult status, and reputation. He could make a comfortable living from touring, put out a new album every couple of years and get by, if not get rich. However, getting by was an achievement for a musician playing something that was out of the mainstream and he'd long since given up on the idea of riches. He was getting by on his own terms, no longer compromising to become bigger and sell more records.

It was an even, balanced state of affairs. John was still drinking too much, but that was unlikely to change. But balance simply didn't work in John's world. There always had to be something to upset life after a little while, or it felt too much like stasis. And if John didn't tip the applecart a bit himself, then inevitably something else would come around and do it for him.

This time around the blame couldn't be attributed to him. If anything, it was a work-related injury. He'd developed a cyst, called a baker's cyst, on the back of his right knee, which had built up gradually over the last seven years. Curiously, he claimed he'd never noticed it growing.

The likelihood was that it had happened through him putting weight on that leg while playing guitar on stage, because of that "fucking great big Les Paul guitar." That had been the reason for him falling down at Cambridge, even though no one realized it at the time.

A baker's cyst is named for the doctor who'd discovered it, not the occupation, and it generally occurs due to problems such as arthritis or a tear in the meniscus. The swelling from that causes a build up of synovial fluid in the knee. After building up over time, it pushes out through the weakest point of the joint capsule around the knee, usually just behind it, forming the cyst, which then swells. Generally, the pain takes the form of a dull ache, which becomes worse with prolonged walking or standing. While rest, and elevating the leg, along with taking pain killers, can alleviate the pain, they don't get rid of the cyst itself. As a general rule, conservative therapy is recommended for treating a baker's cyst – ice, heat, a knee brace, controlled motion, and therapy.

Had John gone to see the doctor, that's probably what he would have been told, but it was easier to ignore the problem than to hear something he didn't like - and it was still manageable.

It certainly didn't stop John touring during 2001. There was a month-long winter tour with the band in January and February, then an event many people had been waiting for – John back on the road with Danny Thompson as a duo. The last time they'd played together had been 1986.

The Sunshine Boys tour, as they called it (a reference to the film *The Sunshine Boys*, about cranky old men), was quite lengthy, running just over a month, from the end of May and right through June. The venues were essentially the same size as the universities they'd played together in the mid '70s. There was less horseplay, both on and off the stage, this time around. Danny no longer drank - and without the encouragement, John wasn't going to get too wild. Many of the halls sold out and it was apparent that the magical, almost telepathic communication between them remained. It was physically an easier tour for John, since he was playing acoustic guitar, he didn't have to stand and could keep the weight off his right knee. By the end of June it was done, which, in theory, left John time to begin working on a new album.

Instead, he had to attend to business. Quite simply, the bank wanted to repossess the church and the cottage – which would have left him with nowhere to live. Fighting the money men was never easy at the best of times, but when it involved the roof over your head – or roofs, in this case, as John owned the church and the cottage next door – it took on a much greater urgency.

Ultimately, there was no way he could win, but he thought it was worth prolonging the fight. He could always retreat to Ireland, where Teresa had a house in Thomastown, County Kilkenny, but his aim was to hang on to his property, if at all possible.

According to a reliable source, what money John had managed to save – and he wasn't a rich man, by any stretch of the imagination – had vanished, along with one of his advisors. With it had gone his security and his future.

He had next to no money and an outlay that exceeded his income – a recipe for disaster. And that was what it proved to be. He even tried a stint in rehab to stop drinking, an extreme step by John's standards, although it didn't work. He did at least manage to cut down – a little. But there was no saving the church. By the end of 2001 John and Teresa had been forced to set up home in Ireland.

In itself, that wasn't too bad. Thomastown, where they lived in County Kilkenny, was a beautiful place that could have come straight from a tourist brochure. Their house was modest, but comfortable, with ample room for the two of them and their Jack Russell terrier, plus guests. The village itself had small, old shops and Carroll's Bar; it was almost as if time had stood still in the '50s. With his guitars, studio equipment, a river for fishing and a bar where he could drink, John had virtually everything he needed.

Except his health. He'd never done anything about his leg and it was reaching a critical point. It came to a head when he received a relatively minor electric shock from an amplifier, and "six hours later I didn't feel at all cool." The jolt had opened the cyst and his leg swelled to twice its normal size. It got infected and the nerves were shot. "One toe pointed in one direction, the one next to it in another, and my heel started climbing up my ankle. Man, it was painful, I couldn't walk."

This time there was no option but to seek medical help. Rest was prescribed, which forced the cancellation of his spring tour. John had never been one for enforced idleness, but this time he did as he was told, albeit with reluctance.

There was also the matter of his remaining property in Scotland, which he'd been hoping to keep, fighting against the bank. By August he'd recovered enough to be able to travel to Scotland, in a last-ditch attempt to hold on to the Roberton cottage.

"He was in a van with some friends," related Spencer Cozens. "There was a pub in the middle of nowhere and they decided to go out there for a few drinks. It was dark and there were no lights. They didn't see the bull in the road."

They did, however, manage to hit it. John ended up with whiplash and a broken nose, but he also reinjured his foot, which proved to be the gravest wound of all, even if it seemed very minor at the time.

It was enough for him to have to cancel the autumn tour, taking away his only source of income for the year - and the last hope for holding onto his Scottish property. He had to declare bankruptcy. The stress had exacerbated his drinking, to the extent that a reporter was advised to "for Christ's sake, see him in the morning. You may not get much sense out of him in the afternoon." And, true to form, when Adam Lee Potter of *Scotland on Sunday* caught up with him, he was on his third Bacardi and Coke – at noon.

On the surface he remained cheerful, his old, gregarious self. But there was a layer of depression underneath and a resentment that he hadn't made it as big as his friends like Phil Collins or Eric Clapton, even though he claimed he didn't care enough, or have the drive, to achieve and maintain that kind of success. It was a curious paradox, but John never claimed to have resolved any of his very human inconsistencies.

CHAPTER TWELVE – Losing the Leg

The one thing John couldn't deny was reality. His leg was getting bad, and the accident in Scotland, according to Cozens, "had only made things worse," to the point where he'd almost become bedridden, only able to get around in a wheelchair. He was unable to gig and unable to get into the studio to work on a new record. For a man who'd spent his life relying on his own resources and his native talent, it was a galling situation, having to rely on others.

Given the number of people he'd alienated during his lifetime, either deliberately or inadvertently while in his cups, he was lucky that there were still many who'd rally around him, good friends who were happy to help him out in so many different ways.

Among them were the members of his band. John had ideas for songs for a new album, but couldn't execute or even develop them properly in his condition. At the same they knew that anything they recorded could end up being the last John Martyn album. His life wasn't in the balance quite yet, but if something weren't done about his leg soon, that could change. So his band members took the unprecedented step of beginning to make a John Martyn album without John Martyn.

It was very different from John's original idea for his next album, but the situation had moved beyond his control now. Before the accident, the plan had been for John to make a mostly acoustic album that harked back to his '70s style. According to journalist Brian Cullman, he even planned to work with John Wood, who'd engineered his classic albums from that period. A friend of Cullman's, keyboard player and producer Glenn Patcher, was to have been involved in those sessions.

"Glenn was staying with me in France, and John Wood called him. John was really excited because John Martyn had approached him to go in and do a proper record of songs. Glenn had just been producing a record with John Wood and Joe Boyd for a Venezuelan singer. John [Wood] was trying to bring Glenn into this project. Because he was staying with me he was telling me, and I was getting excited for him to go to London. I think

Danny Thompson had agreed to come in on bass. I don't remember if they were going to go with a drummer who was a really light jazz drummer. But they didn't want any synths, it was going to be very much of a *Solid Air* sound. Glenn was supposed to fly to Ireland, then at the last minute it was just cancelled, I don't know why."

But after the accident all bets were off. The acoustic record, which could well have proved to be John's big comeback, pleasing old fans and new alike, had to be shelved. John just wasn't in the condition he'd need to be in for such a project, where everything would revolve around him.

He had other, more immediate things on his mind. In the wake of the car accident, the condition of his leg had deteriorated and, after trying to treat it, the doctors had determined one thing: it would have to be amputated below the knee. That was the only way to save the rest of the leg. According to Jim Tullio, the final amputation below the knee only came after several surgeries. At first only the foot was removed, but the doctors had to go higher and higher as John wouldn't stop drinking.

Though John joked about it at home and with friends, there had to be an undertow of worry, along with a pressing need to get the new album as far along as possible before going into hospital. There was little danger in the surgery, but even so....

"You have to remember, John was in pain and about to get his leg cut off," Tullio said. "He just wanted to get well. Before he had the amputation, I told him about a doctor who'd saved the foot of a friend of mine who'd suffered the same thing as John. John sent me his X-rays and I went to see the doctor. The first thing he said was 'This man's a heavy drinker.' He thought he could save the foot, although it would take multiple surgeries and a change in lifestyle, with John stopping drinking. John wasn't willing to do that, although after the amputation he called me and said, half-jokingly, 'Why didn't you convince me?'"

In April 2003, John entered the Waterford Hospital Orthopaedic Ward One for an operation that would alter him forever - and in ways that would go beyond the physical He'd been largely wheelchair-bound for some months; at least a prosthesis could help set him free for some of the time.

It's common for an amputee to feel a "phantom limb," as if it were still there, right down to sensations in the extremities. John experienced that after a successful surgery, during the long, difficult period of rehabilitation. He wasn't helped by the fact that being so sedentary during his period as an invalid had made him balloon up by forty two pounds. Already a big man, he'd become a very big man, which meant he had more weight to carry as he learned how to walk all over again.

Most of his time was spent in a wheelchair, which meant he was relying heavily on Teresa and others. For someone who'd always been very independent, coming and going as he pleased, that was difficult enough. And before he could really use the new prosthesis, the stump of his old leg had to become as hard as his calloused fingertips, "so fucking strong I can stub out a cigarette on it and not feel a thing."

Old friend and singer-songwriter Bridget St. John visited him in Thomastown in the summer of 2003, not long after the operation, as John was going through rehabilitation and just starting to learn how to use his prosthesis. She found him "in good spirits. He was getting about in his wheelchair, zipping around and cooking for us in the kitchen. He certainly wasn't drinking too much, he never seemed drunk."

Of course, John was used to drink. When pushed down to Carroll's by Teresa, he liked to order a cider and double vodka, pouring the spirit into the cider. But he'd drink almost anything if it was there - and there was always a bottle of wine in the house ready to be opened and drunk.

And there was an album to be completed with some guitar and vocals, as the other tracks had been carefully assembled by band members and producers during John's illness and initial convalescence. Much of the time he was on painkillers while he sang. But John had long been recording vocals while under the influence of substances, and the performances were the best he could give at the time, with a very honest, open quality.

There seemed to have been a change in him since the operation. He accepted what had happened with remarkable grace and serenity, thanks in part to his adopted Buddhism, but also to a streak of very

Glaswegian realism. For years he'd hammered his body. He'd defied fate and ignored warnings and finally everything had caught up with him. By rights, according to friends, he should have been dead several times over, yet he was still alive and kicking. He could get around after a fashion, he had a good life, and he could still make music. Losing a leg was a terrible blow, that couldn't be denied, but he'd got off very lightly, all things considered.

The next thing for John to focus on was making music in front of an audience. He hadn't performed in over two years and he'd never been away from the stage for so long before. Making music was what he lived for, his reason for being. Certainly this time it would be different, daunting, and a challenge.

However much he might have wanted it to be that way, there was never a chance of John's return being low-key. Even though the venue – Connollys of Leap – was out in the middle of County Cork, once the dates - November 7 and 8, 2003 – were announced, fans were booking tickets from all over the globe. And what had originally been intended as a solo performance changed when Spencer Cozens and John Giblin volunteered their services, making a small stage even more cramped. But a little support wouldn't hurt.

Cozens went over to Ireland in late October to rehearse with John, and by the time they and Giblin faced the cheering crowd in Connollys, it was the return of a hero, a man who could do no wrong for those who adored him. By any definition, it was a success.

It was just the first step, though. He'd made it that far with flying colours, but no one seemed to know what was going to happen next. Even at the end of January 2004, Cozens could say "the album's finished, but I've no idea when it's going to come out, although I assume it will at some point." There were no more dates planned. Everything was in limbo.

That changed rapidly. During February a string of British dates, starting in late April and running through May, were announced, and it was revealed that the new record, to be titled *On the Cobbles*, would be released to coincide with the gigs. On top of that, BBC4 was set to air a documentary on John in late March. From having vanished into near obscurity, suddenly everything was coming up John Martyn.

The songs for the new album had taken on a radically different colour in other hands. Instead of something stripped-down and acoustic, as originally planned, they were more arranged pieces. Yet that was understandable and born of necessity. Constructed at eight different studios (including John's home in Ireland) with the help of Liverpudlian producer Garry Pollitt, they were built on John's basic tracks to make complete pieces that sounded for all the world as if everyone had been in the studio together.

Much of the credit must go to co-producer Chicagoan Jim Tullio, the man who'd teased the successful *No Little Boy* from the wreckage of *Couldn't Love You More.*

"We talked for years about cutting an acoustic record, which is how *On the Cobbles* happened. He asked me to work with him a few times in between, but our commitments never meshed."

Tullio brought a remarkable sense of cohesion to things, whether the tracks were cut in the UK or, in the case of "Go Down Easy," in Illinois (which was also the case with Tullio's own overdubs and the guest vocal of the legendary Mavis Staples of the Staples Singers – with whom Tullio had recently worked – on Leadbelly's classic "Goodnight Irene").

Some of the pieces had been in existence for a while, like "My Creator," part of which John had been working into "Don't Want To Know" for a few years in concert, or "Baby Come Home," which John had cut in 2002 for a tribute CD to the great Glasgow-born singer Frankie Miller (originally released on *A Tribute to Frankie Miller*), a roaring, mostly acoustic piece, or "Go Down Easy," the revised version of the *Solid Air* throwaway that John had resurrected as part of *The Monsoon* dance score in 1992 while working with Tullio in Chicago. In its new form, it was largely unrecognisable, except for the lyrics. Along with the "Goodnight Irene" cover, that meant there were just six new songs.

But they were six of the finest songs John had laid down since *One World*. The intimations of mortality were all too evident on both "Ghosts" and the fleshed-out band version of "My Creator," the statements of someone who's looked at the prospect of his own death and come away far more thoughtful. Strong as the rest of the material was, those two were the key to the record. "Ghosts" was a man haunted not so much by his past, as by his present and future - a fresh meditation on life borne in very real physical pain, ending with a solemn, muted trumpet. "My Creator" was the spiritual heir to "Solid Air," with its low-key, late-night jazzy feel (and with Danny Thompson making a welcome appearance on double bass). He'd already made an attempt at the track, although it had never fully gelled.

"He'd done 'My Creator' and a few others, some of which never saw the light of day. John came out to Chicago in 2000, not too long after he'd met Teresa, and he wanted to marry her in Chicago," noted Tullio. "They stayed two months, but she didn't want to marry him. He played me the tracks. The recording was chaotic with Danny Thompson and John Giblin on bass. Gaz said the studio they'd been using had been closing down, there was problem; he'd just been doing what he could. So we had to fix this and I said, 'Let's make it more acoustic.' John was reluctant, but agreed in the end. The first thing I did was fix "My Creator." I sent it back to Gaz to re-record the drums, and John's bass had also been on the drum track before, with Alan Thomson on the bass this time. I realised I now had three bass tracks – Alan, Danny and John. I decided to use all three, cutting between them. When we were done I told John it was his new "Solid Air," although it never quite worked out that way."

The record appeared on Indepeniente and Tullio said, "Their A&R guy came out for the mixing. John wasn't there; he was getting his foot amputated. I overnighted John a CD of new mixes every day. Since he was in rural Ireland, it took two days to arrive, then he'd listen and call me. I remember he heard 'Under My Wing' and wanted an alto flute on it. He sang me the parts, he had the Mozart quality, he just knew. I was the one who suggested Mavis Staples for 'Goodnight Irene'; I'd worked on her solo album. It turned out that John was a huge fan of Pops Staples. John was thrilled to have her singing, even if they never actually sang in the same room together."

In fact, "Under My Wing," which sounded as if it could have been lifted from the Paul Weller songbook (although Weller's backing vocals sounded as nervous as a boy in the presence of a master), was a thank you to Teresa and a sign that John was ready to take on some of the strain now, and the light-hearted "Back To Marseilles" (with its gloriously rolling acoustic guitar line), "One For The Road" and "Walking Home" all swayed with romance. The only glimpse of fire and anger was on "Cobbles," but even there the blows seemed half-hearted, more nostalgic than anything.

"Some of the tracks were tough," Tullio admitted, "a lot of editing, and some of the songs weren't properly realised. On 'Back To Marseilles,' which was one of the first tracks we did in 2000, there was a sample that sounded like a squeaky bicycle, so we called the track "Squeaky Bicycle" for a long time. John didn't have any lyrics for it. One day in Ireland he recited the lyrics for us to write down. He sang it later, but it didn't flow, so I did some editing. There's a piece right at the start, and I took that from each take and put it in succession as an introduction. He liked it at first, but he slammed it later. We had a similar problem with 'Walking Home' and 'Cobbles.' He'd just sing stuff, ad-libbing, and I had to add some structure."

While he hadn't made that much-awaited acoustic album, he'd done the next best thing. Much of the time his acoustic guitar featured heavily, a return to the instrument that nurtured him (and certainly an apt time for such a thing). The backing was full, but never heavy-handed. Instruments were used sparingly, as were the guests (former Verve guitarist Nick McCabe's contribution to "Walking Home" was a masterpiece of economy). And John had rarely been in better voice. There was a passion to his singing that had all too often been lacking in the studio work of the past. The slurs had truly become tenor sax swoops and curls, but the enunciation had improved. He used tone more confidently than in the past, able to communicate more with less. It was as if all the lessons of the past had come together on this, pushed along by the illness, to create a crowning achievement, as if he was afraid it might be his last.

And concluding with the wry fatalism of "Goodnight Irene" did nothing to lessen that idea. Rendered as pure gospel, it was John going to church (and apart from his own deconsecrated building, he probably hadn't been in one in many years) in the company of the great Mavis Staples. He was every bit her equal. From deep inside himself, John brought out the spirit.

Maybe, as James McNair said in *Mojo*, it was "an old-fashioned triumph over adversity story" – or maybe it was John gracefully coming to terms with his new reality. Either way, it was his best and most satisfying album in many a long year, one to please both fans who'd stuck around since the glory days of the '70s and those who'd come on board more recently. In spite of, or possibly because of, his health problems, John had re-emerged as a creative, vital songwriter and singer, every bit as good as anyone from the two generations that had come in his wake. With *On the Cobbles*, he fulfilled the sporadic promise of the last ten years.

The album's release at the end of April set the stage for May as the month of John Martyn. He'd just begun his first UK tour since 2001. By his previous standards it was short, little more than eleven dates spread over a few weeks. But for him it was a major comeback, and one many people believed would never happen, especially after losing his leg. Yet there was John, a huge bear of a man, shambling onstage using his prosthetic leg, with the aid of a stick that looked more like a tree branch.

A year had passed since the amputation, one in which he'd been forced to learn all manner of new skills and reassess himself physically, mentally, and spiritually. There were still plenty of bad days in with the good and those could be reflected in the performances. Curiously, he only performed one of the songs from the new record in his shows, and even that one – "My Creator" – wasn't exactly fresh. But along with the well-received older material (all songs familiar to the trio of Cozens, Ahmun and Giblin, who backed him, cutting down on rehearsal time), there was one brand-new piece that was being aired, an unrecorded tune called "I Knew When I Met You."

These days shows were split into two sets: the first shorter, with a longer one after the intermission, including a few acoustic numbers with just John on the stage. Not surprisingly, he remained seated the whole time, even on the encores, and there were moments when he had problems reaching the foot pedals in time. But he was nothing if not a seasoned trouper, able to joke about his misfortune. He wasn't there for sympathy from the audience; he wasn't washed-up or washed-out. The only difference was that he'd lost half his right leg. He could still sing and play and he seemed to relish the opportunity to do exactly that.

Not all the shows sold out, but a fair number were still able to put out "house full" signs. It was a good way to test the waters, going around the country at a fairly even pace, nothing too strenuous, to see if he really could still do it. For all the professionalism and experience, there was almost certainly a hidden layer of doubt inside John, one that he voiced to only a few, if at all. But after so long away from the lights, by far the longest break of his career and certainly not one of his own choosing, he must have wondered whether enough people still cared and whether he still had it inside him to do it.

The answers were quite apparent on both counts. There was demand and desire enough for him to schedule an eight-date jaunt through Ireland in July once the tour was complete and he was certain he could continue.

Before that, and following on from his British tour, the last weekend of May was something of a John Martyn celebration on television. With the band, he appeared on *Later with Jools Holland*, performing "Johnny Too Bad" live in the studio, with sweat pouring down his face. That was followed by the long-promised documentary, *Johnny Too Bad*, postponed from March to May, with a vintage *Old Grey Whistle Test* concert of John's, from 1978 screened later that night.

The documentary, by Ben Whalley and Serena Cross, was as comprehensive as it could be within an hour, while glossing over some of the darker aspects of John's life - in particular, his dependency on drink. There were plenty of vintage live clips, especially from the 70s, and the culmination was John's return to performing after the amputation - at Connollys, in November 2003 — although oddly only part of one song from that milestone was featured.

While exploring John's history, the centre of it all was the amputation, both before and after, looking at the way it had affected him and how he had recovered from it. Many who knew him well were interviewed, but even the best-chosen soundbites couldn't really do justice to someone as complex as John.

Something as traumatic was an amputation would have sent many people into a spiral of depression and inactivity. Not John. He had plenty of grit and was determined not to let something like a lost leg slow him down any more than he had to.

There was touring to be done and he established what would become an annual schedule: a British tour followed by a short Irish tour. It kept him in the public spotlight and brought in much-needed money. Far more than that, according to Jim Tullio, "it was his lifeblood. He could use the money, but he *needed* to play. If he'd really wanted the money, he'd had have sold out long before, and he never did."

Something else he needed was the stability that Teresa brought him. All those who knew the couple felt she was an ideal match for him. She'd give him ample rope, but also knew when to say "enough" – and John would listen. They never married, but there was no doubting the fact that it was a true love match.

"I used to call her St. Teresa," Tullio said. "She was his saving grace, especially after the leg. She was a nurse at one time, but she helped him more than anyone. I don't think he'd have lasted as long without her. She rationed the alcohol he got, she took care of him. He was devoted to her. When he met her it did give him stability."

Where they lived, far from any city, was a help, too. It might have made getting around more difficult after John lost the leg, but, as Tullio noted, "being out in rural Ireland kept him out of temptation, especially in the later years when he couldn't get out alone."

John's yearly jaunts quickly took on the aura of ritual. The amputation seemed to have transformed the way people viewed him. Not that he'd become mainstream – that was impossible – but he'd at least come in a little from the margins, with a name that was more recognisable, drawing larger audiences to his shows. For the most part the crowds wanted to hear the big songs, the ones that had appeared on the various "best ofs" and introduction compilations that had appeared. And John generally obliged - although there were always a few oddities in the mix, a chance to stretch out on electric guitar.

One thing that became apparent from year to year was how much weight John was gaining. He'd always been big, strapping, but he'd carried it well. Now, as he was restricted in his movement, spending most of his time sitting, with no exercise to work off the food he consumed (and John still loved to cook), he'd ballooned in weight. Generally, however, "his spirits were fair to good," Tullio said. "I wouldn't say they were great. I think he was bothered by the fact that his leg had been amputated, even though he chose that over the alternatives. And he really did gain so much weight. I took him around New York in '08 and he said, 'Tools, I fucking hate this.' He couldn't do for himself. But he kept working and he didn't give up."

He also continued to write and record; his Muse hadn't deserted him. Garry Pollitt, who owned a portable studio and good microphones, would periodically travel over to Ireland from his Liverpool home and stay for a couple of weeks at a time, capturing songs, guitar playing and vocals.

The tours were successful enough - but in 2006, John was invited to do something a little different and quite special. The "Don't Look Back" concert series gave artists the chance to present all the tracks from a classic album before an audience. In most cases, many of the tunes wouldn't have been performed for many years; some might never have had public airings.

John was asked to recreate *Solid Air* at the Barbican in London. The portents were good, as the concert would be on his birthday, and tickets went quickly - even at £23.50, all two thousand seats were sold out. He'd have his usual band with him, along with Martin Winnings on sax.

The show was a success, even if John didn't follow the track sequence of the disc. The performance, according to *The Independent*, was "both thrilling and perplexing." Being John, it could never be a note-for-note recreation. Instead, it was seen through the prism of the band - updated and little slicker. But it was a reminder of just how good the record was, no matter in which order it was played. It was a classic.

So much of a classic, in fact, that taking it on tour was a good idea. The *Solid Air* jaunt was fitted in before the annual tour, eight dates that took the band around the country. The opening act, John Smith, seemed a curious choice. A singer-songwriter, he was an excellent guitarist, with a voice that was eerily reminiscent of John Martyn in the early '70s, with the same slur and sustain. It was almost as if John was passing on the torch to a new generation.

Although the shows were well-received and the halls packed, the shows themselves were hit and miss. At some, John was on tremendous form with both his singing and playing. At others, such as the concert at Sheffield City Hall, he seemed to be going through the motions much of the time, his playing lacklustre.

"He'd hurt his hands," Tullio explained. "It goes all the way back to the cow incident when the windscreen glass cut his hands. Gaining weight affected his hands, too. They were swollen, and at the end he was in pain when he played."

CHAPTER THIRTEEN – The Last Year

At the beginning of 2008, something happened that few would have anticipated. At the BBC Radio 2 Folk Awards, John received a Lifetime Achievement. If John had ever been a folk musician, that period had ended thirty years earlier. But he didn't fit easily into any category and he'd survived long enough to warrant some honours – and this was the closest that might fit.

"I was a bit scared to be honest, and almost overwhelmed by the sense of occasion," John admitted at the event, joking "at last, a celeb at last."

Phil Collins – definitely no folkie himself – gave John the award and there were accolades from many others, including Eric Clapton, who wrote a message saying: "So far ahead of everything, it's almost inconceivable."

After so long on the musical margins he more than deserved the attention. He certainly couldn't escape without performing. Along with his usual band – Spencer, Arran, Alan Thomson and Martin Winnings – former Led Zeppelin bass player John Paul Jones sat in on mandolin for a take on "Over The Hill," while John also performed "May You Never," declaring "I was told to do this, so I'm doing it."

It all ended in a well-deserved standing ovation - good therapy for John, who was still recovering from his recent illness. From being the perennial outsider, he'd made it into the establishment. With age, it seemed, anything was possible.

2008 continued to be a year of accolades. On September 1, to celebrate John's sixtieth birthday later that month, Island issued a four-CD box set, *Ain't No Saint*, a retrospective that covered most of the forty years of John's career.

Assembled by John Hillarby, who ran the official John Martyn website and who also wrote the essay in the booklet, it emphasised rarities and live tracks. There were only a few previously-released studio cuts on the first two discs, while the last two were all live, taking in some otherwise unreleased cuts from *Live at Leeds*, all the way up to John's performance of "Over The Hill" at the BBC2 Folk Awards earlier that year.

It was a massive undertaking and an honour that was long overdue for John. With a total of sixty-one songs, over thirty of which hadn't been issued before, as well as unseen photographs, it was a treasure trove for fans and a perfect way to cap what had turned out to be an annus mirabilis.

Although John himself had known months in advance, it came as a surprise to many people that he was awarded the Order of the British Empire in the New Year's Honours List of 2009.

It was given for his services to music and, as Teresa told the *Glasgow Herald*, "he didn't believe it until he saw it in the papers."

John had been looking forward to travelling to London, to being inside Buckingham Palace to receive the award himself. It would be the perfect cap to what had been a great year. Turning sixty hadn't proved so bad, and he'd rounded out 2008 with a tour. There was also plenty planned 2009.

One constant problem for John was trying to find the right prosthetic leg. Although he went through five of them it was difficult, if not impossible, to find one that fitted really well. The problem was compounded by his weight. It was a vicious circle – without a prosthesis that fitted well, John was forced to spend most of his time in the wheelchair. Sitting meant his weight kept increasing, so it became harder to find a leg that could support him properly.

The situation changed in 2008, according to Jim Tullio, when "this doctor in New York called me, wanting information on John. He claimed he could help book a US tour. Apparently he got a few dates and so I put him in touch with John. The doctor went to Ireland to meet John, and periodically he'd call me. John was too ill to do the tour, and I said to the doctor, 'Let's help him get a new leg.' The doctor was working at Columbia Medical Centre and he got on it, he set it all up. John would have to go to New York to have it fitted."

It seemed very hopeful, but there was a catch to it all.

"But unbeknown to John, the doctor booked him to play at Joe's Pub in Manhattan while he was over in October [part of the venue's 10th anniversary celebrations] and then invited Danny Thompson to play with him. John got wind of it and said he didn't want to play – all he wanted was the prosthesis. I said I'd come to New York and bring a guitar in case John changed his mind."

John and Teresa didn't go directly to Manhattan. Instead they started their New York trip in Woodstock, where John had been with Beverley to record several decades before. This was really to visit The Band drummer Levon Helm, who'd remained a good friend.

"While he was there he decided to do the gig so he wouldn't let the doctor down, even though he wasn't fit enough. Then this doctor said he'd contacted Pharaoh Sanders and played him 'My Creator' and Pharaoh wanted to record with him. He even had a photo of Pharaoh holding the *Cobbles* CD. Pharaoh was one of John's big influences, of course, so John was trying to please the doctor. We went to Manhattan. Danny flew in and we all met at the hospital where John was getting his leg fitted, and it turned out to be one that finally fitted right."

With that finally taken care of, John could look ahead to playing the gig; he'd actually play a second night there too, as part of a tribute to Judy Collins.

"John was nervous about doing the gig with Danny," said Tullio. "He told me he didn't think Danny could swing any more, although he sounded fine to me. It was a packed house at Joe's Pub. Danny played well and so did John, although he didn't sing too well."

John was definitely looking ahead to the prospect of recording with one of his idols. He'd been a fan of Sanders for many years, and much of the slurred vocal style had come from the way Sanders played the tenor sax. Recording together would be one of the highlights of John's career.

"While John was still in Woodstock he told me in a café that he wanted to record with Pharaoh in Chicago – Pharaoh lived in Santa Monica, so it was closer than New York," explained Tullio. "I had a new studio and ramps fitted for John's wheelchair. We were going to record in April 2009, with Danny on bass, Phil Collins on drums, and Pharaoh."

John even stopped drinking to be in good shape for the upcoming session, which was a huge commitment from someone who'd spent so long with alcohol as part of his daily life.

"John wanted me and Gaz to finish the record," Tullio continued, "and we wanted to get Pharaoh on it as a tribute, to fulfill his last wishes. Pharoah was going to be playing Birdland in New York in May, and we said we'd go to New York and rent gear. Jimmy McKnight, a friend of John's, came over with Gaz, and then Spencer Cozens met us in New York. But it turned out that this doctor had been lying all along. We went to Pharaoh's gig and he knew nothing about recording. The doctor had talked to his manager and got a picture somehow, but nothing had been set. Finally McKnight called Pharaoh and he said he'd do it for $10,000 and he'd record at his home in Santa Monica. So it never happened. But the New York trip wasn't a total loss. We went up to Woodstock and I recorded Garth Hudson from The Band on accordion for 'Stand Amazed'."

But one thing no one had anticipated was John catching pneumonia - and not just pneumonia, but double pneumonia. He'd survived the amputation, adjusted well to life with one leg and seemed to have the constitution of an ox – but this was something he couldn't fight, certainly not at home. According to Jim Tullio, "When he got double pneumonia, he couldn't fight it. By then he hadn't had a drink in five weeks, and I think his body broke down. He was under a doctor's care for stopping, the doctor visited every other day."

It was evident he couldn't be adequately cared for at home and John was admitted to hospital. But even treatment there couldn't help - and on the 29th of January 2009, John Martyn passed away.

The first announcement came on the website, which stated: "With heavy heart and unbearable sense of loss we must announce that John died this morning." The man who, in his own estimation, had "lived three lifetimes" had run through them all.

The newspapers began to run obituaries immediately, full of praise from those who'd known and worked with John.

"He was uncompromising, which made him infuriating to some people, but he was unique and we'll never see the likes of him again," said Phil Collins. "I loved him dearly and will miss him very much."

Danny Thompson, a friend for so long and one of his road companions, said "I miss him so much, even the early-morning phone calls when he'd ring at 3am and say, 'I love you, man,' ...He'd do this regularly, long after we'd stopped playing together, and I'd say, 'If you love me, why can't you let me sleep?' ...his music was real. You can't lie when you play, because you get found out."

From being largely forgotten, or of interest only to a minority, a cult hero, John had become much better-known in the year he turned sixty and was lauded as one of music's great original thinkers after his death.

John was cremated on Sunday, February 4, after a service at St. Mary's Church in Kells. The church was full of family and friends paying their last respects. John's music was played during the service, with one exception – local singer Mary Moore performing the traditional piece, "The Sally Gardens."

According to one newspaper report, John only left a total of £82,000 in his will. According to the *Sunday Express*, Teresa would receive three-quarters of the estate, with the remainder going to Mhairi, his daughter with Beverley – they'd become closer over the years, and she'd kept the McGeachy surname. There was apparently no mention of son Spencer in the will (according to Beverley, John's son had become homeless and was living on the streets of Brighton, with a drug problem). It was believed that the will didn't include John's assets in Ireland.

It wasn't a huge amount for a lifetime of work that included a few hit albums and years of touring, but his legacy would be the music, always the music - and that would keep on selling, and bringing great joy.

EPILOGUE

Heaven and Earth was never intended to be a posthumous release. It should simply have been the next John Martyn album. Work continued on it in Ireland from the time of John's amputation until shortly before his death, interrupted only by his annual tours.

Garry Pollitt did much of the hard labour. As he was based in Liverpool and had a portable digital studio, he'd been able to travel over to John and Teresa's house in Ireland regularly and stay for a couple of weeks at a time, recording.

That said, not all the tracks that appeared on this disc were new.

"'Heel Of The Hunt' was a track he'd cut before *On the Cobbles*," noted Jim Tullio, "and I still don't really know who played keyboards, although we credited it to Spencer. It was one of the tracks he gave me in 2000. I wanted it for *Cobbles*, but we didn't use it. We put on a different bass and real drums. Both 'Bad Company' and 'Heaven And Earth' were done in the church in Scotland. When I was in Ireland to finish *Cobbles*, we thought the vocals weren't strong enough, so we didn't use the tracks. They're still the same vocals, he never re-did them. 'Heaven And Earth' is one of my favourites off this album. I think 'Bad Company' is weaker vocally, but it has a vibe."

They spent the summer of 2009 finishing all the recording, and then there was a lot of editing. "We had multiple guitar tracks to work with but a lot fewer vocal tracks. It was a labour of love, really, and when we'd finished we were wondering how it could be released. Universal was interested, but in 2010 they had a new regime in place and weren't interested either in John's album or the tribute. Then they called back later, after Jim Snowden put a deal together, and said they were interested – but for a lot less money."

The albums, both John's posthumous release and the tribute, would appear in 2011. But in 2010 John was remembered close to home, at the Celtic Connections festival in his hometown of Glasgow. In 2007 the festival director, Donald Shaw, had persuaded John to perform *Solid Air* in its entirety there. He planned to host a tribute to John a year after his death. It took place at the Fruitmarket venue on January 30th, virtually a year to the day after John's death, and featured the man's songs interpreted by several performers, including Eddi Reader and Martin Simpson, under the direction of Danny Thompson.

Throughout his career, John remained a prime example of the art not being the artist, the life not being the work. Even in death he remains a paradox, a man of uncountable layers and levels whose masks rarely came all the way off. He was a man with a thousand acquaintances, but very few close, trusted friends. The people he stayed close to loved him and retained a fierce loyalty towards him.

In *Johnny Too Bad*, musician Ralph McTell speculated that something bad must have happened to John when he was young to account for the way he'd always cloaked himself. Others who know him well have agreed. If so, it was something he's kept hidden from all but the most intimate of friends and lovers. Or possibly it was something he never even realised himself. It would make sense: the masks, the excess and ongoing problem with drinking, the latent aggression - they all point to a troubled soul. Whether he'd made his peace with himself and the world, only John can say.

And in the end, he left a vital legacy: not only his children, now all grown and living lives of their own, but also those people who loved and treasured him – and who will always remember him.

For the rest of us, there will always be his music.

THE WORKS OF JOHN MARTYN

ALBUMS

London Conversation, 1967

The Tumbler, 1968

Stormbringer, 1970 (with Beverley Martyn)

The Road to Ruin, 1970 (with Beverley Martyn)

Bless the Weather, 1971

Solid Air, 1973

Inside Out, 1973

Sunday's Child, 1974

Live at Leeds, 1975

So Far So Good*, 1977

One World, 1977

Grace and Danger, 1980

Glorious Fool, 1981

The Electric John Martyn*, 1982

Well Kept Secret. 1982
Philentropy, 1983

Sapphire, 1984

Piece by Piece, 1986

Foundations, 1987

The Apprentice, 1990

Cooltide, 1991

BBC Radio 1 Live in Concert, 1991

Couldn't Love You More, 1992

No Little Boy, 1993

Sweet Little Mysteries: The Island Anthology*, 1994

Live, 1995

And., 1996

The Hidden Years*, 1996

Snoo..., 1997

The Very Best of John Martyn*, 1997

The Rest of the Best*, 1998

Serendipity – An Introduction to John Martyn*, 1998

The Church with One Bell, 1998

Live at Bristol, 1998

Another World, 1999

Classics*, 2000

New York Session, 2000

Glasgow Walker, 2000

Live '91, 2000

Patterns in the Rain, 2001

Kendal 1986, 2001

Germany 1986, 2001

Live at the Town and Country Club 1986, 2001

Sweet Certain Surprise, 2001

Live at the Bottom Line, New York 1983, 2001

Solid Air, Classics Revisited*, 2001

Live in Milan 1979, 2002

And Live, 2003

Live in Concert at the Cambridge Folk Festival, 2003

Live at Kirk Galley, 2004

On the Cobbles, 2004

Late Night John, 2004

Mad Dog Days, 2004

Live in Nottingham, 1976, 2005

Live at Leeds And More, 2006

On Air, 2006

The John Martyn Story*, 2006

One World Label Sampler*, 2006

In Session at the BBC, 2006

Sixty Minutes With*, 2007

BBC Live in Concert, 2007

Live at the Roundhouse, 2007

The Battle of Medway: 17 July 1973, 2007

Anthology, 2007

The Simmer Dim, 2008

The July Wakes, 2008

Ain't No Saint*, 2008

May You Never – The Very Best Of*, 2009

Heaven and Earth, 2011

Compilations denoted by a *

VIDEO

In Vision, 1973-1981

John Martyn at the BBC

Live from London

Foundations

The Apprentice Tour

Empty Ceiling

Tell Them I'm Somebody Else

The Man Upstairs

One World One John (2011)

ACKNOWLEDGEMENTS

Follow your heart, they say, and the rest will come. This is a book I'd always imagined writing, but I never believed anyone would want to publish. Several years ago, in a conversation with Sean Body, head of Helter Skelter Books, he asked who I'd really like to write about, I answered "John Martyn" without missing a beat, although it seemed like a pipe dream. Yet within a month Sean had given me the go-ahead, and I'm immensely grateful to him for this opportunity. Then Sean sadly passed from leukaemia, a man greatly missed, and everything regarding the book fell into limbo for a few years. My gratitude to Jim Snowden for being the catalyst in its resurrection and to Ali Muirden and Lorelei King at Creative Content for putting it in the digital domain.

The root of my love of John Martyn dates back to 1972. I'd just finished my A-levels, enjoying that delicious limbo between school and university. My new girlfriend, Laura, (known as Lol) and I were enjoying a wonderful summer. One evening she took me into her family's music room. The thick carpet, grand piano, and wall crammed with sheet music were paradise to someone with dreams of a musical life. She made me sit on the floor, put an LP on the stereo, and came to sit beside me. The record was *Bless the Weather*. Within the space of a track, I was hooked – by the guitar, by the slurred, sensuous vocals. My life changed. She gave me a copy of the disc for my birthday later that month.

By the time September arrived, Laura had gone from my life, but John Martyn's remained ever since. I bought *Solid Air*, *Inside Out*, and *Sunday's Child* the day they were released. I was lucky enough to live in Leeds and be at the concert that became the *Live at Leeds* album.

Since then I've bought every album John Martyn has made. Call it an act of faith, or one of those artists that resonates within me. I've preached the gospel of John Martyn for years. And now I have the chance to do it again. Life doesn't get any better. So thanks to you, Lol, although I doubt you'll ever see this.

It's a book begun on one continent and completed on another, and that means thanks to many. I'm always grateful to the Leeds United e-mail list, for its pleasures, laughs, and distractions. And there's Kevin Odell in London, Kevan Roberts in Seattle, stout friends indeed. Mike Murtagh might not be with us anymore, but he was a JM fan too, giving me one of my treasured possessions, his copy of the "Anni" single. SN, who provided knowledge and so much more; thank you so much. Pepper, Esme, Jess, Silvi, and Mardi (not forgetting August, too). Graham, who might one day understand why I love this music so much. And Linda, who has probably been bored to death by my raving about John over the years, but loved the two performances she saw. Penny loves the music, as do others, and some I've introduced to John's work. Jim Snowden brought this book back to life, to my surprise and pleasure.

Thanks, especially, to all those who took the time to be interviewed for this book. I take it not as a testament of my persuasion or ability, but of the love and regard they have for John. In New York, the splendid Bridget St. John reminisced for a wonderful hour in Greenwich Village, and I'm grateful she's become a friend. Bill Young took me around Ca Va Studios in Glasgow, in London Spencer Cozens talked about his years with John. Chris Blackwell gave of his time while in Seattle to talk happily about John. Back problems prevented me meeting with Alex Boyesen in London, but e-mail and phone calls substituted, as they did with Robin Frederick and Joe Boyd. Claire Martin, Dave Mattacks, Phill Brown, Clive Palmer, Jim Tullio, Neil Ardley, Arran Ahmun, and Claire Hamill were all happy to chat on the phone about John, and share their insights and memories. Writing a piece on Yes brought me to Jon Anderson, who reminisced about the time they toured America together. Thanks too to those who led me to the sources – Dan Cohen, Meg Friedman, Jon Kertzer, and various webmasters and webmistresses, with a big nod to Hans van den Berk, who has been generous with information. I'd been fortunate enough to interview John himself at length in 1993, and have drawn on the transcript of that; I'm grateful to *Discoveries* for allowing me to use the material.

For someone who's been around for such a long time, there are relatively few interviews with John. But a fair proportion of what's been printed has been reproduced on the Big Muff website (www.johnmartyn.info). They've also been useful source material for this book. So, fair attributions to: "Heaven Can Wait" by James McNair in *The Independent*, "Battered and bruised...but still standing" by Adam Lee Potter, *Scotland on Sunday*, "I'm Still Standing" by Aidan Smith, *Scotland on Sunday*, "Root Love" by Steve Burgess, *Dark Star*, "John Martyn" by Gerard Nguyen, *Atem*, "Blood, sweat and cheers" by Vivian Goldman, *Sounds*, "A Happy Man" by Andy Childs, *Supersnazz*, "Been Gone So Long" by Bob Stanley, *Mojo*, "Talking with John Martyn" by Andy Childs, *ZigZag*, "Up to date with John Martyn" by Andy Childs, *ZigZag*, "Martyn & Garfunkel" by Angus MacKinnon, *Street Life*, "Singing in the rain" by Malcolm Heyhoe, Paul Hunter, *Licquorice*, "The Stormbringer comes into the sun" by Ian MacDonald, *NME*, "John Martyn: A fingerpicking Brityn" by Dan Hedges, *Guitar Player*, Dotmusic interview, "The talented Mr. Martyn" by Andy Robson, *Classic Rock*, "From art school to recording artist" by Mike Conway, *iCast*, Interview by Mitch Myers, *Magnet*, "Felling Gravity's Pull" by Rob Young, *The Wire*, "The triumphant return of John Martyn" by Lahri Bond, *Dirty Linen*, "John Martyn Interview" by Kevin Ring, *Zip Code*, "Piece by Piece" by Trevor Dann, "Piece by Piece" by ?, *Well-Kept Secret*, "Same Again" by Mark Cooper, *Q*, 1990 Radio 1 interview by Nicky Campbell, "Grace and danger" by Paul Tingen, *The Guitar Magazine*, "Martyn's moments make the music" by Dave Hoekstra, *Chicago Sun-Times*, "The acoustic-electric...John Martyn" by Rick Batey, *Guitarist*, "John Martyn" by Keith Grant, *International Musician*, "Digne Martyn" by Francois Gorin, *Rock & Folk*,

Fans should also note that there's an excellent John Martyn website – as close to "official" as any of them get – to be found at www.johnmartyn.com and also Big Muff at www.johnmartyn.info

This book and other John Martyn merchandise including the amazing Tribute project featuring 30 artists reimagining the works of John including: David Gray, Lisa Hannigan, Beth Orton, Robert Smith, Phil Collins, The Swell Season, Snow Patrol, Beck, Skye, Bombay Bicycle Club and Paolo Nutini.

Are available at www.johnmartynmusic.com

If you enjoyed "Solid Air – the life of John Martyn", you might also enjoy:

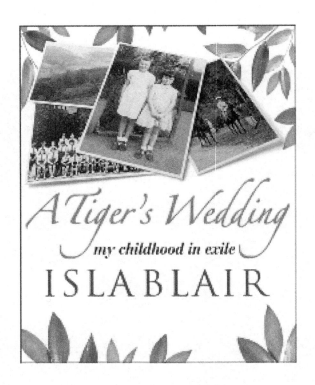

"A Tiger's Wedding – my childhood in exile" by Isla Blair

Published by Creative Content

Our website: www.creativecontentdigital.com

Visit us on Facebook: www.facebook.com/CreativeContent

Follow us on Twitter: www.twitter.com/CCTheLowdown

Printed in Great Britain
by Amazon

48300456R00149